I Live Again

ILEANA, PRINCESS OF ROMANIA
ARCHDUCHESS OF AUSTRIA

ANCIENT FAITH PUBLISHING
CHESTERTON, INDIANA

Published by:
  Ancient Faith Publishing
  A Division of Ancient Faith Ministries
  P.O. Box 748
  Chesterton, IN 46304

Original text first published in 1951 by Rinehart & Company, Inc.

ISBN: 978-1-944967-47-5

Printed in the United States of America

25 24 23 22 21 20 19   17 16 15 14 13 12 11 10 9 8 7 6 5 4 3 2

CONTENTS

To my friends and countrymen,
to all those brave souls that have remained behind
to face all that man can bear, and yet have not failed,
to them in love and humble admiration
I dedicate my book.

INTRODUCTION

It is with much joy and appreciation that our monastic sisterhood greets the republication by Ancient Faith Publishing of *I Live Again*, which has been out of print for decades. We believe that the autobiography of our monastery foundress, Mother Alexandra, Princess Ileana of Romania, will speak to the hearts of modern-day readers in a most inspiring way. Her honest and reflective writing offers a glimpse into her loving heart, determined spirit, and deep faith in God. And all of us, the nuns and the pilgrims to the American monastery she founded as well as those living in her beloved Romania, can reap the spiritual fruit of her labors, prayers, and tears.

As you read the book, you will gain an insight into European history, told from the inside (from the 1920s to 1948). You will also gain insight into how a Christian woman can turn trials, adversities, failures, and even persecution into steps for spiritual growth and opportunities to live one's life according to the Gospel of Jesus Christ. I am sure you will be moved and impressed. And I trust you will also be inspired to live your own life with a greater zeal and determination to do the will of God, no matter what circumstances He may hand to you.

We wish to thank the publishers at Ancient Faith Ministries, along with their helpful and skillful staff: among them, John Maddex, CEO, who has given us much help, assistance, and encouragement for many years. Also Katherine Hyde, Editorial Director, has directed our Mother Magdalena in the task of gathering and refining the material and photographs needed for this new edition, as well as editing the current work. We thank V. Rev. Dr. Remus Grama for his insightful Prologue, which will guide you in reading the book within an appropriate historical context. Granddaughter Ileana Habsburg-Snyder offers a moving personal reflection, as does Protopresbyter Laurence Lazar, whose family knew Mother Alexandra for many years.

Our special gratitude for his offering here of a personal and reflective Epilogue goes to our beloved Archbishop Nathaniel of the Romanian Orthodox Episcopate of America, who was a spiritual friend and advisor to Mother Alexandra during the years of our monastery's founding.

May all who read *I Live Again*, the autobiography of a woman of the world—and a woman of God—learn to do as she did: to live life to its fullest, keeping the commandments of God and doing what Christ asked of her at each moment. Holiness, as Mother Alexandra once said, is mostly doing whatever is in front of one's nose right now, and not getting in God's way.

Very Reverend Mother Christophora, Abbess
The Feast of Holy Pentecost, 2017
The Orthodox Monastery of the Transfiguration
Ellwood City, PA

PROLOGUE TO THE NEW EDITION

As one who was blessed to know and minister to the author in her years of retirement in Ellwood City, I am honored and, I must confess, equally humbled and apprehensive even to come close to this subject. However, given the importance of this new edition and my deep respect for Mother Christophora, the Abbess of Transfiguration Monastery, I agreed to offer a few personal thoughts.

I Live Again springs forth with an energizing grace, like a brook of fresh water straight from the depths of the Carpathians. It is a book of the deep and prayerful personal reflection of one who experienced greatness and humility with a rarely encountered dignity. In the pages of this book, Princess Ileana embraces the reader with her typical love for life, with an amazing honesty, yet with a noble and spiritual discretion. In other words, this book invites you to breathe history, with all its dramas, from love to sacrifice. It takes the reader into the intimacy of the royal chambers of Romania's castles, where the young Princess Ileana, or *Domnitza*,[1] as she was endearingly called by her people, was brought up. Her personality was formed and refined in the quintessence of the best that European monarchic culture could offer: studying politics and arts, traveling, learning foreign languages, driving, navigating, and flying, riding horses and hiking the ridges of the Transylvanian Alps, and certainly brushing shoulders with the potentates of her world. Yet she was close to the Romanian peasants, whom she adored and whose folk costume she wore with a deep sense of pride and identity.

She was born in 1909 to parents who soon after were crowned King Ferdinand Hohenzolern-Sigmaringen and Queen Marie of Romania.

---

1 *Domnitza* means "Lady," and in the Romanian language the word designates a royal descendant.

They ruled Romania from 1914 to 1927. Her father, Ferdinand, was the nephew of the previous childless king, Carol I Hohenzolern, and his wife Queen Elizabeth (1866–1914). Queen Marie was born in Edinburgh, a princess of Great Britain and Ireland, granddaughter of Queen Victoria. She was also first cousin to King George V of England, while her mother was a first cousin to Tsar Nicholas II. By blood, Princess Ileana was therefore related to many monarchies. Further, in her immediate family, she was sister to King Carol II of Romania (1930–40) and aunt to King Michael of Romania (1940–47), who was forced by the communists to abdicate in 1947. And the story does not stop there. Her sister, Elisabeta, was the queen of Greece, having been married to King George. Another sister of hers, Marie, became the wife of King Peter of Yugoslavia. Thus, with a mother who was rightly surnamed the "mother-in-law of the Balkans" and with grandparents, aunts, and uncles in all major countries of Europe, she in her turn married Archduke Anton of Hapsburg in 1931, by virtue of this receiving the title of Grand Duchess of Austria.

The cruelty of World War I caused much suffering in Europe. If some countries were wiped out from the maps by the Germans, Romania was squeezed into a small territory in its eastern province of Moldavia. The great casualties of war and the inadequate conditions in overcrowded hospitals had generated epidemics and hardship. In the midst of these desperate conditions, Queen Marie became a moral symbol of encouragement for the wounded soldiers as well as for the afflicted population. The queen's compassion deeply impressed and shaped Princess Ileana. Writing about this she says, "it was perhaps at this time that the foundation was laid for my interest in nursing and hospital work" (p. 46). By God's mercy and Queen Marie's graceful influence in European politics, after the war Romania emerged united with all its historical provinces. President Woodrow Wilson and Romanian-Americans were keenly aware of the queen's role in preserving their country. To honor her for this, at the president's invitation, in 1926 Queen Marie and Princess Ileana toured

America for the first time, being given full royal honors, including a tick-er-tape parade in New York City.

The 1920s were years of prosperity for the young princess, when she lived in the sphere of light of her parents, growing in spirit, wisdom, and beauty. She was painted by artists and loved by the plain people for her simplicity. Later, in the years of her exile, she would long enormously for the peace and sense of protection the peasants ever inspired in her heart. The royal palace of Cotroceni had a church, and Peles Palace was close to Sinaia Monastery, where she prayed and came close to God. She also loved the monasteries which Queen Marie had praised in her Ode to Romania. In fact, Bran Castle, which she would later inherit from her mother, also had a wooden church nearby. The royal family founded cathedrals, choosing the historical Curtea-de-Arges church, of the legend-ary Master Manole,[2] to be their burial place. In broad lines, this was the world she grew up in.

In the 1930s, when her younger brother, King Carol, usurped his own son, the popular and much-loved Princess Ileana moved to her husband's country, first living in Munich and then in Modling, near Vienna, Austria. In the first ten years of marriage, she gave birth to her six children. With the dawn of Austria's occupation by the Germans and Anton's draft into their air force, life would get much harder. But Prin-cess Ileana always found the resources to help others, from the poor and needy of Sonnberg, where her family acquired an ancient castle, to the wounded Romanian soldiers in Vienna. The unexpected death of Queen

2 According to a famous legend, Master Manole is the builder of this historical church. The tradition has it that his work done in the daylight kept collapsing every night, until one night when he was enlightened by a strange dream. To prevent this disaster, he was directed that the first woman to come to the con-struction site must be built up within the walls. Manole's beloved wife was indeed the first to come. To the Master's anguish and in spite of her pleading, she was first jokingly, but then somberly, walled up in the growing temple. Upon completion, the king removed the scaffolding to prevent the masters from building a nicer monastery and, thus, Manole and his builders had to die also. This myth conveys the moral that nothing may be accomplished without a sacrifice.

Marie in 1938 brought deep pain to Ileana. The queen's legacy, however, continued to live in her altruistic daughter. In World War II, when Austrians endured Germanization at the hand of the Nazis, Ileana was often under the scrutiny of the Gestapo. In spite of this, she turned her serene castle into a hospital and became the self-appointed caregiver—"not by training, but by calling," as she would often confess.

When the political uncertainties increased, in 1943 she returned to Romania, where she felt safer and at home. By this time King Carol had been replaced as ruler by Marshall Ion Antonescu, and Romania was engulfed by war, bombardments, and much misery. Having settled in Bran Castle (a wedding present to her from her mother), she first worked the hot soup line in the Brasov railroad station. Her tenacious sacrifices for the wounded and needy taught her a profound lesson of faith: "I have learned that where there is faith in the Lord, His work can be done" (pp. 82–83). Her passion was to help those in need and heal the hurts of her people. Driven by this inner force, she opened a hospital near her castle and placed it under the protection of the queen's heart. The reader may be surprised to learn that in her last will Maria, the "romantic queen," left her heart to the Romanian people. Placed in a silver case and first kept at her summer residence in Balcic on the Black Sea, the precious gift was brought by the princess to Bran and placed in a shrine built into the rock of the nearby mountain. This was done so that the peasants could easily visit their beloved queen.

Like her mother, Princess Ileana was also very attached to Romania and its people. She writes, "We Romanians are attached to the very soil of our land, and we never can feel the same in any other" (pp. 49, 51). Because of this, during childbirth she always put a bowl of Romanian soil under her bed to make sure that her children were born on it. Testifying to her love for her country, she also writes, "I grew up part and parcel of my country. . . . Romania was and is the love of my life, the reason for my existence" (p. 48).

But this connection with the land was brutally cut off when King

Michael was expelled from Romania by the communists in 1947. This "condemned me, not to death, but to living death" (p. 368), and she had to overcome all this in the subsequent years. With a few belongings in her luggage, after she prayed on her knees together with the peasants, she and her children had to leave her beloved Bran Castle, finding haven first in Buenos Aires and then in the United States of America. Driven by her inherent Orthodox Christian faith and courage, and by an unabated optimism, she lectured extensively throughout the US and wrote about Romania and her faith. Having suffered the loss of her world and especially the loss of her daughter, Maria-Ileana, who died in a terrible accident, and after her other children became adults, she reached a time of deep discernment. This culminated in her decision to become a nun. Leaving New England for a monastery in France, she received the angelic habit, being tonsured with the name Mother Alexandra.

If the Romanian exiles previously looked up to their domnitza for encouragement, now all Romanian-Americans regarded her even more highly, as their beloved Mother Alexandra. She visited parishes and continued to mingle with Archbishop Valerian, clergy, and faithful at Vatra Romaneasca and other places. Inspired by an altruistic faith, she continued to serve others. Thus, she opened the first Romanian women's monastery, in Ellwood City, Pennsylvania. In these hills she found a sort of a transfigured city of Bran, where she sought to lead others through the steps of the many transfigurations she had already experienced. I met her here in 1982, when—in contrast to the well-established monastic site of today—the dwelling was still very modest.

I once visited Mother Alexandra in St. Elizabeth's Hospital in Youngstown, Ohio, and she gave me a book. She shared with me her dream to erect a wooden *troitza* in memory of the victims of communism. She wanted to inscribe on it some of the most symbolic Romanian names. We concurred on names such as Ion, Petru, Vasile, Gheorghe, and Niculae. At the time she was also deeply occupied in translating the poetry of countless Romanian victims of communism, which she published.

Later on, I was once blessed to interview her and Father Roman Braga of blessed memory, on prayer.

In 1990, after the fall of communism and after ten years of separation, I visited Romania. She asked me upon my return to tell her if it was safe for her to go. She had not been back to Romania since 1948. After my positive report, and perhaps other deeper advice, she felt she had to go back to visit Romania, and she did. When she came back, she told us about her emotional pilgrimage to Curtea-de-Arges and Bran. It stands out in my memory that a peasant offered her a basket of red apples, picked from the same tree from which his father gave fruits to His Majesty King Michael upon his departure in 1947. As she continued the story, she became emotional and said, "Dear Father, I sank my teeth into this apple, and then I felt I was finally reconnected with the country." Two sparkling tears shone in her blue eyes. Not even three months later, an accidental hip fracture led to her quick demise. Mission accomplished. The burial was presided over by then-young Bishop Nathaniel, whom she held in such high esteem.

I Live Again sums up not only the dramatic ups and downs of the life of a princess but the epic poetic story of the triumph of true faith in the face of adversity. In this sense, its title is most revealing. *I Live Again* was written with the American reader in mind. It reveals the life journey of the young princess, from the peace of her royal chambers to the stinking, lice-infested rooms of wartime hospitals. It confesses the loss of that bygone world and the struggle to regain the essential meaning of life in service. It could represent a strong document for a future canonization of this Romanian princely Mother Teresa, who also found meaning by living out the Gospel. It particularly inspires one's faith, and it transfigures the reader with its dramatic realism. With strength of character, Princess Ileana challenged the cowardice of the godless communists, whom she had painfully to watch become the masters of her country. She once reproached a non-believer, "God you may deny, but you cannot elude Him."

For this reason, this book is not the fairy-tale, romanticized story of one member of the royalty. It is in fact an inspiring scenario for a yet-unproduced movie and a profound insight into the first half of the twentieth century in Europe, in which the Romanian epic and her drama are the red thread. The story of Domnitza Ileana, who became a nurse and beggar for the wounded soldiers, who served hot soup in the Brasov railroad station, and who then served as a nun in America, carries a deep message of faith.

Like the doctors without borders of our time, her calling was to serve: her Lord, her king, and her people. Her service was aimed to transform and to give meaning to the simple, the wounded, the lowly, and later, to the exiles. All this came to a head in her life after the death of her daughter Maria-Ileana, when she decided to withdraw for discernment to a monastery in France. It was then that she chose to follow her Lord even more deeply, in total service to Him and others. It was her mission in this world to carry on the legacy of her beloved mother, Queen Marie, with the *noblesse* and selflessness of her entire ancestry, grafted so ontologically onto the Romanian ethos of the legendary Master Manole.

V. Rev. Father Remus Grama

FOREWORD

To many she was Princess Ileana of Romania and Mother Alexandra, but to me she was Granny, my grandmother and my friend. As a child I admired her, feared her, and respected her. I loved her as any child would love a grandparent, but our relationship deepened when at seventeen I read her book, *I Live Again*. I saw her through adult eyes for the first time. She was a royal who deeply loved Romania and its people. She was a humanitarian who opened her home as a hospital to those wounded during wartime. She was an advocate for her people through her painful exile as she railed against the abuses of communist rule. She was a child of God who accepted a difficult calling to found an Orthodox monastery in America. I soon understood that I had a granny like no other.

As I reached out to her, we grew close. She had an extraordinary and rare depth of experience and faith. She provided guidance through every crisis and milestone in my life. Her advice was often unexpected, direct, and brutally honest. Her responses were rarely to console me, but to teach me and impart her vast wisdom, and eventually her faith.

Over thirty years our relationship deepened as we shared life's joys and disappointments. On her deathbed, she could not speak but only look in my eyes. I told her how much I loved her and thanked her for being not only a grandmother but a wonderful friend. It was many years after she passed away that I came to faith and realized how much she prayed for me all those years.

Her legacy lives on in my heart, in this book, in her other writings, and in the beautiful monastery she founded in Ellwood City, Pennsylvania.

Ileana Habsburg-Snyder, granddaughter of Princess Ileana

WITH ALL MY MIGHT

Long ago, during the First World War, in Jasi, my mother wrote *The Country that I Love*. In it she depicted those parts of Romania which had fallen to the enemy, which none of us knew if we would ever see again. I remember sitting on the floor at her feet busily drawing while she read aloud what she had just written. I was eight years old at that time, and I felt my heart would burst with grief as the tears ran down my cheeks. It happened that sixty-one years later I picked up this book again. The pictures it brought to mind were unbearably vivid; Mama had such a gift with words that made all come so alive and burned deep into my heart. But tears flow no more. What I feel now is beyond a grief that can be assuaged by tears, let alone be washed away by tears.

How can one express the longing, the hopeless desire of passionate love for a way of life bound to the country of one's birth—I am not alone in loving the Romania of yesterday, the Romania we lived and worked for. The country and the people now so cruelly separated from us, not by conquest alone but by a devastating power of oppression negating all that was, forming a moat larger and deeper than the ocean which geographically parts us.

Romania is the great love of my life, and if those who read these pages do not understand that this love is the leitmotif of my story, they will be unable to understand my story. I have a story which crosses several ages of our time—this century of ours has seen many ages come and go. Modes of life, cultures, forms of government, new countries have appeared as others disappeared—the changes have followed each other in close succession; thousands of lives have been uprooted. The world is bespattered with unknown graves of those who have gone to face their Maker far from home and friends. Some people have survived thrown up on foreign shores, and one of these lives is mine: a royal child born in a white palace overlooking the capital, to end, so it would seem, in a simple wooden nunnery in the hills of Pennsylvania. In between lie seventy years of joy and grief, of love and hate, of loss and gain, and especially of change—change in all but my faith in God and love of my country.

Mother Alexandra
Orthodox Monastery of the Transfiguration, 1978

LOST SPIRIT

In the cold and empty night, empty of all life and light, my wandering spirit walks abroad.

Heavy snowflakes chasing through space fall noiselessly to the ground. White drifts are driven against that house of my parents in which I was born. Through a broken window moaning upon rusty hinges I try to look into those halls now empty of all but the beautiful and stately memories of the past.

Terrified, my spirit runs along the streets and alleys, looking for known faces, but encountering none save visages full of fear and pain. Shuffling feet now drag heavily where before the crowded, lighted streets echoed to the ring of happy steps. O Bucarest, beloved lost city, how sad has been your fate!

I search to find rest in other places: in a fold of the mountains. Here someone will receive me; I will knock at this door or that; the warmth of a peasant house shall wrap me around; here they will not be afraid.

I see myself go from gate to gate: the snow falls unceasingly, covering all traces. I knock at the windows; I call. Nothing. But here they knew me once! Nothing. The night is cold and silent, my spirit freezes. I let out a cry of hopelessness. Silence. The snow falls unfeelingly: I have not left a single mark where I have walked: I am but a poor lost and wandering spirit, searching paths once well known and loved. But now, today, how can a spirit without a voice be heard?

I had forgotten. I left these places long ago, and I died . . .

Buenos Aires
January, 1950

ONE

I AM ALONE in my peaceful white kitchen. The pots and pans shine brightly. The curtains are gay. I who have lived behind an Iron Curtain, who have faced the accidental death of war and the purposeful death of assassination, have found sanctuary. My life has been spared often by what has seemed sheerest chance: the chance that the bomb fell in the *other* end of the trench where we crouched; that the Communist under anesthetic for an operation in my hospital babbled of the plans for its destruction. Now, in New England, the peaceful shadows are gathering outside as they also are gathering in the silent house, for I am alone, though not lonely; so many thoughts keep me company.

In this big, old New England house there are two rooms I would like to show you; two rooms which hold my present and my past, the substance from which I must create my future. Which will surprise you most—my shining modern kitchen, with every device for American housekeeping, or my bedroom upstairs, with its unrelated collection of things from another life? I do not know. I cannot judge how these things will seem to you.

When at seventeen I visited the United States with my mother, reporters used to ask me, "What is it like—to be a princess?" and I could never think of anything to say to them in answer. How could I compare it with something else when I had never been anything except a princess? One is what one is; and it is not so simple to describe oneself as it is to describe one's surroundings! I can easily compare one place with another; one way of life with another. In Romania, for example, there was a trumpeter who blew a lovely call—a succession of quick, golden notes—when any of us entered or left the palace. Here I come quietly into my own drive; a passing neighbor may nod pleasantly, my key unlocks the door into my silent hall. In Austria a formal and official letter to me would be addressed: *Ihre Kaiserliche and Königliche Hoheit die Durchlauchtigste Erzherzogin und Frau*—"Her Imperial and Royal Highness the Most Illustrious Archduchess and Lady." Here the delivery boy says briskly and cheerfully when I open the door to his ring, "Habsburg here?" as he looks over his parcels. But these are outward things, and of little importance. How one is addressed is a matter of custom. Romanian trumpet and American doorbell both came into being without my advice being asked.

"What is it like—to be a princess?" Shall we find the answer in these two rooms I am inviting you to look at? Perhaps we shall, but there are reservations in that "perhaps." Let us suppose that you have two homes, one in the city and one at the seashore. Quite suddenly while you are living in your city home you are told that in twenty-four hours you must leave it behind you forever. You can take hardly more than you can literally carry—a few boxes perhaps; no more. And even so, some things you are forbidden to touch. Meanwhile at the seashore a few of your neighbors quietly and surreptitiously try to spirit away some of your possessions which they can hide until you come for them. When you have finally assembled again these treasures selected under the pressure of anxiety and grief you will sometimes wish that a few of the choices had been different ones.

It is so with me—and yet these treasures from another world, another life, look very peaceful here. There on one wall of my kitchen is a picture of my mother in Romanian dress among her flowers. For the background of the picture stands Bran, our fairy castle upon a rock, where once I lived. On another wall I have an old icon of Christ, the symbol of that faith which has carried me through all my troubles, and has landed me here on my feet in New England, with the strength to live again.

Yes, to live *again*, because after I left home, which for me has always been Romania, I was as one dead. Not circumstances alone were hard to bear, but the need to live at all. I did not doubt for a moment the physical necessity of my presence for my six children; my love for them was as strong and potent as ever. But inside, the "me" that was me independently of the mother, the wife, the friend—the essential "me" upon which all the rest is built—suffered a mortal shock when my life was severed from my people. So I had to start again, not only outwardly but especially inwardly. Getting down to brass tacks in my kitchen helped me greatly. The need to busy my hands quieted my mind. The effort to cope with simple things and to do them well helped me to start afresh.

How shall I ever forget that first day, when I stood in my grand, new kitchen with no earthly idea of how to cook a meal! I had no inkling of how things were either stewed, boiled, broiled, roasted, or baked.

"Ah!" you say. "*That* is what it is like to be a princess! Not to learn any useful work! What a life of leisure that must be—when one has never even learned to cook!"

It was some such feeling, doubtless, that made one of my recent American acquaintances say to me, "But how good it must feel to you—to know that you are at last leading a really useful life!"

It is difficult for me to think of words positive enough to explain how wrong such a viewpoint is in my case. I was born to the sound of the twenty-one gun royal salute to the daughter of a long line of kings and emperors; therefore, it is true that I started life in one sense from above—from the top, you would say. But the twenty-one gun salute meant also that I was born into an occupation already established for me. Duty was the keyword of my childhood and youth. I was trained to do my duty to my country in all things, to be respectful and loving to my parents, to be loyal to family and friends. "Princes are born in public and die in public"—and between those two occasions they *live* in public. It was my duty to serve others along the lines rigidly laid down for those in my station: to be there when called upon; to listen to the needs of others; to weep with them or to rejoice with them, as they might require. It is only now, when I have lived in other countries, that I can look at all objectively at my training; that I can see how anyone might think it odd that I would feel I must attend a scheduled state banquet on one special evening when, as a young girl, I thought my heart was broken; or that I would drive across the city of Ploesti during a bombing raid to keep an appointment at an important school function where I had promised to preside. These things were duties, but housekeeping was not included in those duties. It would have been egotism on my part to take the time that belonged to the country in order to learn to do things which were already being done efficiently and well by others. Royalty has always got into difficulties when it insisted on leaving its prescribed duties for something it chose to do for its own pleasure.

It is true that I had some leisure time—not much, but a little—which I could spend as I liked. During some of their leisure my older sisters had toyed with cooking. I smile when I think of the paraphernalia brought up to their rooms upon silver trays carried by liveried footmen: the spirit lamp, the dishes, spoons, and utensils; the collection of ingredients properly washed and prepared. But it was only a game, and one that did not happen to interest me as much as it did them. I spent my own leisure in other occupations: learning something about painting and sculpting, and beginning those activities which led later to my serious training in nursing. Even after my marriage, when I found it difficult to cope with the cooks and servants of a strange country, my duty seemed to lie with my children and with my little infirmary, which served the neighboring villages. I solved my housekeeping problems then by bringing in Romanian servants to help me—and that is why, in spite of a disciplined and busy life, I could stand in my shining Massachusetts kitchen utterly ignorant of cooking. Fate had brought me into a new situation. "Duty" had completely changed its face. Lunch for six hungry children had to be served.

Perhaps because as a child I always had a governess near me to remind me of my duty if I forgot it, or to scold me if I failed in it, I have the habit of talking to myself—of encouraging or reproving myself in what I am doing.

"Well, Ileana, my girl," I said to myself, "what now? Let's see what you can do. There was a time when you might not have believed you could face bombardments—but you learned. When you first studied nursing it would have seemed incredible that one day you would desperately but quite calmly operate on patients in need—but you did. And the patients lived, too! Come! Surely you are not to be stumped by a kitchen stove!"

A kind friend had left me ingredients. I had an old cookbook, and I made a stew and it was good. The family approved. Thus I embarked upon my career as a cook. Old memories of appetizing dishes served from my mother's kitchen came to my mind. By dint of thought and other recipes, these slowly took shape. At first I was overwhelmed by all I had to do. Fatigue took possession of my body and my mind. A hundred times I ran up and down stairs; I made the wrong gestures; I burned my hands and arms.

This sounds as if no one had wished to help me, but many did. The kindness that was shown me, the presents I received to start with, were heartening indeed. But I felt I had to stand on my own feet and learn the hard way, for the hard way is the only way. I know from bitter experience where it leads to, to lean on others. It is only when one has learned to stand on one's own feet, when one has found a solid foundation, that it is wise or good to accept help. So I declined much of the kind assistance offered me. I determined to make a home for my children by myself with my own efforts, to be steadily cheerful, and to make them want to help and be part and parcel of this united effort to start living again in a new world. An ambitious undertaking, but the first steps could be taken in my kitchen. So, leaning upon God alone and using those wits He had given me, I pulled through—not only through that first meal and that first day, but through the succeeding meals and days. I learned the ways of the white stove, and then I dared to tackle the automatic laundry machine and the electric mangle.

Yes, I have spent a lot on this kitchen. It may perhaps surprise you to find such complete equipment in a house for which I had at first no furniture outside the kitchen except seven beds and seven chairs. (And—which seems to amuse some of my new friends—a large Oriental rug which was a wedding gift to my mother from her uncle, Czar Alexander III.) But in making my new life I meant to have the best tools from the start, and to wait patiently until I could get other things less essential. Did not your pioneer ancestors do the same when they began their new life in a new world? Tools were the important things for them too. Indeed, in many ways I think they would more easily understand my problems than you do. For they left a civilization dear and familiar to them in order to find something still more precious—the freedom that men down through the ages have discovered must always be pursued, attained, and then defended! Those men and women who stood on the shore at Plymouth, watching the *Mayflower* disappear over the horizon on her return trip to Old England, would understand how one may love the present while still cherishing the past. They who with unaccustomed hands used strange tools to conquer a new land would understand my white and shining kitchen! I feel very close to the spirits of those ancestors of yours, who also learned to live again, as I sit back and gaze upon this cheerful, practical room in which I began a new life by starting quite naturally from the simple essentials of life and of every day's need. Soon I shall gather up and wash the dishes of my frugal meal and go into that other room to which I have invited you.

My mother, Queen Marie of Romania

There, too, I feel close in spirit to your ancestors—those who brought across an unknown ocean a cherished bit of china, a piece of silver, a family miniature—for there I have gathered a few precious belongings from my other life. Come and look at it with me, for the bedroom with its white walls is my castle, and it is also the whole story of my life.

Over my bed hangs a beautiful Spanish crucifix my mother left me in her will. It had remained in Sonnberg, my home in Austria. A Russian soldier during the occupation threw it out the window; a peasant child found and hid it for me, and finally it came back to me. Here I have also the icon my mother was given at the time of my youngest brother's death. She carried it always with her, and since her death it has never left me—although only through the unexpected sympathy of one of my Communist guards was I finally permitted to take it with me when I left Romania.

In this room I draw the curtains, which are yellow with large blue-brown designs. How strange to look out between them on twilight in an American town! They come from the very first house I ever arranged—a hunting lodge in faraway Moldavia which was left me twenty-three years ago by my father. How it shocked the old caretaker to have the heavy plush draperies replaced with such bright ones! The little rug on my floor is an old Chinese one—a soft, perfect blue—which used to lie on the floor of my mother's room in the castle at Bran. From the wall, looking down on her rug, is a watercolor of tulips painted by my mother, who loved flowers; and there is also a wonderful print of the sea. This is both old and new. I once had the same picture, and found a print of it here in the house of one whom today I call friend, and who gave it to me; and thus it is a tie with what was and what is.

Guardian of my days and nights stands a carved statue of St. Benedict, bent in reverent and dignified prayer. Once he stood in a blue-tiled room in the castle at Sinaia beside a marble fountain gushing mountain waters. The windows behind him looked out upon the Carpathians. As a little girl, after bidding my parents good night I always paid a visit to St.

28

Benedict, whose perfect impassive face fascinated me. Did he know that the child who with awe-filled love kissed him good night would one day wrap him in window draperies and desperately win permission from the Russian invaders to take him across an ocean, to a strange continent? So he came here with me, and is as a living presence in my room.

On the mantelpiece are a few beautiful jades—hidden from the Russians in a chimney in Austria for four years. Beside them is a round, flat, gilded box. This holds my greatest treasure—a handful of Romanian soil brought over the Romanian frontier past Romanian guards who had betrayed their country, and who turned away and could not face me when I showed them what the little box contained.

Around me tonight there is peace, contentment: so much to look back on, so much to be grateful for, so much to look forward to. I am not, then, lonely, even though I am alone in this house I have invited you to visit. Besides, tomorrow the children come back from school. There will be happy cries, rushing and stamping up and down stairs, radio and gramophone going, questions and demands, arms entwined around my neck, laughter—and probably a little scolding! It will be home and a happy family life. And there are friends old and new within reach. I can call them if I choose, or they may call me.

But tonight I would rather be still and pause a moment before I look forward to the future or backward at the past. Like Brother Lawrence, "I have need to busy my heart with quietude."

Ileana MSI

TWO

THERE IS one thing I cannot show you in either of my two rooms: one very important thing which I was allowed to bring with me from my old life, and which made the foundation of my new one. You can see it in a photograph of my mother there on the table, but no picture can give you any idea of the living glow and the rainbow fires in the sapphire and diamond tiara she is wearing.

"A tiara!" you say. "Now *that* is what one expects of a princess!"

Yes, I can agree with you. This was truly a royal diadem. Nicholas I of Russia had it made for his wife, the Princess Charlotte of Prussia, when he became emperor in 1825. Through his granddaughter, my mother's mother, it descended eventually to me. My mother wore it at her coronation in 1922. She chose it also to wear on state occasions during the visit she made to this country. And so the tiara and I both entered the United States twice, and together: once in 1926, when I was one of a royal party receiving an official and impressive welcome in New York City, and when the diadem was suitably packed and guarded; and once in 1950, when I flew from Argentina to Miami—hoping to avoid any public recognition—with the tiara wrapped in my nightgown!

Perhaps this is not your idea of how a princess should care for her jewels? It was certainly a surprise to the customs officer! To the tiara, however, it was only one more in a long series of adventures. A few of these I know about: for example, that it was smuggled out of Russia in 1918 during the revolution there. My mother had given it to me when I was married in 1931. I lent it to her to wear at the Jubilee of King George V of England, and she left it in her bank in London because of unsettled conditions at home. After her death I had no small trouble in claiming it, but I got it away from England just before World War II actually began. I kept it in Austria until 1943, when I smuggled it into Romania, and there I saved it from the Communists when I left in 1948. It went to Switzerland with me, and then to Argentina, where I pawned it to put money into an unfortunate business that failed. Its adventures as a single piece of jewelry were then almost over, for it became evident that I must try to sell it in order to pay our debts.

Because by this time I was suffering severely from arthritis, I received permission in May, 1950, to come to the United States for medical treatment. As I gathered all my forces, physical and financial, to make this trip, I felt desperately that I was nearing the end of my endurance. I pawned everything I had of value in order to leave my family in Buenos Aires the money to live on, and in order to redeem the tiara. I could not afford to insure something whose "breakup" value had once been appraised at eighty thousand dollars, so I decided to wrap it in my nightgown and keep it with me in a small bag. Thus with three hundred dollars, a ticket to Boston, and a hidden tiara, I prepared to enter the United States for the second time.

It was a thirty-hour trip by air—over the Andes and finally over the Caribbean—and I had plenty of time to think. Bursitis in my left arm made me barely able to move it, and my back and feet were one continual ache from arthritis, yet I enjoyed that flight. Since my husband is an enthusiastic aviator, he had for many years flown his own private plane. Our trips to England, to Hungary, and to Romania were made by air as matter-of-factly as you plan to travel in your automobile. Indeed, when there are small children and babies in the family, traveling by air is easier than any other method I have tried.

I remember thinking of this with great feeling in 1941! Pregnant with my sixth child, I drove the other five children (the oldest not yet ten) eight hundred miles across Austria, Hungary, and Romania during wartime. Then I often remembered wistfully how short and easy such a journey had been in the plane—the smallest baby riding comfortably in our aluminum *albie*. Perhaps I should explain that an albie is a large, shallow, oval bowl hollowed out of wood, which the Romanians use not only for washing clothes but often as a cradle. When I wanted something in which a baby could rest in the plane, I went to a metalworker in Bucarest and asked him to make me such a bowl out of aluminum, with straps so that it could be carried or could be hung in a car or plane; and we found it very useful.

While I needed no albie on my flight from Buenos Aires to the United States, I felt that I was in a very real sense carrying my children with me, for on the results of my journey their whole future might depend: Six months earlier my two older children had received scholarships in prep schools—one in Pennsylvania and one in Massachusetts—and their letters had been showing a growing confidence and contentment. For most of their lives they had been the victims of war and its accompanying anxieties, first in their father's homeland and then in mine, and the younger children could not remember any other conditions. My husband and I had sought security and a new life for them in Switzerland and then in Argentina, but we had not found it. Could it be that somehow, in the friendly country I had visited as a girl, I might find a new home for them? What princess who is also a mother would not give up a diadem to gain a home for her children!

Anxious, weary, in pain, but strangely hopeful, I finally arrived in Miami, where the long flight was interrupted. I lined up for customs inspection, glad to see that no word of my arrival had preceded me on this second entrance into the United States. I had not realized how public the inspection would be, and when it was my turn and I answered that I had something to declare, I asked if I could unpack my bag in private. The officer was good humored, but a little impatient with my hesitation. When I insisted on it, he made it clear that he thought I was being a nuisance.

"What have you got there, anyway—a corpse?" he asked me.

However, when he finally led me to an office and I opened my bag, it was my turn to feel a little superior. It was obvious that he did not know quite what to do when a tiara turned up in the luggage he inspected. He touched the central sapphire a little gingerly. Since it weighed 125 carats it was nearly the size of a man's pocket watch. Was it real? he wanted to know. When I assured him that it was, he looked still more harassed, but finally he decided that he would send it to Boston "in bond." Together we wrapped it in a newspaper and put it into a box, which he duly sealed and ticketed. It was with a qualm, I confess, that I watched it put into the luggage compartment of the plane for Boston before I myself embarked. If it should somehow be lost, I was losing everything I had, and it was now out of my hands!

Arriving in Boston, I was told that, since it was Sunday, all offices were closed and I would have to wait to claim my "package." I knew no one in Boston except the friend who, with her husband's help, had arranged for me to come to this country. Since she could not be sure of the time of my arrival, I was to let her know when I got to the airport. I found a telephone and stood looking at it stupidly, giddy from my thirty hours' flight and full of pain. I had no idea how to use an American dial telephone, but I was in the United States, where people are kind. A friendly gentleman found the number for me and called my friend. While I waited for her to come and fetch me I tried to forget my present anxiety by looking back across the years since I had seen her—twenty-five of them, to be exact.

I had been fifteen years old then, learning my way in social work, and an enthusiastic member of the Romanian Girl Reserves. Helen Jackson—dark haired, with a gay, round face and twinkling eyes—had come to Bucharest to help start the industrial section of the Y.W.C.A. there. Her songs and fun put us all at ease, and I loved the opportunities to be with her group of girls. Both they and I were free in the evenings, they from work and I from study—but those pleasant times were far in the past. Helen, her job completed, left Bucharest to carry on elsewhere; I grew up; the years passed, with their joys and griefs. Through mutual friends we had again got in touch with each other, and after twenty-five years we met at the Boston airport. Helen was now Mrs. John Beale, with hair turned gray but kindness still unchanged. I—no longer a teenager joining the factory girls of my country in games and songs—was the mother of six children and a lonely wanderer, parted from all I knew and loved. Helen and Jack Beale opened the doors of their home to me until I found a home of my own.

Their solicitude and kindness on that afternoon in May were almost too much for me after so many difficulties. They drove me to Newton along the Charles River, and I found it beautiful—so green and sunny, so clean and free. Then and there I fell in love with New England; it was love at first sight.

In the joy of seeing my two older children again—so changed and grown in the months they had been away—in the need of rest and immediate medical care at the Lahey Clinic (for once I had found a temporary haven I seemed for a time almost to collapse from the long anxiety I had suffered), the diadem was temporarily pushed to the back of my mind. When I did think of it I felt confident of its safety in this friendly country.

Ten days of rest and hospital treatment, however, made me able to find my way to the customhouse and inquire for my "parcel." It took some time for the officials to trace it, and I felt some stabs of alarm until it was finally located in a safe in another building. But even within sight of it there was a further delay—I must get a "customhouse broker"! I had never heard of such a thing, and when it was explained to me I naturally asked:

"But whom shall I get?"

"Oh, we are not allowed to recommend any particular broker, but there are plenty around here," replied one of the gentlemen, waving his hand casually in the direction of the window. I looked out, and my eye fell on a sign across the street: "Stone & Downer, Custom House Brokers." *Why not go there?* I thought to myself—so I did!

Everyone was very matter of fact about the whole thing, both then and the next day, when we all met by appointment in an office of the customhouse on Atlantic Avenue. Everyone was very matter of fact until the parcel was opened, and the officials saw what had been lying about the office for ten days—for even I, who was so familiar with it, felt always a thrill of delight at the radiance of blue and white fire when the tiara was suddenly brought into the light. The faces of the men revealed their shocked amazement. They gasped. Then one smiled, relieved.

"But of course you have this insured!" he said.

"Oh, no," I told him calmly. "Why should I? It has escaped the Nazis and the Communists safely. Naturally I did not expect to lose it here!"

They were evidently uncertain whether to laugh or to scold me, but from that moment we were all friends. One of the men asked me to autograph a visitors' register he kept—"with all your titles and things!" he explained; and I was tempted to draw him a little sketch of the tiara as a souvenir. The age of the jewel was found to make it free of customs, so eventually I walked off with it under my arm—still in its somewhat battered cardboard box. When it was rewrapped with the help of Mr. Irvine, who represented my "Custom House Brokers," I tucked it under my arm again and walked up State Street to the post office, where I mailed the package to a jeweler in New York. That was not its last journey. Sometimes it was guarded by police, at other times my son carried it about in the subway! Finally, after much trouble, worry, and heartbreak, it was sold for a sum much below its value. It was both beautiful and splendid, but my children were in need. As it stood, it neither fed us nor clothed us nor warmed us. I could not even wear it!

So I was grateful on the day when it was gone, even though I felt a traitor to the past and all the proud heads that had worn it. I wondered if my ancestors were turning in their graves—and then I remembered that hardly any of them have graves any more. Does this sound strange to you? It is because the Communist and the revolutionist fear the dead and destroy their bodies. Those graves of heroes which have been shrines for the people, those tombs of rulers which bear testimony to the proud history of a nation—all of them are violated. The remains of bodies are dug up and burned, their ashes are scattered, and the ground is leveled. So it may well be with the graves of my parents, although when I was exiled in 1948 theirs had not yet been touched.

Even then, however, there had begun a violation of which this destruction of graves is but a symbol. Before I left Romania I talked about this with Emil Bodnaras, then Communist Secretary of the Cabinet. I asked him why the Communists were circulating slanders which they knew to be false.

"But surely you can see why this must be," he told me calmly. "You and your class must go. The past must go. As we destroy the very ashes of the dead so that nothing remains, so we must destroy every vestige of love and respect for their memory in the hearts and minds of the people. What your mother did for the people—what you have done for them— must first be tarnished and then blotted out."

Well, the graves have been destroyed. It remains to be seen if the past can be wiped out so simply and completely. Perhaps it will be like my tiara, lost to me in one form but still helping and protecting me in another. Surely this is what our beloved dead would wish for their children—and for the country that was also like a loved child to them. What they have left us, whether it is a diadem or a tradition, they wish us to use for our good. If the forms they found useful must be altered to fit our changing times, their blessing is on us while our purposes remain, like theirs, on the side of right and goodness.

So it was with no permanent regret that I gave up my diadem. It had been a gift from my mother, and what it enabled me to do I consider also her gifts: to pay my debts of two years' standing; to make a first payment on a home in New England; to go back to Buenos Aires and bring the other four children to the United States; to put them into the schools where they had been given scholarships; to take a respite in which I could regain my health and find a way of earning my livelihood. *"Il faut faire face à la vie, car la vie aime les braves."* It is necessary to confront life, for life loves the brave: so my mother once wrote in a book she dedicated to a friend. Many years later, in a time of great trouble for me, I found and opened that book—and the message was as if my mother had spoken to me in that hour.

My parents' early training of me has been of great value, as has been the gift of cheerfulness and natural love for people that God has blessed my nature with. But the real strength to carry on my life, to face disappointment, and strangers, and loneliness, to determine to "live again," comes from something much deeper within me—from the inner force which absolute faith gives. It has sustained me through the past, and I have firm confidence that it will sustain me through the future. But it is only of the past I can speak as I pause in the present to describe something of what it was like to be a princess—a princess with a sapphire and diamond diadem!

THREE

IF YOU are to recognize in my story the people and places I am talking about, I must sketch a background for you and introduce you briefly to the members of my family. I may as well begin by telling you frankly that a princess spends very little of her time wearing a diadem! Although the court functions at Bucarest were always dignified and beautiful, by the standards of some courts they were simple and sober ones. I myself wore the lovely sapphire and diamond tiara on only one state occasion, and that was at a large ball which the Legitimist Party gave in the Hofburg in Vienna, four years after I was married. I went to only one "court ball" in my life, and that was at my own wedding; but there I wore a much smaller diadem given me by my father-in-law. (It was, however, an appropriate one for the occasion when the title "Archduchess of Austria" had been added to my name, because the diadem had originally been a present from Napoleon to Maria Louisa, who was also an archduchess of Austria.)

You must understand that while I was growing up Romania was struggling to take her rightful place with the rest of the civilized world in what proved to be a tragically short period of national independence. There were less than seventy-five years in all; seventy-five years of freedom between Turkish dominance and Communist enslavement—yet the Romanian dream of independence as a nation is nearly two thousand years old. Romans under Emperor Trajan had colonized Dacia Felix, the old name for Romania, in A.D. 101. After the fall of the Roman Empire the inhabitants of the colony retreated to the forested Carpathian Mountains to hide from the Asiatic hordes that swept into Europe. There the people guarded so well their Christian faith and their Latin language and customs that to this day they are a Latin people. They are related to the Italians, the French, the Spaniards, and the Portuguese, and not to their immediate neighbors, who are Slavs.

When the Asiatic conquerors withdrew, toward the close of the thirteenth century, three distinct provinces came into being: Wallachia, Transylvania, and Moldavia, which included Bucovina and Bessarabia until 1812. Occasionally these provinces would win a short period of freedom, but usually they were under a foreign rule. Times without number they were used as battlegrounds in wars among their three great belligerent neighbors—Russia, Turkey, and Austria-Hungary. Without an opportunity for education, forced into the hard and difficult occupations of the peasant, and denied the benefits of the progress developing in other countries, the Romanian people nevertheless tried uninterruptedly to become one country. It is a tragic but an inspiring story, too long to tell here, which came to a climax in 1859, when Moldavia and Wallachia managed to join together under Alexandru Ion Cuza. Still virtually Turkish provinces, and considered by the Treaty of Paris to be "vassal states," they called themselves hopefully the "Romanian United Principalities." When for domestic reasons the principalities decided seven years later to call a foreign prince to rule over them, my family entered the story, for they chose my great-uncle, Prince Carl of Hohenzollern-Sigmaringen.

It was a young Romanian patriot and revolutionist, Ion Bratianu, who was largely responsible for persuading this German prince to leave the magnificent castle of his family, which stands not far from the Black Forest, where the Danube has its beginnings. Down this river Prince Carl traveled to Romania, disguised as the valet of Ion Bratianu to escape the vigilance of the Turks, who were strongly opposed to his election as prince. When he first set foot on the soil of his new country he said solemnly, "Now I am a Romanian!" For him that statement was a sacred pledge, and he devoted the remaining forty-eight years of his life to fulfilling it.

The new Romanian was not only politically intelligent, but he was personally brave. He wrested independence for his country from the Turks in 1877, at the Battle of Plevna. When a shell burst near him, his companions were startled to see him doff his cap and bow in the direction of the explosion, saying, "This is the music that pleases me!"—a gesture which I often remembered during the bombardments I experienced, but which I never felt myself able to imitate.

With the defeat of the Turks, Prince Carl was crowned King Carol I of Romania in 1881. When he had arrived in Bucharest in 1866 someone had said to him, "There is the palace!" and he had asked in honest bewilderment, "Where?" The low house, on a muddy street in which pigs were comfortably wallowing, certainly bore no resemblance to the palaces he had known in Germany. With freedom Bucharest grew surprisingly fast into a modern town, but although the palace was to some extent enlarged and improved, it still remained small and modest. When time and prosperity permitted, King Carol built in Sinaia a beautiful castle, called Peles after the rushing stream that courses through the meadow of the Carpathians upon which it is built, but the palace in Bucharest remained the same. Plans were drawn up after World War I for a bigger and more imposing structure, but my parents felt that other projects for the country as a whole were more important. During my father's last illness the palace burned, and although my brother Carol began rebuilding it in 1931, it was never entirely finished. As I said earlier, the splendor of court spectacles has always been given a subordinate role in Romania. A whole country was fighting for its individuality as a nation, and neither king nor subject had much time to pose in costume!

King Carol I and his poet-wife, Queen Elisabeth (Carmen Sylva), had no children except a daughter who died in childhood. The King's nephew, Ferdinand, my father, had been born second son of the Hereditary Prince of Hohenzollern; but after he was chosen as heir apparent of King Carol, in 1889, he counted himself a Romanian with the same seriousness of devotion that his uncle had shown. At the death of his uncle in 1914 he became King Ferdinand I, and he reigned until 1927. Because of world-changing events, during his reign the Romanian dream was realized to its fullest extent. World War I destroyed much: countries disappeared, thrones crumbled: but to my country it brought the deeply longed-for unity of all Romanians.

In 1916 Romania joined the Allies in World War I—a fact which in itself proves that her royal family no longer thought as Hohenzollerns, but as Romanians. When the Russian Empire fell as a result of the Bolshevik Revolution, Bessarabia, which had been a Russian province, was able to break free and to join the mother country of Romania in March, 1918. Eight months later the disintegration of the Habsburg monarchy freed Transylvania from the Hungarians, after seven hundred years of servitude. In 1866 my great-uncle had been chosen to lead a precarious union of four million Romanians. Fifty-six years later, in 1922, my parents were crowned King and Queen of Romania Mare (Greater Romania), a union of eighteen million Romanians for whom the prospects of permanent status as a nation looked bright and promising.

In 1893 my father, then Crown Prince of Romania, had married Marie, born a princess of Great Britain and Ireland. She was a granddaughter of Queen Victoria—the eldest daughter of the Queen's second son—and so a first cousin to King George V of England. Since her mother was a grand duchess of Russia, sister of Czar Alexander III, my mother was also a first

My father, King Ferdinand I

cousin to Czar Nicholas II—whose visit with his family to Romania in 1914 is one of my most vivid childhood memories.

My parents had six children, the eldest of whom is my brother Carol, born in 1894, who became King Carol II. He abdicated in 1940; and his son, King Mihai I (or Michael, as his name is in English), abdicated under duress of the Russian Communists on December 30, 1947. The second child of my parents is my sister Elisabeta, who was Queen of Greece until she divorced her husband, the late King George of Greece. Next comes my sister Marie, whom we call Mignon, who later became Queen of Yugoslavia. Her husband was murdered in Marseilles in 1934, leaving three sons, the eldest of whom is King Peter of Yugoslavia, deposed in 1941. My next brother is Nicholas, now living in Switzerland; I was born in 1909; and I had a younger brother Mircea, who died of typhoid during World War I. There are great differences of age between us all—fifteen years, for example, between Carol and me.

In the changing European scene the royalty of my parents went undisputed. Their coronation as rulers of Greater Romania had taken place in Alba Iulia—a city in Transylvania dear to the hearts of Romanians because it had been the headquarters of Mihai Viteazul, Michael the Brave. This prince had for a brief period in 1601 gathered together and led Trajan's Dacia Felix, but his murder by his enemies had ended the union of Romanians for another three hundred years. To my country, my parents' coronation at this shrine of Romanian independence was symbolic of their position as the embodiment, the inspirers, and the executors of an age-old dream. To my parents, it emphasized their position as the first servants of the state—and they continued to see to it that their children performed a fair share of the work!

I was the youngest and, because my sisters were both married before I was thirteen, I was the only girl at home during the active years following World War I. The years of my teens were those when my country also was "growing up" as a unified nation. Since I was born five years before World War I, my early childhood had been peaceful, but in a way I remember it now only as a far-off dream of a story I was once told. For in December, 1916, the Romanian army, with the King, his ministers, and Parliament, were forced by the Germans to evacuate Bucarest and withdraw to Jassy, in Moldavia. The collapse of Russia made the position of Romania still more difficult, and it was not until November, 1918, that we were able to return to our home in Bucarest.

During those two years of difficulty and danger I was not too young to understand what was happening. More than 300,000 refugees were crowded into Jassy, a town of 50,000 people. There was little fuel, and never enough food. I can remember being always hungry, and yet wishing I need never eat; for the limited amount of food we were able to get had little variety, and was often so spoiled that in normal times it would have been considered uneatable. Epidemics of typhus and typhoid raged through the town and countryside. In the hospitals where my mother and sisters worked I saw two and often three patients in one bed, while many people died in the streets.

For years I saw in nightmare dreams the funeral "procession" I so often saw as a child in Jassy: the bony horse drawing an ordinary farm cart loaded with dead bodies, piled as high as possible; a rough board put across the wagon bed to make a seat where beside the driver sat a priest in his vestments, and an army trumpeter to sound his call over the mass graves. One day while it passed our house I watched from a window, wondering how such a starved-looking animal could pull the heavy wagon. Suddenly the horse stopped and quite slowly collapsed between the shafts, dead. His fall overturned the wagon, and the naked bodies spilled stiffly out over the street. I remember catching sight of our Romanian cavalry guard rushing out to help as I turned away from the window to run for comfort to the little wooden horse I had brought with me from Bucarest—the favorite toy of my baby brother Mircea, who had died only a month before we were driven from our home.

I remember our Romanian guard also on the day the Bolshevik revolution was declared in Jassy. The house into which our family was crowded stood next to the Russian headquarters, and I looked out of my bedroom window to see the Russian officers lined up against their garden wall, while Russian enlisted men prepared to shoot them. Between our yard and theirs was a dividing wall, with wood stacked against it; and while I watched, frozen with horror, our guard, who had heard what was happening, came rushing around the house. Drawing their swords, they dashed up over the woodpile to the top of the wall and jumped into the Russian garden in time to rescue the officers—but not all scenes of violence ended so happily.

Many of my memories of those two years in Jassy are pleasanter ones. I was the constant observer of my mother's work with our people, and I grew to feel close to them in a way which might not have been possible under more normal circumstances. When I was only seven years old I went about with Colonel Anderson, the head of the American Red Cross work in Romania; and I took great pride in being his interpreter as he distributed supplies and organized relief work in towns and villages. The British and American army officers stationed there also were very kind to me—even though they were unintentionally the cause of my losing my belief in Father Christmas, who is the Romanian Santa Claus.

To guard against my being disappointed when I received no presents, my parents had told me that Father Christmas would not be able to get over the German lines and come to Jassy; and I passed along this information to my British and American army friends at a little Christmas tree party to which they had invited me. They seemed quite shocked at such an idea and said they were positive I was mistaken; they were quite sure Father Christmas would be able to get through the lines. That night in our crowded sleeping quarters I was awakened by confused noises, and peeping through my half-closed eyes I saw more than a dozen of my officer friends filling a Christmas stocking for me while my mother watched. Somehow I knew at once that there had never been a Father Christmas; that always before my own family had filled my stocking; but I knew also that I must seem not to know this! So I lay still, pretending to be asleep, until they had gone and I fell asleep again in earnest.

The stocking I explored the next morning was probably one of the strangest collections of gifts an eight-year-old girl ever received for her Christmas. I remember there were two tobacco pouches—a leather one

Mother and I in national dress, 1927

and a rubber one; a wooden cigarette case; a little gold piece of American money; a small bar of chocolate; a regimental badge (which I still have); tiny British and American flags; and other similar things I have forgotten. I loved every one of them, in spite of the disappointment I still felt at losing my belief in Father Christmas; and I was careful to tell my officers that Father Christmas *had* come, after all! I know now that I spoke more truly than I realized, for the effort these harassed and anxious men made to do a kindness to a little foreign girl in a land strange to them was surely the true spirit of Christmas.

When Colonel Anderson left Jassy he gave me a small sum of money to administer by myself, and I remember how deeply proud and responsible I felt to have charge of this little fund which I could use to help others. It was perhaps during this time that the foundation was laid for my interest in nursing and hospital work, for the great need of our people for help of this kind was burned into my heart. It was impossible to forget those years in Jassy even when we returned to Bucarest and a more normal family life. I was a loved and happy little girl, with many things in my life to enjoy. I still remember, for example, how pleased I was with the lovely dress I wore at the coronation in 1922—cloth of gold, with a blue velvet cape! And I never felt aggrieved or unhappy because the next years were ones of work and study, with none of the freedom and the gay social occasions that I find are taken for granted by teenagers in the United States.

I had little unscheduled time. My life was bound to the growth and progress of my country. So many things were being founded, organized, and developed! I threw myself enthusiastically into all the youth movements then coming into being, and in this way I grew to know intimately the young people of my country. I became a Girl Reserve of the Y.W.C.A. so that I could learn about their organization, and soon I was head of the group in Romania. At school in England for a year, I joined the Girl Guides and took their training courses, so that I was able to help set up the Guides for Romanian girls. I became a part-time student at the

School for Physical Education in Bucarest, getting up at seven o'clock in the morning to make time for my classes there. I learned to know the peasant, the student, and the soldier; the schoolgirl, the factory girl, and the daughter of the courtier. I knew the slums and the peaceful convents. I grew up part and parcel of my country: its aspirations and its developments were an integral part of my very being. Romania was and is the love of my life, the reason for my existence.

I have said this much about my early life because it may help to answer that question I was so often asked on my first visit to the United States: "What is it like—to be a princess?" Perhaps you will be disappointed at my answer, as an American girl was who wrote and asked me for my picture. When I sent her one she wrote politely to thank me, but she added sadly, "I *did* hope it would be one of you in royal garb!" Unfortunately I did not wear "royal garb"! In organizing and later visiting the different sports clubs and youth groups, I traveled up and down the country wearing a uniform, or the peasant dress of the district, or simple modern clothes—whichever was most convenient. The boys' and girls' clubs for the working class of young people kept me out almost every evening, and so I seldom even went to a movie. Although at home we wore evening dress for dinner, that occasion was usually also a responsibility. I was expected to use my education to talk intelligently with our guests, whatever their fields of interest might be. I was not being entertained, but living up to my duty of entertaining others.

I have said that a princess spends little of her time wearing a diadem. And yet, although it did not show in any of my pictures, and although neither I nor anyone else was conscious of it at that time, I know now that I actually *was* wearing a diadem! Only during the most recent years of my life, when I returned to my country in a time of danger and suffering, did I come to realize this. For at every difficult moment I found at my shoulder a friend to help me in my work for my country. The soldier at the station canteen who lifted me quickly to a safe position where I could stand while I distributed food to the crowds of refugees who were

Archduke Anton and Princess Ileana, newly married, 1931

maddened by hunger; the marketwoman who roused a mob to prevent the kidnapping of my two sons; the official who used devious means to get supplies for my hospital—all these and many more who sprang to my side in every crisis would say softly later, "But, Domnitza Ileana, do you not remember when we worked together in—?" And they would name a group or a place which had been a part of my youth, and of theirs. It was only then that I realized I had indeed been wearing a diadem: the diadem of leadership, given me by the love of my people; a diadem which is my most precious possession, and which can never be lost or destroyed!

This is what it was like—for me—to be a young princess. This is why I became so deeply and eternally a Romanian in my mind and heart and soul. Even when in 1931 I married Archduke Anton of Austria, of the Toscuna line of the house of Habsburg, and lived abroad for a time, there were reasons why nothing really changed the old allegiance.

During the first ten years of our marriage we had six children: Stefan, born in 1932; Maria-Ileana (whom we call Minola), born in 1933; Alexandra (Sandi), born in 1935; Dominic (Niki), in 1937; Maria Magdalena (Magi), born in 1939—one month after the war broke out; and Elisabeth (Herzi), born in 1942. For a year after our marriage we lived in Munich, and then we moved to Mödling, near Vienna; but in 1934 I bought the Castle of Sonnberg, which became our most beautiful home. There we led a peaceful life devoted to our growing family and to the people around our estate. I was prevented from taking part in constructive work for my new country, not only by the needs of my children but also by the political changes and the uncertainty of the national situation in Austria. This kept me from feeling that I was really a part of Austria, as I felt I was a part of the country of my birth. Besides, we Romanians are attached to the very soil of our land, and we never can feel the same in any other. So strong was this feeling in me that I had a pottery bowl of Romanian earth under my bed when my children were born, so that they also should be born on Romanian ground!

Circumstances of which I shall speak later took me back to my country in 1944. It is especially of that time and of the years immediately following that I wish to tell you. They stand out most strongly: we lived through so much in those five years! The fight for survival was so strong, so poignant. Although this is my story, it is closely knit with Romania's fate and with that of all Eastern Europe, for what touched one touched all in these latest great historical events of our times. And I had the unparalleled opportunity of seeing it all from close quarters; of knowing personally, and often most intimately, people out of all walks of life. Their tragedies became my tragedies, their hopes and losses mine. Death and violence, plot and espionage, treachery, torture, cowardice, and incredible bravery—these were part of everyday living. My hand trembles even now when I think of all there is to write and to say about those days. For the changes that came about were not merely changes in rulers, governments, or occupations. These changes are aimed much deeper; they are directed at the soul of a people, robbing them not of political liberty alone but of the very decencies of life. The force now dominant in the country of my birth ruthlessly destroys not only those who oppose but also those who do not march in the lead of the new order of things. This force is not against a class, it is against a whole mentality. It stands not for the freedom of the masses, but for their subjugation.

I know how bravely my people stood up against this horror; how their spirit rebelled and rebels still. Their endurance is unbelievable; their sufferings cry out to the skies from which as yet no answer comes. They bend to the storm, but my deep conviction is that they will not break. As long as they can remain on their native soil they will remain true to it!

All this is a far cry from the quiet of my New England kitchen. Let me look back a moment to the last peaceful period of my life: those years in the Castle of Sonnberg. Now the castle stands lifeless, a deserted, empty shell; but let me try to think of it as it was when I first saw it. I would like to tell you something of my life there. Once there was a princess—the story could begin—once there was a princess who lived in a castle!

FOUR

ONCE THERE was a princess who lived in a beautiful castle. But while she was away an enemy invaded it, and her faithful servants hid some of her treasures in an old chimney which they hurriedly walled up. . . .

It is no fairy tale I tell you. Do you see the beautifully carved pieces of jade here on the mantelpiece in my New England bedroom? They came to me from my mother, and are a part of a lovely collection she had; but for three years they were walled up in an old chimney, in a room where Russian occupation troops were staying. The Castle of Sonnberg, more than four hundred years old, had of course many chimneys running through its massive walls; but when I first bought it I did not think of the unused ones as places to hide treasures. Instead, they were merely something to reckon with in our plans for renovating what was a badly run-down building.

Anton and I, like many young couples with small children, wished to find a home in the country. Our problems were the usual ones, with perhaps a few complications which one would not experience in the United States. In the first place, Anton was what is called in German *heimatlos*, which means, literally, "homelandless." This made our first two children also heimatlos, or without citizenship; our next two were Austrian citizens; and our last two were born German citizens—all without our having any choice in the matter.

When Emperor Charles, of the House of Austria, abdicated in 1918, and Austria was formally declared a republic, my husband's parents were among those relatives of the Emperor who refused to recognize the new government. They and their children were therefore declared heimatlos, and compelled to leave the country. Anton's parents took their children to Spain, where they continued to live until the Spanish Revolution began, in 1931. The fact that Anton and his family were forced to leave Spain, just about the time my engagement to him was announced, changed our plans for our future life. For a short time after our marriage we lived in Munich, in Germany; but the Austrian government finally gave us permission to live in Austria. We leased a house in Mödling, near Vienna, and there our first two children were born—still, however, officially without citizenship.

When one lives in times of national crises, one's memories of political events tie in oddly with one's memories of family life. For example, the thought of the Socialist uprising in Vienna in February, 1934, is for me bound in with my deep anxiety for my little son, Stefan, who was seriously ill at that time. He was barely eighteen months old, and his baby sister was less than two months old. Anton had gone to the airdome on the other side of Vienna when I heard the guns begin—first scattered shots, then the continuous fire of machine guns, and finally artillery fire. My anxiety for my sick child, my fear for Anton's safety whether he remained at the airport or tried to make his way home, and the necessity for calming and reassuring the servants when I was far from feeling any assurance whatever myself—all this comes back to me when I think of that difficult period in Austrian history. Chancellor Dollfuss was killed in a similar uprising five months later, but in the meantime he had declared an amnesty for the royalist sympathizers. This restored Anton's citizenship, and also gave Austrian citizenship to our two older children. The next two children were born as Austrian citizens; but the seizure of Austria by Hitler in 1938 meant that our last two children were registered as German citizens, and became Austrian only after the defeat of Germany in 1945.

These later events, however, were not foreseen when in 1934 our quest for a house in the country ended at the Castle of Sonnberg. Although it was thirty miles from Vienna—farther than we had expected to go— and had lapsed into a deplorable condition after having been to some extent modernized and remodeled about twenty-five years before, we liked it so much that we decided to buy it. We began the process of putting it in order by having it cleaned; and at least twenty carloads of rubbish— papers, magazines, wrecked furniture, rags, broken glass and dishes, and plain, ordinary dirt—were hauled away!

As so often happens, everything took longer than we had expected; and since our lease expired at Mödling before the work was finished, we moved into the castle while there were still twenty-four workmen on the premises, and nothing was completely in order. Our heavy furniture was brought in vans, and our car was loaded with small oddments—including, oddest of all, a pony! When one lives in the country, of course one wants a pony for the children. Ours had come from a circus—a Czechoslovakian circus which I had often seen when it toured Romania, and which I had been delighted to see again in Vienna. When I asked the proprietor if he had any extra ponies he would like to sell, he proudly presented me with a *Romanian* pony, named Medias for the Romanian town where the circus was playing when the pony was born. I was of course much pleased with Medias, but I confess that he added no little to our transportation problems on moving day!

In Romania, and in fact in all countries of the Eastern Orthodox Church, no one would think of establishing a household, even for a short time, in a house which had not been blessed. The fact that others who lived there before you had the ceremony performed makes no difference. Each new start made in that house has its own service of blessing, which consists of prayers and readings from the Bible, and includes the story of the First Miracle at the wedding in Cana of Galilee. Then a container of water is blessed, and this water is sprinkled upon all the walls of the house. Asking God's blessing on every beginning is something our church considers important. Not only homes but all institutions—hospitals, schools, factories, everything—begin their activities with this service of blessing. With this same service my children and I began our new lives in our New England home, on the name day of my elder son, Stefan. One's name day, which is the day of the saint for whom one is named, is to us more important than one's actual birthday. I was therefore happy when at Sonnberg, the repairs finally finished, we were able to have our ceremony of house blessing on the twenty-first of May—my Saint's Day, which has always been especially dear to me because it is also a special festival in the Romanian Church.

Many things of course remained to be done in the castle. In parts of it central heating had been installed, but this had to be repaired. Wanting to be entirely modern, we converted the coal heater to oil; but we had scarcely time to enjoy it before the war cut off oil supplies to private citizens, and we had to reconvert the heating system to coal. In all of this, as well as in the maddening struggles to repair and to install electricity and plumbing in a castle built before either had been thought of, Anton was able to plan for and direct the workmen. An experienced pilot who not only flew but could repair his own plane, he was a trained engineer, much interested in mechanics. He was able many times to show the workmen how something they considered impossible could be done; and later, as supplies for repairs became harder to get, he kept our equipment in good running order. The responsibility for directing and maintaining even so small an estate as Sonnberg is something quite different from living on a similar scale in the United States. How can I make you feel that you have visited us in Sonnberg in the middle 1930s?

There is, first of all, the castle to show you. It and the eighteen acres of ground around it were perhaps best described by Anton's sister when she said:

"In the center there is a well; around the well stands the castle; around the castle is an island; around the island is a moat; around the moat is a park; and around the park runs a river!"

While this sounds like a child's riddle, it is actually quite an accurate description of Sonnberg. The castle had been built in the sixteenth century. Square, and without ornamentation except for its tower, it had its rooms arranged around an open courtyard with a well in the center. Originally this location had been swampland; a marshy area which a little river, dividing and then reuniting, had made an island. Some sixteenth-century knight had seen the possibility of locating a fortified dwelling here by digging a deep and wide circular moat in the center of the marsh, heaping up the dirt to create an "inner island" on which the castle was built. The swampland outside the moat was tiled and drained, so that except in very wet weather excess water was carried off into the river. We lived, then, upon a double island, and crossed two bridges when we left our castle.

The nearest town, or what you would call our "shopping center," was nearly two miles away; but the little village of Sonnberg was at our gates. There were still standing some of the very houses that had been built close to the castle for protection four hundred years before. The village included the little church and the schoolhouse, which served not only Sonnberg but also two other neighboring villages, and there was a small general store as well as a baker's shop. When one drove through the village and crossed the little river on the castle bridge, the driveway continued across a narrow section of the "outer island"—which was a parkland of woods and meadows—to the moat. Here one crossed on a longer bridge, of six arches, where the original portcullis had been located; and then the driveway led to the entrance of the castle, with the tower rising in the center of the front wall. On this "inner island," around the castle, we laid out our gardens.

Tradition says that the castle was originally three stories high, with the tower two stories above it, but that the weight of the building had gradually caused it to sink into the "made land" on which it was built. Whether that is true or not, we found it only two stories high, with the other floor hardly more than an unusually light and airy basement. The castle walls are of course of stone, four feet thick; but while the floors of the corridors around the inner courtyard and some of the other passageways were also still the original stone, parquetry had been laid over the floors of the rooms.

Houses in Austria are taxed according to the number of rooms in them, and we were taxed on thirty-five rooms. Does this seem a large number? It did enable me to set aside five rooms for my mother on one of the sides of the "hollow square" in which the castle was built; but our own household required a good bit of space. When the six children had been born, there were eight in our own family; and in addition to this number we had a staff of nine servants: cook, kitchen maid, nursemaid, three housemaids, laundress, housekeeper, and chauffeur. The gardener was also the farmer, and had his own house: but at the castle, besides our occasional guests, there were always from thirteen to seventeen people living; and when my mother visited us she brought with her a staff of five or six people, in order to relieve me of responsibility instead of adding more.

You must remember that our household was not run at all like a modern American establishment, which can have laborsaving devices and make use of convenient and economical stores and services. Our laundry, for example, was done by hand; and washing and ironing for a household of that size was enough to keep a fulltime laundress busy. Much of our food was produced on our own place, and when the war brought increasing food shortages, we added to the number of our livestock. Eventually we had about a hundred chickens, as well as ducks, pigs, seven sheep, a cow, and bees, all of which paid their way in an entirely practical manner and were not regarded as amusements or hobbies. The farmer, the house-keeper, and I sheared the sheep; and after the wool had been washed I spun it into yarn—using a distaff, since I have never learned to use a spin-ning wheel. This yarn was then knit into jerseys, socks, and other articles of clothing for the household. I did much of this knitting, and I also did most of the children's sewing—always by hand, since I had learned to do it that way and not with a machine. Besides the usual vegetables and fruit, we raised potatoes, wheat, and corn on our own land, some of which was leased to the farmer. There was not only the cooking to be done, but the canning, preserving, and drying which stored up our winter food.

In addition to supervising and sharing these practical and everyday duties, I found time for the gardening, painting, and sculpture which I so loved. I wanted to make the highest tower room into a chapel; and in preparation for this I designed cut-stone insets for the eight windows. For each window I used a different flower in the central panel: iris, rose, lily, delphinium, tulip, thistle, hyacinth, and water lily. I had got as far as cutting out the designs in wood with the jigsaw in Anton's workshop, and having them copied in stone by a workman I knew in Balcic, in Roma-nia, when the war came and interrupted this project.

I loved those eight panels! I had worked on them with devoted care, happy in the thought of the use for which they were designed; and I had felt—as one so seldom does about one's own work—that I had done them well. Sometimes I wonder if by any chance they have survived the destruc-tion of our home. I wonder if—stacked at one side of a basement room as they were when I last saw them—they were overlooked when our lovely Renaissance furniture was broken and burned; when our glass and china were smashed on the flagstones of the courtyard; when the portrait of my mother painted by de Laszlo was ripped to pieces and burned; when all of our treasures except those few hidden by our horrified servants were either looted or wantonly destroyed by the Russian soldiers. I did not return to Austria after the war to see the empty shell that had once been our beautiful home, and perhaps this makes it easier for me to go back now in memory to 1935, and '36, and '37, when in spite of threatening war clouds life seemed peaceful.

Besides the care of our growing little family of children (for, as I have said, our six children were born during the first ten years of our marriage) and my necessary occupations for the household, and besides the luxury of working on unnecessary but fascinating projects for beautifying the castle and gardens, I found much to do in the village. My children's nurse and I started a small dispensary for infants and children, which was open one day a week. Many of the treatments begun there had to be followed up at the homes, and I made this my responsibility. When a trained nurse was required by those who were especially needy, I arranged my other work so that I could take over that duty as long as it was necessary. During the six winter months I established and managed a canteen to provide food for about thirty of the poorer school children, getting an old woman from the village to do the cooking. I happened also to discover a small and struggling troop of Girl Scouts in Vienna, and I began working with them—organizing summer camps for them in our park. We even had the joy of having English Girl Guides come to teach us the latest ways of camping, which was an adventure for both groups of girls. Throughout the year there were also the festivals to be celebrated. At Christmas of course there was always the Christmas tree party for all the village children, with gifts for the younger ones and candy for the older ones, which I prepared and wrapped.

Perhaps you can see from this that my days were pleasantly and usefully full. In the evenings I found time for my special recreation and joy, which is reading, while my husband busied himself with his short-wave radio transmitter and receiver, for he is an enthusiastic "ham." We seldom went into Vienna, since we both found our home satisfying. In the summer we took our children to a house on the Worthersee, a beautiful lake in Kernten. Across the lake there were only the Karawanken

Mountains between us and the home of my sister Mignon, Queen of Yugoslavia—a journey of perhaps thirty miles as the crow flew, but much more difficult to achieve by road. With Anton's plane, of course, we were not bound to roads. Sometimes we flew to England; always we spent a few weeks of every year in Romania; but our great events were the visits of my mother, and she found it pleasant to spend a month or two with us now and then.

As I have said, one of the four sides of the castle's "hollow square" was entirely my mother's, and she arranged it according to her own taste. We adored having her with us, and since she brought her own staff her visits lightened my work a great deal—something I was especially grateful for because I did not recover quickly from the births of my children. You will remember, I confessed earlier that cooking and planning menus had never been my strong point. For this reason I appreciated my mother's bringing her cook with her; and she put me at my ease by reminding me laughingly that she, too, as a young housekeeper had urged her father to bring his cook along when he visited her. He had protested a little, saying that he had been invited to bring his gun, his horse, and even his yacht when he visited friends, but never before had he been invited to bring his cook!

My mother's presence radiated life and light. I cannot here find words to tell what she was or what she meant to me: that would in itself make a book. Everyone loved her. Everything was nicer when she was there— even the village children's faces took on a new look, for she was always interested in each one. I remember that one year for Christmas she crocheted a little cap in bright colors for each child. You can imagine with what pride these small Austrian peasants wore a headcovering made by a queen's royal hand!

But those peaceful years ended in 1938, the year when Austria was engulfed by Nazi Germany. For me the anxieties of that time were at first submerged in a more personal grief, the death of my mother. I remember so well how she had looked at the death of her own mother, and how she said to me, "It is a terrible thing to be nobody's child!" I was a little girl then, and I puzzled over what she had said. How *could* one be "nobody's child" at *any* time? But in 1938 I discovered that with Father and Mother gone, one's whole life pattern is altered. There is still life to be lived; there are still responsibilities to be carried forward; but in this world there is no longer the loyal and loving security upon which one relies, often without conscious understanding and appreciation of how much it means. In castle and in village alike—"It is a terrible thing to be nobody's child!"

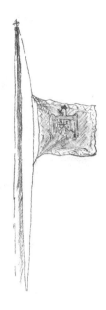

FIVE

HERE IN my New England home I find that the winters are very much like those in Romania. On chilly nights I sometimes put across my bed as an extra covering something which, if I show it to you, may seem an odd sort of blanket. It is an evening wrap made by Revillon in Paris: a full-length cape of ermine bordered all around with Canadian red fox. Yet, beautiful as it is, it has never been worn as an evening wrap in its fourteen years of existence as a cloak, while it has often been used as a robe to throw over a bed.

I have this ermine cape, when so much that would be of more use to me has been lost, through those odd chances which affect one's life in war even more than they do in peace. It had been sent for summer storage in Vienna in May, 1944, just before I left Austria for what I did not know then was the last time. It was stored by a furrier whose premises did not happen to be among those sacked and looted by the Russians;

and four years later he sent it to me in Switzerland, after the Russians had compelled me to leave Romania. Though, as I have said, it occurred to me both then and later that chance might have preserved many things which would be more useful than an ermine wrap, I confess that I feel a bittersweet happiness when it brings me warmth on a frosty night. I have so often seen it thrown over my mother's bed as an extra covering, and I remember so well how it came to serve this purpose.

In 1936 my mother spent Christmas with us in Sonnberg, and we had our usual happy family festivities, shared with the village. Stefan was almost four and a half, and Minola three years old; both of an age to feel the happy anticipation of the holidays. Sandi, like any small girl of nineteen months, enjoyed the bright lights and gay colors in her own way. In the Catholic and Orthodox countries of Europe, Christmas is celebrated a little differently than it is in the United States. For Austrian children, St. Nicholas—the original of your Santa Claus—comes on the fifth of December, which is his day. He is usually dressed as a bishop, in the best-looking robes and miter that can be provided for him. (I remember at our last Austrian Christmas, in 1943, how I used this very ermine cloak to make our St. Nicholas more resplendent; and how I hoped the children would not notice that the saint wore very obvious soldier's boots, which showed below the fur!) St. Nicholas brings with him Knecht Ruprecht, a kind of captive bad spirit who is prepared to punish any naughty children the good saint may find. Knecht Ruprecht is usually impersonated by someone dressed in dark, furry clothes. He has a tail, and he is loaded with chains which he rattles loudly and fearsomely. Since I never wanted the children frightened, our "Knecht Ruprecht" was represented only by a rattling of chains outside the door; and he was at once dismissed by St. Nicholas because there were no *naughty* children present! Gifts are left later that night by the saint, after he has interviewed the children; and he leaves them either in stockings hung up or boots left standing by the hearth. On the twenty-fifth of December Christmas is observed as a solemn church festival, although a Christmas tree—supposed to have been brought by the Christ Child—is lighted in every home, and carols are sung by the family.

I do not think my pleasure in that Christmas of 1936 could have been more deeply felt had I known it was the last Christmas we would spend with my mother, and that within those holidays I must find and store up my last treasured pictures of her when she was still well and strong and gay. Those bright days were not clouded with this knowledge. Instead, my pleasure was spoiled only by my resolve to keep my mother from knowing that I was again pregnant, for I knew she would worry at the prospect of my having another baby so soon when the other three births had been such difficult ones. There were occasions when it took all my will power to conceal how very ill I felt, but I managed it somehow, and she left without knowing that in July she would have another grandchild. One of the most vivid memories I have of that holiday season is the picture of the graceful figure of my mother gliding over the ice, for she was an accomplished skater, and the moat at Sonnberg provided a wonderful skating rink. There was nothing to warn me that this was her last visit to the castle.

In the spring of 1937 she had the first indication of the illness to which her death over a year later was finally ascribed. Because of a strained family and political situation about which I will not speak at this time, I was at first not allowed to go to Bucarest to see her; but in April I was finally permitted to spend a week there. She continued to improve slowly until she could at last be moved to the castle at Sinaia; and when Dominic—Niki—was born on July 4 she was able to come briefly to the telephone so that she herself could talk with Anton about her new grandson, and about how I was feeling.

When Niki was a month old we went as usual to the Wörthersee for the summer. This time Niki occupied the albie in the plane, and we had as additional passengers a dozen chickens to ensure fresh eggs for the children. However, I remained anxious about my mother. I continued my urgent requests to be permitted to come to Romania to see her, and during the last of September we were allowed to join her at the Castle of Bran. We went with her to Balcic, where she had another hemorrhage in October, and had to be moved to Bucarest. There she seemed to be recovering gradually, and we celebrated her sixty-second birthday with her on October 29—an occasion when so many of her people expressed their joy at her recovery that she was almost overwhelmed by it. It was during those weeks that she saw a picture of the ermine cloak sketched in a Paris fashion magazine, and said sadly to me:

"How I would love to have this if I were well! But I shall never wear anything of that kind again."

I decided inwardly that she *should* have it; that perhaps it would supply a little impetus to her fight for health and strength if she felt I expected her to grow well again and to wear an evening wrap. I ordered it for her Christmas gift before we left Romania for Sonnberg in November, and it arrived to give her surprise and pleasure—but a pleasure marred because she was not well enough to come to us at Christmas, and I was not permitted to spend Christmas with her in Romania.

Not until February of 1938 could I see her again, when she was well enough to be taken to Meran, in the Italian Tyrol. I joined her there, and it was there I first saw the ermine cloak thrown across her bed as a robe, for there was still no possibility of her wearing it as I had hoped to see her do. Her condition was the result not only of illness but of the anxiety and strain in the family which she saw only too clearly were affecting her beloved Romania. My constant worry about her prevented my following the mounting Austrian crisis as closely as I would otherwise have done. It was therefore with deep shock that I heard over the radio on March 12 the news that Nazi troops had crossed the Austrian border, to complete the following day what Hitler hypocritically called the *Wiedereingleiderung*—the "again-interlinking"—of Austria with Germany.

My responsibility for my children at once took precedence over everything else, in my mother's mind as well as in my own; and she sent me immediately in her car to Innsbruck, where I took the first train for Vienna. As we drove through the Brenner Pass to get to Innsbruck, which is in the Austrian Tyrol, we crossed the frontier, and there I first saw the reality of what I had been hearing on the radio, for the Austrian coats of arms had been torn from the customhouse, and were thrown on the ground.

The journey across Austria, which normally would have occupied nearly the whole day, took even longer because of the "glorious liberation" Austria was suffering. At irregular intervals the train was stopped and entered by bands of hoodlums which included young men and women in their late teens and early twenties, irresponsible and reckless in the general disorganization that was taking place. They would demand that the conductor show them the passports of all the passengers, and would talk loudly of the treatment being given to anyone "disloyal" to the Nazis. I realized very quickly that the name "Habsburg" on my passport would be certain to win instant and unfavorable attention, but before I had much time to worry about what to do I received a reassuring look from the conductor. In the instinctive way one sometimes senses the presence of a friend—or of an enemy—I understood that he would help me; and I noticed during the day that when he was ostensibly showing the passports to the self-appointed "loyalty investigators" he managed to shuffle them in such a way that mine was apparently never seen. It was a kindness for which, of course, I could not thank him for fear of endangering him if I were overheard, since already I began to realize how conditions were.

If I had not realized this before, I would have done so at once at the station in Vienna, where Anton met me when the train finally arrived, for a Nazi flag was prominently displayed on our car. When I expressed my horrified unwillingness to drive with such an insignia, Anton explained grimly how it had happened. Early that morning fifty men of the SA had arrived at the castle, prepared to take over the premises in order to prevent any Habsburg from trying to interfere with the glorious entrance of Austria into the Reich. Their "moving in" had of course frightened and disorganized the servants, which in turn had upset the children; and

Anton had had his hands full all day. There had been moments when their frank suspicions of all archdukes, combined with sudden absence of law and order, had made them a definite danger. When the wire came announcing the time of my arrival, they at first refused to consider allowing Anton to drive to Vienna to meet me—something which was necessary if I was to get to Sonnberg that night. Eventually, however, as he pointed out patiently and repeatedly that no one was running away, but that instead I was *returning* to the Reich, as it were, they agreed to let him leave with the car. After all, they had the children and all our possessions as hostages! But—Anton explained to me—no car could move anywhere without the Nazi insignia. It therefore remained on the car as I returned to Sonnberg and our fifty unexpected house guests.

For ten days those men slept in our house and barns, followed us about suspiciously, and—which made us honestly afraid of them—showed themselves so obviously unfamiliar with the firearms they carried that they were a menace to their own safety and that of everyone around them. It soon became plain to us that they were in general the riffraff from neighboring villages, including a few from our own Sonnberg, who had never been willing to work honestly, and who had been encouraged to believe that the new regime would put them "on top" with no effort on their part. Hastily armed and irresponsible groups like this made everyone afraid to do anything which might seem "uncooperative" with our self-appointed "liberators," and life became difficult in both small and large ways.

That first evening, for example, when I telephoned my mother in Meran to tell her I had arrived safely, and that Anton and the children were all right, there was considerable confusion because the operators in Austria insisted that we both talk German instead of the English we had always used. This sudden and arbitrary order, plus the poor telephone connections, confused and worried my mother, who must have complained about it to someone. At any rate, many weeks later when she was moved to the Weisser-Hirsch Sanatorium in Dresden, Hitler's aide-de-camp was sent around with a tremendous ring of orchids and Hitler's humble apologies that a "foreign queen" should have been forced to speak German in order to telephone her daughter. But by that time the Nazis had done so many terrible things in Austria that this particular offense seemed to me an extremely minor one for which to apologize.

At Sonnberg we "entertained" our fifty SA men for ten days, after which they were sent somewhere else. During the first month of the "liberation," in addition to the constant strain and anxiety caused by our "guests" and the fear that more might come in at any time, we were subjected to three or four *hausdurchsuchungen*, or house searches, each time by a different group of men from the black-shirted Storm Troopers, or from the Gestapo. These house searchings had their own technique of accomplishment, and I gradually learned the corresponding technique of meeting them.

Room by room the SS men would search the castle, turning out drawers and closets and throwing their contents on the floor, where everything was left to be put in order later—*if* the household passed the inspection and the householder therefore remained in residence! Books were leafed through, papers and letters looked over, furniture was searched for secret hiding places, and the entire house was left in confusion and disorder. At Sonnberg we were told that they were looking particularly for any evidence of "monarchistic" activities on our part; or for indications of lack of confidence in the Reich, which might be shown by our sending money or property abroad or by our receiving letters from friends outside which might indicate that we had in any way plotted against or even criticized the government.

The technique of meeting the house searchings, I found, was to remain entirely calm and friendly; to assume that the SS men were doing their duty with the best and most helpful intentions possible; to rise to meet them as if they had been welcome guests; to continue one's normal activities except when asked to go from room to room with them; to make no sudden movement, even to save some precious thing from destruction; to keep one's hands quiet and relaxed; to do nothing which could be interpreted as trying to conceal or hide anything; to answer questions easily and frankly. My life of discipline once more stood me in good stead here; for after the fourth hausdurchsuchung in as many weeks, the leader of the last group of SS not only told me that we would have no more of such invasions, but he added:

"If all princesses were like you, how pleasant it would be!"— a compliment which I received with mixed emotions.

Late that spring my mother was moved to a sanatorium in Dresden, Germany; and I was able to get permission to leave Sonnberg to see her. Dresden is almost directly north of Vienna, but a large section of Czechoslovakia lies between Austria and Germany at this point, and my journey was in consequence made much longer because of the necessity of staying within the borders of the Reich. Since conditions were still unsettled in Austria, Anton and I took the children with us for the long trip; but for our second journey to Dresden, in June, we felt that it was safe, as well as much more comfortable for them, to leave them at home. On this occasion, by special permission from both countries, we were allowed to fly over Czechoslovakia, which shortened the trip for Anton and me—a detail which I mention only because the free and unrestricted travel in the United States may prevent your realizing how complicated even short journeys can be in Europe.

In Dresden I had my last glimpse of my mother when I turned to wave good-bye as we left the sanatorium, and from her bed at the window she lifted her hand to us in farewell. From Dresden, still very ill, she was taken back to Romania in early July, and from there I received my last message from her directly—a telegram telling of her arrival, and ending "God bless you all." One of my greatest griefs has been that although I was a nurse I was not permitted to be with her and to assist in caring for her. Anxious and unhappy because of this, and not reassured by messages she sent me through other people, I postponed our usual summer trip to the Wörthersee. It was on July 18, 1938, that I received a telephone call telling me my mother was dying.

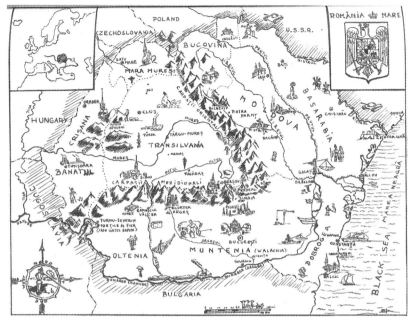

Map of Romania drawn by Stefan, Archduke of Austria

Here the difficulties of the political situation in Austria, which had been a constant undercurrent of worry through all my concern for my mother, met us in full force. You can imagine receiving such a message; perhaps you have at some time received exactly that same message; but in the United States you cannot imagine being unable to respond to it—yet that was my situation. Austria had been taken over by Germany, and therefore there was no longer any such thing as Austrian citizenship. Our Austrian passports were worthless, and the new German passports had not yet been issued. Not only were we unable to leave the new "Reich" without a passport, but it would be hopeless to attempt to cross the Hungarian frontier and travel across Hungary without one. It was with the power of desperation that I started the wheels moving: it was through the kindness of many individuals who recognized my grief and desperation, and who from sheer human kindness dared to deviate a little from the official pattern, that passports for Anton and me were issued within an hour.

I still remember the last frantic mishap. The Hungarian Consulate in Vienna had been notified that we would be coming for visas on our new passports, and they were kindness itself about agreeing to wait. Inside the Consulate sat an officer ready to give us our visas—but at the door of the Consulate stood a porter who had not been notified of our arrival, and he refused to let us in.

"The Consulate is closed!" he announced firmly, and shut the door in our faces.

All the representatives of other countries were of course being besieged night and day by members of the oppressed minorities, and by those in political disfavor, for visas which would enable them to escape the Nazis; and the porter undoubtedly had orders not to admit people after hours. When he closed the door in my face, I felt for a moment that insanity of despair which is the special cross of the oppressed and the downtrodden. Then, rallying my forces, I pressed the doorbell again, keeping my finger on it until the porter in a towering rage opened the door a crack to threaten me. Throwing myself against it, I thrust my foot and my arm into the crack, and said with passionate determination, "But I *shall* go in!" And on this wave of determination I was indeed inside, with neither the porter nor I knowing exactly why he had given way, and in a short time I had the Hungarian visas.

With no further news of my mother, Anton and I set out in the car for a nineteen-hour drive across Austria, Hungary, and Romania. In the very early morning we came to the Romanian frontier, and I asked the guards if they had any word from the palace, but they said no—no word. When I returned to Austria ten days later they begged my forgiveness.

"But we could not bear to be the ones to tell you of the Queen's death, Domnitza!" they said.

Yet on that first morning I think I knew in my heart what had happened, even though I refused to acknowledge it to myself until we came to the town of Cluj after sunrise and saw the flags all flying at half-mast. My mother had died at five o'clock the day before—while I was still desperately struggling for permission to come to her. And she left me, among other outward symbols of an inner love and tenderness and understanding which are rare even between mothers and daughters, the fairy castle of Bran which we had both cherished so deeply, the sapphire and diamond diadem which has enabled me to begin a new life for my children, and an ermine evening wrap which lies across my bed on frosty nights.

SIX

S NOW FELL relentlessly and slowly out of a leaden sky. I watched from the low window of our Vienna apartment and saw with anxiety and a certain exasperation how the drifts piled ever higher in our sodden little garden. It was February 24, 1942, and I was making my first visit to Vienna after the birth of my sixth child, little Elisabeth, now over five weeks old and snugly asleep in her cot. She and I had made our first journey as separate entities, though we were still bound together by the flow of life my breasts held for her. I had intended to stay in town only a day or two for medical checkups and the necessary errands for the family, but twice our attempts to reach Sonnberg had been prevented by high winds, storm, and snow. Once we had managed to get some distance out of Vienna before the impassable roads forced us to go back, with the waste of gasoline lying heavily on my conscience.

I was anxious to return to the other children, and I felt both a physical and a mental depression. The journey had shown me that I had by no means recovered my normal strength, but this was not all. After the sober months at Sonnberg, where I had been preoccupied with the effort to produce food and to keep up the morale of our household and of the village while I awaited my child's birth, I found that Vienna jarred strangely on my nerves. Friends had taken me to the opening of a fashion collection, and I had been astonished not only at the amount and variety of beautiful materials, but at the conversations around me. It seemed to me incredible that people could spend thought and money on such nonessentials in wartime. I felt indignant at their agitation because of the restrictions on beauty parlors and other luxuries. Oddly enough, my indignation was increased rather than lessened when I succumbed and ordered things for myself! I felt ashamed that I, who knew better, should forget even for a moment the sacrifices being made at the front.

At Sonnberg war seemed very close to us always. When I heard that the son of one of our neighbors had been killed in battle I had written in my journal:

> Only nineteen years old! He was not a friend—he was hardly more than an acquaintance; but I can see him as he was two years ago on the Wörthersee. Tall, strong, sunburned, full of fun and laughter, enthusiastic and clean-spirited. I weep for this sacrificed youth—for the youth everywhere being sacrificed. He fell at Kertch. Suddenly this battle has a face for me—Jurgen's life-filled face, now suddenly still.

In the quiet countryside, where everyone was a friend or an acquaintance, there were few battles which did not wear the face of someone known to us. In the country, too, the lives of all women were changed more completely and obviously than was usually the case in the cities. The restrictions in fuel for both house and car meant immediate and radical changes in living where other transportation was not available. The rationing of food and clothes meant that farm produce must be more strictly accounted for; that certain crops must be increased and certain alterations be made in the number and kind of livestock one owned. The mobilizing of all men, until only the very old or crippled remained, meant that farm tasks must be taken over by women. All these things made life strange and difficult for us who were suddenly saddled with the entire responsibility of the estate as well as of the household. Anxiety, privation, and difficulties of all kinds at first made a nightmare of the decisions between unknowns which were constantly being forced upon us.

Responsibilities pressed upon one so constantly that there was hardly time for the normal activities of living. I remember how in October, 1939, there had come finally an afternoon when I admitted to myself that the birth of my fifth child was near. Yet I denied the feeling as long as possible so that I might put all in order. I went about the estate, checking to see that everything was well organized for the time I must remain in bed. I drove my car into the garage, which was some distance from the house, and emptied it of water because the nights were getting cold and I must not risk damage to the engine. I went to the kitchen to see that all was well there, and made a tour of inspection throughout the house before turning my attention to my increasing pains, and calling the doctor to come. For in wartime, as in peace, I wished my children to be born at home. It is something about which I feel strongly, for birth is a family event. I loved that hour when it was possible to call the other children in to see the newest member of the household.

This first of my two children born in wartime was also a daughter, Maria Magdalena, whom we called Magi. Her christening service had to be postponed because her father, like so many other fathers, was at the front and did not even hear news of her birth immediately. Anton had been conscripted in the fall of 1938 at the time of the Sudeten crisis, and had been stationed for three weeks at the frontier, which was only about an hour's drive from Sonnberg. I remember going to see him once, and having someone point out to me how the little houses of the frontier guards had been put on wheels so that they could be moved with ease as the frontier was changed from one place to another—something which seemed to me to show how artificial are many of the boundaries between men and countries. It is not those which can be so easily moved which need concern us unduly, but it is our failure to discern the basic and eternal boundaries before we have crossed them which leads to many of our difficulties.

The Sudeten crisis temporarily over, Anton had been dismissed and had come home in time to help me deal with the billeting of a medical detachment in Sonnberg—the first of thirteen such billetings upon us, lasting from three days to six weeks. This first time a part of the command, including about ten officers, was assigned to the castle itself; and another readjustment of the household had to be made. In such a case one was required to furnish linen and blankets, rooms, beds and other necessary furniture, and also to arrange that the kitchen and living quarters of the house be shared. A few of these close contacts with the army made us realize that universal conscription was very near, and Anton decided to volunteer so that he might choose his service—that of the air. After completing his infantry training, which was required of every soldier, he was assigned to the air forces, first as Kurierstaffel, or flying courier, and later as flying instructor. While I knew intellectually that in war each post is a part of the whole, I confess that it was emotionally a certain consolation to me in those dark days to feel that Anton never actually carried arms or was obliged to kill, for I was torn between my conflicting loyalties at this time, as I shall explain later.

Driven by a feeling that I wanted to be of service, as soon as I had stopped nursing Magi I entered a systematic course of Red Cross training to supplement and complete the courses I had previously taken in England and in Romania. I did not join the German Red Cross because to do so involved swearing fidelity to Hitler, and this I could not do. Therefore I never received a certificate for this nursing course, but the training added a great deal to what I had already learned from both theory and practice. Except for this training course, my life became an irregular one of wartime responsibility and anxiety, with the family calendar keyed to Anton's furloughs. When he had leave which was too short to allow him to come home, I made long journeys across country to be with him. I remember especially one time when I made a fifteen-hour train trip to Berlin to meet Anton, who had a twelve-hour leave there. An infection which I had been fighting was aggravated by the long, cold trip, and Anton had hardly gone back to the front before I became so ill that I went to the Romanian Legation, where I was put to bed with a high fever. I was in such pain that when there was a bombing raid during the night I refused to let them try to move me to the shelters in the basement. It was not until morning that I learned how one of our Romanian couriers, in from Bucharest, had refused to allow his princess to remain alone during the raid, and had sat outside my door all during the night. After I had recovered I was informed by the Romanian Minister of our loss of Transylvania to Hungary and of Bessarabia to Russia, then an ally of Germany. It was also his painful duty to inform me of the abdication of my brother, Carol II, and of the distress and confusion in my country—matters of which I will say a little more in a later chapter.

Some incidents of those years, however, were less serious; and we seized on these with exaggerated gratitude because they allowed us to pretend for a moment to forget the horrors of war. I remember a brief vacation at the Wörthersee in 1940, during Magi's first summer, when we floated her in an old airplane tire, which was just the right size for her, while the other children swam about in delight at her being able to be with them in the water. It was this same summer, when Anton joined us during a longer furlough than usual, that I drove a car which had the Romanian registration of "6 B," with the "6" made in a rather square shape. The first thing we knew the police were investigating us! A citizen of the town had gone to them in great excitement to report that a German officer had been associating with a woman who was obviously an English spy, since she drove a car which was plainly marked "G B" for Great Britain! When the police assured him that he was mistaken, confronted him with us, and reproached him for jumping at such a farfetched conclusion, he was quite unrepentant, and said with righteous indignation: "Even with all the wartime restrictions, one ought still to have *at least* the right to *denounce!*"

It was in March, 1941, that I had my nearest approach to any contact with Hitler, and that was an extremely remote one. I had gone to Vienna from Sonnberg on business, and unfortunately chose quite by accident the day when Hitler had come to sign the Tripartite Pact. The streets were crowded with people hoping to see him pass, and I was forced to park my car many blocks from where I needed to go, and to walk a long distance to transact my business. My life was a strenuous one, and I never seemed to have strength enough to get through my days. Somehow this walk was in the nature of a last straw, and in addition to my general dislike for Hitler's policies I felt an absurd but overwhelming resentment of the fact that his presence in Vienna was making life even more difficult than usual. I took great care—and a certain pleasure—in making sure that I did not go near any place where I might catch even a glimpse of him or his car!

Of such great and small incidents were the years after my mother's death made up—of such incidents, all occurring against the almost monotonous background of daily living under increasing difficulties and growing sorrow. With five small children, I was not spared the ordinary diseases of childhood, which had to be tended without neglecting my other duties, and with less help than in normal times because of the increasing demands of war. Some of these illnesses were more serious than others. Alexandra, who was six in 1941, had a severe infection in both ears, and it was finally decided to send her to Sinaia in Romania for a few months, where my own childhood nurse could care for her. After the usual delays of red tape, her passport and visas finally arrived, but this was not until her new sister Elisabeth was nearly two weeks old.

It was partly to telephone Sandi from the Consulate in Vienna that I had come to town that February in 1942; but when I had heard from her that she was happy and contented, and from my nurse that Sandi was already gaining in strength and weight, I felt the impatience about which I have spoken. I felt alien to those acquaintances in Vienna who were trying to ignore the war, and my sympathy with those friends who had lost dear ones only made me more conscious of the fact that I was doing nothing constructive in the city. Indeed, as I looked out on the falling snow which was keeping me separated from my other children, I felt with growing frustration that I was really doing little that was constructive at Sonnberg. There we had gradually achieved a certain system under which I was no longer needed personally as much as I had been at the beginning of the war. Surely, I felt, there must be something more I could do which would satisfy my longing to be of real use. Small Elisabeth, whom we had already begun to call Herzi—Little Heart—slept placidly on in the gathering twilight. And just then, as if in answer to this deep wish of mine, the telephone rang.

On the wire was an acquaintance who had been visiting one of the soldiers' hospitals in the city. She thought I might be interested to know that quite by chance she had heard of a wounded Romanian officer among the patients. I took down the address of the hospital and made a quick mental calculation. Did my gasoline permit my taking the car or must I go by streetcar? I decided to risk the automobile, since it would be so much quicker, and without difficulty I located the small and unimposing hospital, established in an old school building. I inquired at the desk for a Romanian officer. Yes, there were even *two* Romanian officers, I was assured—but this was not a visiting hour! I exerted myself to waken the sympathy of the officer in charge for these men who were wounded and in a strange country, and presently I was taken to them. They were not too seriously hurt, but they were unhappy because they had no clothes or personal possessions, no way of writing to their families, and no idea of how long they would be kept in this particular hospital. They had been sent to Vienna with thirty wounded soldiers, but assignments to different hospitals had separated them from their men, and they could find no one who would help them get in touch with one another.

They were delighted to meet "a Romanian lady" who could speak to them in their own language, and they told me their troubles promptly and in detail, but obviously with little hope that I—whom they considered simply another fellow citizen somehow stranded in Vienna—would be able to do much about it. I wanted them to feel reassured about this, but I felt a little hesitant about just how to introduce myself without making them feel shy. Finally I decided to leave them the Romanian paper I had got at the Consulate that day, and had had no chance to read. Its address included my full title, so I asked them if they would like to have some news from home, and left the paper on one of the beds when I turned to go. I was hardly outside the door before I was called back; and after quick apologies for their failure to recognize and address me as *Altetza Regala*—Your Royal Highness—they helped me to make more specific plans for finding the other thirty Romanians. Learning who I was not only made them feel I might be able really to do something about their troubles, but also—I was happy to notice—made them feel with relief that they had found someone from whom they had a *right* to expect help. It was moments like this that made me glad I was a princess!

I do not remember exactly how many offices and hospitals I visited before finding those thirty soldiers, but eventually I located not only these men but other groups of Romanian wounded—some who were in serious condition. The roads to Sonnberg continued impassable for nearly a week, but in that week I found and entered upon another road, which led into one of the richest periods of my life. When I now look back upon that snowy February day, I realize what a long, long way I have come and how much I have learned. I know now that love and pity, implemented with the will to serve, can transcend all things and work incredible miracles; that one can overcome shyness, fatigue, fear, and even what seems uncontrollable physical repulsion, by a simple overwhelming longing to serve and be of use. I have learned that there is an entrance to most men's hearts, be they foes or friends, regardless of political opinion or national convictions. Before death and pain men are equal, and most men realize this and are ready to help one another. I have learned that where there is faith in the Lord, His work can be done.

The road along which I learned these lessons, and which led me into more deeply moving personal contacts than any I had had before, seemed a short and simple bypath as I took my first steps upon it. In the beginning it was easy to find out and satisfy the needs of our Romanian wounded. Most important at first, I found, was to talk with their doctors and nurses; to translate the soldiers' requests and questions, and the answers which were made in a language unknown to them; to give them a feeling of security by showing them there was someone who cared what became of them in a strange land. I thought much of my mother during those days, and of what she had done for our soldiers during World War I; of the endless hours she spent in the hospitals in Jassy, going fearlessly not only among those who were wounded, but among those dying of typhus. I felt I knew what she would want me to do, now that she must work through the hands of others. I knew a call had come that I must obey; that I must find a balance between its demands and those of my family life; and in large measure I succeeded.

Still nursing little Elisabeth, I made frequent visits and increasingly longer stays in Vienna, taking her with me. More and more Romanian wounded arrived in Vienna, and besides visiting the old hospitals I spent long hours locating and visiting those which were rapidly being improvised in all parts of the city. The work became too much for me alone, and since the officials at the Vienna Consulate began to feel I was making too many demands on them, I went to the Romanian Legation in Berlin. While at first they were inclined to feel that this was not so important an affair as the political crises with which they were dealing, eventually–like the tiresome widow in the New Testament–I was heard because of my importunity. Despite the interruption of an operation which I myself had to undergo that summer, the machinery for helping our wounded was set up so that we could not only take care of finding and sending home the less seriously hurt, but could assemble in one hospital most of those who must stay for longer treatments, such as plastic surgery.

Put together in a few short paragraphs, this work which I felt had been given into my charge sounds impersonal and even undemanding. What do you think of when you read these pages? Of my visiting the wards as a dignified and royal Lady Bountiful, distributing small gifts? In a wartime economy the smallest gift of extra food, of tobacco, of clothing, of money for stamps and personal needs, represented thought and effort, and was obtained only by constant appeals to friends both in Austria and in Romania. I became a beggar of the first rank, regardless of royal dignity! Do you picture me sitting calmly, presiding over the files of records, so that friends might find one another and news from the home villages might be properly distributed? When the wounded arriving from many points are men of many nationalities and languages, records have a way of being lost; and it is only by constant inquiry and careful piecing together of information that any sort of system and order can be attained. The Viennese could be pardoned for feeling that their own nationals should be given first preference, and it required tact and patience to win assistance for my Romanians—who were, after all, only "foreigners" in Austria. In the end, dozens of people were helping with the work, but their efforts had to be coordinated in order to be of real value; and there was little "calm presiding" done by anyone! Do you think of me sitting graciously beside the bed of a wounded soldier—his wounds of course located in some part of his anatomy where they are out of sight and can give no offense to anyone—and writing at his dictation a tender letter to his mother or his sweetheart? The number of such pleasant bedsides is small compared to wounds which cannot be hidden; and most of these dictated letters one writes with anguish, knowing the anguish they will carry to a loving heart. And there are other letters which must be written; letters which can no longer be dictated by the soldier at whose bedside one has sat.

Actually there was no formal and regular pattern to the work I did during every bit of the time I could spare from Sonnberg. Often one thing led to another, so that from one simple errand connected with one particular soldier I would be led to another task, and another, and another. I found myself doing things I would not have believed I could bear to do, and accepting calmly sights and sounds more horrible than I had ever imagined could exist. I began to realize that my childhood in Jassy had a purpose in my life; that those heartbreaking experiences had prepared me for what I must now do.

I remember one young Romanian student, dying of tuberculosis which he had developed at the front. He asked so little for himself, he was so patient and uncomplaining, and he faced death with such courage that he gave help and inspiration to me whenever I visited him. We had talked much of our beautiful Romania, where flowers which must be cultivated in other countries grow wild and cover the fields with carpets of brilliant color. He died on a cold and dreary day, and I felt suddenly that I must try to find at least a few blossoms which could be buried with him as a symbol of the beauty we both loved. When I returned to his ward with them, his body had already been taken to the hospital morgue. Could I take the flowers there? I wanted to know. But certainly!—that is, if I was sure I would not be afraid to do it?

I saw no reason to feel afraid. I had seen death: I had covered the still face and made the sign of the cross while I prayed as our Orthodox Church taught us—a prayer which in English is like this:

God of all souls and all the body, who hath trodden upon death and hath put the devil in bondage, and hath given life to all Thy world; even Thou, O Lord, rest the soul of Thy slumbering servant in a place of light, in a place of greenness, in a place of rest, from whence hath flown all pain, sorrow, and sighs.

Without conscious thought I pictured vaguely some secluded room in the hospital where the sheeted bodies would lie waiting for the further preparations; for the uniform to be put on for the last time; for the hands to be crossed on the breast. And with this expectation furnishing a background for my conscious thoughts of the letter I must write to my soldier's family, I walked through the halls of the hospital and into the morgue.

Time suddenly stopped for me as I stood there, inexpressibly horrified

85

by the stiff and naked bodies piled on tables and shelves with a neatness and order which somehow only made the sight more shocking. And on a table in the center of the room two men were matter-of-factly wrapping another naked body in brown paper, as if it were an unusually large and unwieldy parcel to be tied up. There were other such parcels as well, already wrapped and tied. Uniforms? I suddenly remembered a skiing party many years before. We were a lighthearted group, but most of the young men had served in World War I. When one of them tripped and fell in the snow his friends called to one another laughingly:

"Well, if he's seriously hurt, don't forget to take off his boots!"

Afterwards I asked one of them about it, and he explained—with evident care for my feelings—that if a soldier was killed on the battlefield his companions took his boots, because they were always so badly needed by someone else. At the time I had not thought much about it, except to be consciously grateful for what I then felt sure was lasting peace. Now it came back—their jesting acceptance of a fact which suddenly had meaning for me. This was wartime. Living soldiers shivered with cold, and there was not enough cloth and leather to keep them warm, nor men to make clothing and boots, nor transportation to carry supplies to the front. What soldier, done at last with the vulnerable flesh, would ask that it be covered with anything that might still be of use to his friends? And so I went into the room to wait until it was time for me to put my flowers into the quiet hands before they were covered with the stiff brown paper.

Later there was the service; a mass service for the rows of bodies now hidden in coffins covered with the flags of many countries; and even there I found that my knowledge of what was inside the coffins was not a disturbing one. A soldier could accept it. Could I do less?

Perhaps this experience helped me later, when I had to learn to make a supreme effort to realize that the body is only an outward clothing of the soul; that it is not the man himself. I had been asked to look up a soldier who had been a friend of my family for many years, and I had found him. There he lay, who had been strong and cheerful and handsome. He was a skeleton with one leg, and from the stump of the other leg came a nauseating smell of rotting flesh. Because of unhealed wounds and bedsores he could have no clothing on him. Only his eyes in any way resembled the man he had been, and when those eyes recognized me his tears flowed. Filled with compassion and horror I talked with his doctors, who told me it might be possible to save him if a place could be made for him in "the baths."

That was the first time I had heard of the baths, and I immediately used every effort to find out where they were, and then to see that he was moved there as soon as possible. They were not a cheerful sight, those baths! In a cellar whose very air was filled with the stench of decay, soldiers suffering from gangrenous infections in their worst form were placed in cots under moving water. It was a place of living death; and while incredible cures took place, so that one marveled at the recuperative powers of nature, many men died—and not quickly.

I visited our friend there as often as possible, and he proved to be one of those whose wounds finally healed, so that in two months' time he could be moved to another hospital and eventually sent home. It had of course been impossible for me to talk *only* with him when I came, or to give to him alone the occasional precious cigarettes I could obtain. Few visitors ever came to the baths, and the soldiers there craved this contact with the outside world almost unbearably. I had known this without really thinking about it, but it was impressed upon me when my friend was moved to another hospital. I had not been sure just what day he would leave, and since I was on another errand in that part of the city I stopped in at the baths to find out if he was still there. He had gone, and his place was already filled by another soldier in even worse condition than his had been, but the man in the next bath spoke to me.

"Ah, Your Highness, we were all hoping that you would not hear your friend had been moved until you had come *once* more!" he said. "Without your visits we shall have nothing to look forward to. I had hoped that I might die before they ended!"

And so it was that I added the baths to my regular calling list, and spent much time there. The man who had spoken to me was a paraplegic; one who had been wounded in the lung and spine, so that he was almost wholly paralyzed. An illegitimate child whose mother had abandoned him, he had been adopted out of pity by an old marketwoman. He had been drafted, wounded, and now lay dying; for the baths failed to help him, and pieces of flesh now and then fell from his legs as they slowly rotted away. For nine more long months he lived; and the last three days of his life I stayed beside him constantly, awaiting his wakening "in a place of light, in a place of greenness, in a place of rest . . ."

Do you find it difficult to imagine scenes like this? So I also would have found it had I not experienced them in two world wars. There were many times when I felt I could not endure it. There were times when my body rebelled against what it must see and do, and I would return to my children for a time and refresh myself in caring for them and living in their world; or I would make a trip to Romania to transact necessary business there, and to beg for more parcels for the wounded. Then I could return to the hospitals—not only to give but to receive.

For the road of the wounded which I took that snowy day in Vienna brought me many gifts in return for that which I gave of myself. There were soldiers who were deaf and blind to everything but the pain or the horror of their condition. For them I could do little except to make some of the time pass more comfortably. But there were many more who stood on the threshold of an open door which was still closed to me, and who gave to me something of the vision they were granted of a new heaven and a new earth. With such men it was easier to ignore those dreadful things which the body can endure before it is laid aside, for they were more consciously aware than most of us of the fact that the body has no lasting connection with the real and eternal self. They knew that in the last analysis it is unimportant—as unimportant as the stiff brown paper one might use to wrap that body once it is finally useless and discarded.

SEVEN

HERE I think I must tell you a little about the reasons why my own life and my personal duties were so changed after 1938. It is not my intention to relate the political history of Europe during World War II. Nevertheless, it is almost necessary to review briefly some of the events outside Romania's own borders which affected her, and which altered my own life as it altered the lives of half a world, if you are to understand my story during the ten years between 1938 and 1948.

To the average person in the United States, Central and Eastern Europe, I find, are simply a section of the map where there are strange-sounding names and where the boundaries are always changing. There were few people in this country, it seems, who followed with much interest what was going on in that part of the world, either before or after Pearl Harbor; yet there events took place which involved all of us. Why is it, you ask me, that after fighting with the Allies in World War I,

Romania fought with the Axis in World War II? Why did I find Romanian wounded in German hospitals, when in the preceding war, hardly more than twenty years before, the two nations had been enemies? It is not a simple question, and a complete answer would have to include more of the history of Romania and of Europe than you wish to hear. Yet I think a few facts will help you to understand some of the reasons why Romania, for centuries a battleground for the quarrels of Germany, Russia, Turkey, and Austria-Hungary, found herself in this latest war a target for English and American bombs also.

In March, 1938, Hitler's troops marched into Vienna, and Austria ceased to exist. In September, 1938, Great Britain, France, and Nazi Germany signed the Munich agreement of "appeasement," and Romanians knew that the peace of Europe was ended, and that once more they were in the center of what would be a battleground. In October, 1938, Germany snatched the Sudetenland from Czechoslovakia; in March, 1939, the German armies marched into Prague. In August, 1939, when the "Nonaggression Pact between the German Reich and the Union of Socialist Soviet Republics" was signed, there was added to this Hitler–Stalin agreement a secret additional paper. This paper provided for a "territorial and political rearrangement" of Central Europe, and provided that part of Romania would be given to Russia. And in September, 1939, Hitler's armies entered Poland.

During those years Romania had not failed to plead for help. In 1938 the government of Romania had asked Great Britain to take a more active part in implementing her relationship with Romania—Britain's last ally in Southeastern Europe. In February, 1938, a planned visit to Bucarest by the chief economic adviser to the British government was canceled because Mr. Chamberlain wished to avoid irritating Hitler by seeming to take an interest in this part of Europe. In October, 1938, Mr. Churchill, speaking in Parliament, said:

We are in the presence of a disaster of the first magnitude which has befallen Great Britain and France. Do not let us blind ourselves to that.

It must now be accepted that all the countries of Central and Eastern Europe will make the best terms they can with the triumphant Nazi power. The system of alliances in Central Europe, upon which France has relied for her safety, has been swept away, and I can see no means by which it can be reconstituted. The road down the Danube Valley to the Black Sea, the road which leads as far as Turkey, has been opened. . . . There was always an enormous popular movement in Poland, Romania, Bulgaria, and Yugoslavia, which looked to the Western democracies and loathed the idea of having this arbitrary rule of the totalitarian system thrust upon them, and hoped that a stand would be made. All that has gone by the board.

Romania, then, had every right to feel that she had been abandoned by her former allies to "make the best terms" possible "with the triumphant Nazi power." When Poland fell, in September, 1939, and France and England officially declared war on Germany, Romania, as their ally, was faced with a decision. She could have declared war also—and been promptly overrun by the Soviet and German armies which were destroying Poland at her very borders. France and England were farther away, with time to prepare for war and with no enemy at their gates. Romania therefore acceded to Nazi demands that she remain neutral; a state which, after all, permitted her to offer shelter to Polish fugitives. This she did in spite of strong German and Russian protests, as many Poles have gratefully testified; and not a few of those she befriended escaped to Allied lands and later joined Allied armies.

Such a state of affairs was of course not long allowed to continue. After a thwarted attempt on the part of the Nazis to capture Romania in a *putsch* planned for September, 1939, Germany and Russia moved in to the kill with a succession of complaints from Russia of alleged Romanian "incidents." In June, 1940, the Romanian government was given twenty-four hours in which to cede Bessarabia and Northern Bucovina to Russia, warned by both Germany and Russia that only by so doing could war with both these powerful nations be avoided. There was no help for Romania from her former allies, Great Britain, France, and the United

States. She acceded to the demand, and was given four days to evacuate a territory of more than fifteen thousand square miles, with a population of three million. Furthermore, at Hitler's demand, a German military mission was "invited" to come to Romania; and the Romanian king (then Carol II) was warned that, as a punishment for Romania's attachment to France and Great Britain, further territorial concessions must be made to Hungary and to Bulgaria. In August the Romanian Foreign Minister was summoned to Vienna and told that by the next day the decision to accept these demands must be made or Hungary and Russia would at once loose total war against Romania, with Germany's approval; and Romania would be wiped out. If, however, this concession was made, Germany would guarantee that Romania might keep the balance of her territory! Once again there was no help offered. A few days later, in August, 1940, nearly twenty thousand square miles with more than two million inhabitants were given to Hungary, and more than twenty-five hundred square miles with four hundred thousand inhabitants were given to Bulgaria. National bitterness at this ruthless dismemberment of the country completed the ruin of Romania's internal government. King Carol II abdicated in September, 1940, and his nineteen-year-old son Michael, about whom I will speak later, was declared king.

Romania's position, already terrible enough, was now made even worse by a growing coolness between Germany and Russia, as these two nations began to disagree over their spoils. There is not time to list the entire succession of events; but by November of 1940 Molotov was reproaching Hitler to his face for having guaranteed Romania against further territorial losses, and he finally demanded that this guarantee be withdrawn—a demand Hitler refused for the time being. Continued disagreement between Russia and Germany led Hitler in December, 1940, to draw up a secret plan for a military campaign against Russia, which included the "co-operation" of Romania. In January, 1941, a number of German troops were moved into Romania, an action which Russia strongly protested. By the last of February, however, the Germans announced to the Russians that they had 680,000 troops stationed there, with "inexhaustible reserves in Germany" backing them.

With Romania as only one pawn in the complicated chess game between Germany and Russia, a game which included Bulgaria, Greece, Yugoslavia, and Serbia in equally bitter moves and countermoves across the board, events moved forward to June, 1941, when Germany attacked Russia on all fronts, with Romania as one of its allies.

Perhaps even from this brief outline it will be possible for you to see that in June, 1941, Romania could not choose between war and peace. If she remained neutral she would receive instant annihilation as a country. Instead, she had to choose whether to join Russia or to join Germany when these two powerful nations began fighting each other on the very soil of Romania herself. At this moment a survey of the situation showed that every continental European nation that had opposed Hitler had been wiped out as a nation. The United States had elected a president who had promised his country solemnly that no American youth would be sent abroad to fight; and the Romanians believed that this represented the firm intention of the United States to stay out of the war in Europe. No help could therefore be expected from that quarter. Had Romania elected to join Russia, the German troops then stationed in Romania could probably have ended the fight before it began. England, who had suddenly become an "ally" of Russia, would have had no power to protect Romania from either "enemy" Germans or "friendly" Russians. Russia made no guarantees whatever to Romania during the tense spring of 1941, in spite of numerous Romanian requests for assurance that Russia would at least promise not to attack Romania if Romania entered the war against Germany. No such assurance was given. On the other hand, Germany offered a chance for Romanian soldiers to march into the stolen provinces of Bessarabia and Bucovina to liberate their fellow Romanians from the Russians. This was a cause which seemed so obviously a righteous one that the average Romanian accepted it not only with approval but with enthusiasm, and with the hope that Germany would be grateful enough for Romania's help to allow her to keep her reclaimed lands if she won their freedom from Russia.

In addition to the overall picture, one must remember that Romania had had close contacts with both German and Russian armies in World War I, as well as in those first years of World War II. Both German and Russian soldiers were hated by the fiercely independent Romanians, but no one on the ground could fail to realize that German ruthlessness was limited while Russian savagery had no limits. For more than twenty years, over the border between Romania and Russia had come fugitives with tales of brutality and oppression; and these had been augmented during the past year by fugitives from the provinces of Bessarabia and Northern Bucovina, which Russia had stolen. Stories of property confiscation, of the methods of the secret police, of the bloody extermination of any who objected to the system, of the desecration of the churches, of the deliberate destruction of family life, and of the immense and horrible forced-labor camps—these things, which most of the world has only recently begun to hear of, were common knowledge in Romania for more than twenty years before 1941. Besides, it is one thing to hear of atrocities from a book or a magazine article which can be read in your warm, protected home; it is quite another thing to hear of them from the fellow countryman who sits at your hearth, dazed and scarred from the brutality to which he witnesses. It would have been a difficult thing to have convinced a Romanian in 1941 that the safety of "democracy" demanded his joining forces with the Russians; those Russians who had invaded Romania ten times between 1700 and 1900, whose ancient and modern brutalities he knew at first hand, and whose dangerous political ideology he also knew. Much of what is now being openly stated about communism in the United States—its utter opposition to freedom of every kind, and its entirely cold-blooded justification of any means to attain its end of worldwide domination—was common knowledge twenty years ago among Russia's close neighbors. These are some of the reasons why in 1946, when the Russians took over Romania, there were less than one thousand members of the Communist Party in the whole country, as the Russians themselves stated.

In 1941 there was actually, then, no choice for Romanians to make. There was only the hope that in spite of their desperate situation, which compelled them to join forces with the Germans, they might still exist as a free people. Therefore, so long as Romanian soldiers were fighting on Romanian soil to free Romanian people there was unity within the country on the war against Russia. When Romanian forces had won back their provinces, and crossed the Russian border to fight beyond it, internal disagreement grew. Nazism was not popular in Romania, and the people did not like to think they were helping to fight the Nazis' war for them! Great Britain declared war on Romania on November 30, 1941, and this increased Romanian anti-Nazi feeling. To appease the threatening German dissatisfaction with this attitude within his country, Romania's leader, General Antonescu, declared war on the United States on December 12, 1941. The declaration of war made him increasingly unpopular, even though it was generally understood that he took this action because he was forced to, and even though he promised that no American citizen and no American property would be harmed—a promise which was faithfully kept until the Russians took over Romania and wiped out all promises. Romanians actually felt that America's entrance into the war was really a triumph for them, since it would ensure the preservation of democracy and freedom, and straighten out the whole shambles brought about by the totalitarian governments. An astonishingly active—and largely unpunished—resistance movement spread and grew, so that on August 23, 1944, Romania came to terms with the Allies. An accord was signed and a fourteen-day notice to leave Romania was given to the Germans, but Hitler persisted in ignoring this, and ordered the Germans to make a prolonged and terrible bombing attack on Bucarest. Romanian armies then turned on the Germans and drove them from Romania; something which was often a bitterly difficult thing to do from the purely personal standpoints of men who had been comrades-in-arms a few weeks before, and were now ordered to fight one another.

The whole story of this three-year period, from June, 1941, to August, 1944, has not yet been told. When it is, it will be an epic of patriots who differed in convictions but not in devotion to their country; an accusation of the self-serving and time-seeking men who exist in every country, and who betray each party in turn; and a moving tribute to the countless "little people" who suffered without understanding. During the last months of this period Romania made desperate attempts to ensure that her surrender to the Allies would be truly a surrender to the Allies *as a whole*, and that she would not be turned over, helpless, to Russia. Winston Churchill had said in September, 1943, that "satellite states, suborned or overawed, may perhaps, if they can help shorten the war, be allowed to work their passage home." This was radiocast to all the satellite states, including Romania. The Voice of America and BBC alike appealed to Romania, as to the others, to turn against the Nazis and "work their passage home." Romania's underground of resistance was supported and aided by British and American encouragement. But when the final surrender was accomplished, Russians insisted that the Armistice be signed in Moscow rather than at a central meeting place for the three Allies. Russians signed "for" the British and Americans; the carrying out of the Armistice was left to the Soviet army. In the game of power politics, in a series of moves which I do not wish to list here because to those who are not students of such things they might seem unbelievable, Romania—with her freedom-loving people, and with her woods and farmlands, her oil and coal and other mineral wealth—was turned over to Russia, and in Russia's control she has been ever since. I have tried in this brief outline to speak without bitterness. I have not referred to internal Romanian politics or to the political considerations that swayed the other countries involved, although these are even now to some extent a matter of record. For those who are interested in a further study of Romanian history and the Romanian people, especially during the past fifteen years, I recommend a book by the late Reuben H. Markham: *Romania Under the Soviet Yoke*. From this book and other reliable sources, some still unpublished, I have tried to verify the dates of events inscribed on my memory. I have also made use of the small section of my journal which happened to survive the almost total destruction of family letters, records, and photographs.

Mr. Markham, a staff foreign correspondent of the *Christian Science Monitor* for more than twenty years, spent most of his adult life in the Balkans and in Eastern and Central Europe. I knew him and Mrs. Markham for more than fifteen years, and often talked with them during that time. A citizen of the United States, he had a perspective we Europeans lacked; but, on the other hand, he inevitably misunderstood some things because of his different background. I do not agree with all the interpretations he gives the facts in his book on Romania, but the facts themselves have been carefully collected and verified. His admiration and friendship for Romania are beyond question. He will always be remembered with affection and gratitude by us who knew him, and by all who are able to understand how much he did for Romania—something, incidentally, which he modestly minimizes in his book.

For my own simple story, I think that this short summary of dates and events will be sufficient to explain why the Castle of Sonnberg ceased, soon after my mother's death, to be the busy, pleasant, country house of a growing family. It will enable you to understand why my life changed and why the castle became in turn a museum, a barracks, and a hospital—and finally only the poor, stripped ghost of the happy home it had been.

EIGHT

IN THE spring of 1951 in New York City a young Romanian asked friends of mine to introduce him to me. He had, he said, a message for me, a message from Dachau. It was strange in such a setting, and at the beginning of a new life, to be reminded so suddenly and vividly of another life; it was strange to reflect that I might have received that message much earlier and more directly, for it was from a Romanian student I had known in Vienna.

In 1944, when Romania came to terms with the Allies, you can understand that Romanians caught outside their own country became suddenly enemies of the German Reich, and were hated with a bitterness which was in proportion to the fear of defeat that was slowly seeping into that Reich. In Vienna the Romanian students studying there were given a choice between disowning their country and going to prison camps. From one such camp the student I had known and this young musician

I met in New York tried to escape. They were caught on the Italian frontier and sent to Dachau, and there my friend died of hunger and the ill treatment for which Dachau has become a synonym. When dying he gave his companion his last messages for his family, and he asked that if his friend should live he would deliver those messages, and also one to me. He wanted me to know, he said, that the most beautiful and precious experience in his life had been working with me in Vienna for the Romanian wounded.

The young musician in New York had been among those fortunate enough to survive until the Americans came to Dachau. He had been among those fortunate enough to find sponsorship and come to the United States. He, too, "lives again," but there are many more students huddled in the crowded camps of Europe who have no opportunity to learn the ways of freedom. I think of them often, for ever since my own girlhood I have known the young students of my country.

In Austria they were for me a link with Romania. We had an apartment in Vienna, a part of an old palace which had been converted into flats. It was a convenient place to stay when we must come in from Sonnberg, especially when the war made traveling difficult and gasoline a commodity to be used sparingly, so that we must do as many errands as possible on one trip. It had a kitchen, a living room, a bedroom, two smaller sleeping alcoves, and another large living room which we found little use for, except that it was a pleasant sitting room and looked out on the garden. Here I had sat on that February day in 1942 when the telephone rang and a friend told me about a wounded Romanian officer; and here in this large room which had known the formalities of the days of the empire I had made a meeting place for the Romanian Student Club of Vienna.

There must have been sixty or seventy young men and women in Vienna in 1942, studying medicine, music, or law, or enrolled in technical schools. They felt for our country the same concern that so oppressed me, as events forced her more deeply into the destruction brought on the world by the two totalitarian powers, Russia and Germany. They found some relief for their concern by tightening their belts as conditions grew more difficult, and by working even harder to gain the skills that they felt Romania would now need more than ever. When I found a certain relief for my own anxiety by throwing myself into the work of helping our Romanian wounded, the students were pleased to join their efforts to mine.

By Christmas of 1942 I was beginning to realize that my work for these soldiers must somehow be organized on a wider scale. Those were memorable holidays; so different from the Christmas of six years before when my mother had been with us at Sonnberg that it was like another world, another planet. In the first place, I had met earlier in the winter a young Romanian officer who had been wounded at Odessa by a bullet which had gone in one temple and out the other, destroying the sight of both eyes. It was not so much the fact that Sandu had survived such a wound which made him an object of interest and concern in the hospital where he was, but his whole character and personality. He had been a brilliant student, standing at the top of his class before he went into the army. In fact, blinded as he was, he later earned his Ph.D. in Bucarest. But besides this he was such a fine and lovable young man that when the doctors had at first some hopes of restoring his sight by transplanting a cornea in one of his eyes, his own batman begged to be allowed to donate an eye. The doctors of course refused to accept this sacrifice, and since the nerve had died no operation could be attempted, but no one forgot the nobility of such an offer or the character of the young man who had inspired it.

Since Sandu was one of the first blinded soldiers I came to know, I remember well how I felt when I met him. I made the usual remarks of greeting, but suddenly I realized that he could not see me smile nor be put at ease by observing that my manner was informal. I felt an overwhelming sense of helplessness at my inability to communicate with him, and a sudden comprehension of the strange world of darkness in which these blinded men must learn to live. It awakened me to the need of doing something for them, and I made a special effort to find out how training could be given them. It was an effort which eventually led to Romanians being sent to Austria to learn the latest methods of such training, but that was many months later. In December of 1942 I could only invite to Sonnberg for the holidays this young officer, two other blinded soldiers, and a fourth wounded man who had his sight and could help care for them.

The fourth man was, however, also considered in rather desperate straits. He was a captain who had been wounded in the throat in Russia, and been hidden from the Russian soldiers by an old Russian peasant woman—for it is an instinct with women to save life. When his Romanian comrades found him he was nearly dead, but since the bleeding from his throat had stopped they fastened him to the front of a tank and in this way transported him to the hospital train that brought him to Vienna. There at the hospital it was discovered that the bullet had pierced both the jugular vein and the aorta—the great artery in the neck; that the blood had clotted in the wound, but that the vein and artery had healed with an opening between them. Blood going to and from the heart intermingled at this point with a little gurgling sound, quite plainly audible, and his heart was overworked because of the condition. Later a surgeon was able to separate and sew up the vein and the artery, and he lived, but at this Christmastime the doctors in Vienna felt that the chances of his surviving such an operation were almost nonexistent.

These four Romanians, I felt, we could make room for in our household so that they might have Christmas with a family and children. I had earlier added to the staff at the castle a young Romanian whose uncle had been aide-de-camp to my mother. In 1941, while I was at Bran for a short visit, he had been detached from his post in Bucharest to act as my secretary and chauffeur, and he had been allowed to drive me back to Sonnberg. He had proved such a splendid companion for Stefan, then nine, that I had asked if he might stay until after my sixth child was born; and as my work for the wounded came into being and increased, his assignment with me was continued. In the end, Arnold Bittermann was with us until we finally left Romania for Switzerland, when I insisted that he must return to his profession of engineering and make a new life for himself, something he has successfully done in Holland, after getting his mother and sister safely out of Romania.

With me also was my friend, Frau Ilse Koller, who had come to me before Magi was born, and who also remained with me until shortly before I was forced finally to leave Romania. She helped both with the care of the children and with some of the details of the work with the wounded; but during that December of 1942 she herself became very ill of mastoid, so that twice the bone had to be scraped. The children's governess developed pneumonia at the same time, and Sandi had an ear infection which finally meant that she must be taken to the hospital in Vienna to have both eardrums pierced. I began to feel that the holidays were not going to be the cheerful ones I had planned, but I was desperately anxious that in spite of difficulties my arrangements for the wounded in Vienna should not be interfered with.

It was here that I called on the Romanian students for additional help, and they did not fail me. I had estimated that there would be only about two hundred Romanian wounded in Vienna over the holidays, since I knew that one large group of several hundred was to be sent home before Christmas. I felt that those who were left behind would need special cheering, so I planned to wear Romanian peasant costume and to take each man a small Christmas package. The students helped by making quantities of *cozonac*, a special date bread which is a part of every Romanian Christmas, and by organizing groups which went to each hospital to sing Romanian carols to the wounded there.

To our horror we discovered almost at the last moment that we had badly underestimated the number of Romanian soldiers in the hospitals, and that instead of two hundred there were more nearly five hundred. Still overwhelmed by this, and working madly to collect packages for these extras, we learned also that the ship with four hundred wounded, who were to have been sent down the Danube to Romania, had been caught by a sudden freeze and was trapped in the ice. The boat was a former excursion steamer, pleasant enough for peaceful summers on the river, but by no means designed to make a comfortable hospital ship. When I visited it I found that the men were sleeping in tiers of three bunks, an arrangement which makes it most difficult to care for them, and that the flimsy materials used to enclose what had been open decks were hardly weatherproof. In order to keep these enclosures above freezing, so much heat had to be forced through the pipes that the inner rooms were almost as hot as Turkish baths, and neither condition pleased men who were in physical pain from their wounds and in mental pain because of their disappointment at not reaching Romania in time for Christmas.

All those who were helping me redoubled their efforts. In some miraculous way we managed packages for nine hundred men, and I was able to carry out my plan of bringing a small feeling of home into the holidays by delivering them myself, in Romanian dress. This was not, however, the most sensible costume to wear in the unusual cold. Going in and out of the hospitals for several days, passing from heat to cold and cold to heat, and working long hours as I had to to make my rounds, I finally caught a lung infection myself. January of 1943 found me ill in bed, but with a certain feeling of satisfaction that I had at last begun to follow in my mother's footsteps. And with that feeling of accomplishment came an idea for the future.

In spite of the difficulties of the holidays, the soldiers who had stayed with us quite evidently had been more relaxed and happy to be out of the crowded hospital atmosphere. I knew that always there were men who must wait about in a semiconvalescent stage, either for one operation or a series of operations. They were lonely and in a foreign country; they needed to be together. Sonnberg was large, I had my nurse's training, and some of the household staff had assisted in work with the village dispensary and could help me. I was quite sure the servants would prefer a settled arrangement to the difficulties of having troops billeted unexpectedly upon us—something which had already happened thirteen times.

Therefore, why not a hospital at Sonnberg for those Romanian soldiers who must wait in Austria for operations?

While I was recovering from my illness I made plans and wrote letters, and when I was allowed to go to Hof Gastein for convalescence I stopped off in Vienna to see those who could help me. I remember also on that journey visiting the school at Salem where Stefan and Minola were students; the beautiful school on Lake Constance which the Duke of Edinburgh's sister and her husband now own. I remember feeling impatient because I could not, without feeling breathless, walk up the hill from the little station at the pace I usually did! I was anxious to be entirely strong again: there was so much to be done.

By April, 1943, the Romanian hospital was established at Sonnberg. The five rooms that had once been set aside for my mother had been taken a year earlier by the Kunst Historische Museum—the Historical Museum of Art—of Vienna. By that time museums throughout the country were scattering their possessions in castles and estates, hoping that some would escape the heavy bombing of the cities. This particular museum specialized in period furniture, and I remember the beautiful pieces that had belonged to Maria Theresa and were sent out to Sonnberg. They included her cradle, a chair and a writing table she had used, and many other historical heirlooms of her period.

It was odd to have the Empress's furniture sent to Sonnberg for sanctuary, when it had been one of her roads—the road from Vienna to Prague—which had ruined Sonnberg nearly two hundred years before. As I told you, the little village at our castle gates was a small one, but there was a larger town, a "shopping center," about two miles away. This larger town had once been a tiny village indeed, named Ober Hollabrun, or, the town "over the holly-bush well," and Sonnberg had been a much more important center. But Maria Theresa's new road bypassed Sonnberg and went through Ober Hollabrun, and before long Sonnberg was only a village of no importance, while its neighbor had become large and flourishing; so large that the holly bush and the well disappeared. Eventually the "Ober" was dropped from its name because when so few people remembered the bush and the well, no one remembered what the town was "over," and what was the use of such a long name anyway? Now, in 1942, some of Maria Theresa's furniture left the big road and came to Sonnberg after all, but it found no real security. For when the Russians occupied Sonnberg they smashed and burned the Queen's furniture as enthusiastically as they destroyed everything else.

But that day of destruction was still a few years in the future in April, 1943, when thirty wounded soldiers were finally settled into their beds at the castle. Much had been done to accomplish this. I had talked with the Military Attaché at the Legation in Berlin, and he had arranged the necessary approval both from Bucarest and from the German authorities. Since Vienna was more and more the center to which our wounded were sent from all fronts, a Romanian Military Bureau was arranged at the Consulate in Vienna, and put in the charge of Dr. Gligore, an excellent doctor who was in Vienna doing special work on diseases of the heart.

With the bureau to keep records and reports of the wounded, the work I had been doing was much more easily systematized. While their numbers were continually increased, the Romanians were being reached much more quickly and efficiently than they had been before. There was still, however, an immense amount of personal work to be done, and here the Romanian students continued to be my chief assistants. There were letters to be written, errands to be done, the never-ending translation of Romanian to German and German to Romanian, the blind and helpless to be read to and fed. In all these services the Student Club was amazingly tireless, patient, and efficient, and we worked together in a fellowship which brought back to me my own student days in Bucarest; a fellowship which I shall never forget.

The number of students and their willingness to help in the Vienna hospitals made it possible for me to spend much time at Sonnberg during that spring. It was a simple convalescent hospital, actually, with no elaborate equipment and with an almost nonexistent staff. There was no resident nurse or doctor at first. Instead, we had a doctor at Hollabrun who called on us at regular intervals and whom we could call in an emergency, and I myself ran the hospital with the help of an orderly. The army furnished sheets, blankets, bandages, and drugs, while I provided the building, the beds, and the equipment. All services were provided either by my own household or by the men themselves. My servants did the cleaning, and I hired extra washerwomen to do the hospital laundry, while the soldiers who were able to move about helped care for themselves and for their more helpless companions. Those who were able washed themselves and helped make the beds, while I bathed and fed those who were not able to do these things for themselves: those who had no hands, for example. Since I had learned massage from a Swedish friend before I was married, I was able to carry on treatments of this kind, as well as to change bandages and dispense drugs.

Usually my day began with the problem of food, a problem which became more serious as time went on, since wartime shortages were numerous and difficult. The wounded, of course, had their army rations, which had to be kept completely separate from our own civilian food rations, even up to the last bit of leftovers. However, since the soldiers who were able to do so were happy to make themselves part of the household, and to help with cooking and table setting, I am quite sure there was a certain amount of surreptitious sharing of the extra food! Our regular food rations were plain and uninteresting, even though fairly adequate, while the army rations included more attractive foods—even some of the frozen fruits and vegetables, which I then saw for the first time. I remember that most of the soldiers did not care for the frozen applesauce which was once sent, and refused to eat all of it, so that I was able to give some to the children and even have a taste myself!

To make things more complicated, the families of the soldiers and interested friends of mine in Romania used to send us food parcels full of things simply not available in Austria: things like suet, ham, bacon, sugar, cheese, and the rich conserves of Romania which are like no others anywhere; conserves so delicious that a spoonful is served, with a glass of water, when in the United States you would serve ice cream or sherbet. There were also dried soups and other staples, all of which "extra" foods enabled me to supplement the rations of the wounded, and to have special dishes prepared for those who needed to be tempted to eat or who required a special diet.

It was this extra food from Romania which finally led to a "strike" of the washerwomen soon after the hospital had opened. They came to me one day to demand that they be given some of the food we were serving the wounded at the castle. I realized how hard it must be for them to see foods prepared which were not available to them, so I told them that if they would turn their ration cards over to me I would "trade" some of their staples for the special foods and see that they had full meals which would include some of the Romanian "extras." But it developed that this was not at all what they had in mind. They had no intention of giving me their ration cards; they were demanding extra food as a bonus. This was of course against the law, but they assured me that others of the "highly born" were doing it and that I would have to do it too if I wished to get help. And what would "The Party" say, I wanted to know, about their making such a threat—and to a hospital too! But they were not to be frightened by this at the moment; they were too sure I needed them. I must either promise extra food, on this "black market" basis, or they would walk out immediately, *and in the middle of the washing!*

I knew as well as they did how inconvenient this would be, for we had no supply of extra linen, and the laundry for the household and thirty additional men, all of which must be done by hand, was no small item. But they were wrong, and no good comes in the end if one agrees to what one knows is not right, so I remained firm, and the washerwomen did indeed walk out in the middle of the washing. There was only one thing to be done: I must show that I was independent of them. So I marshaled all my available help and we finished the laundry! The children's governess was horrified when she found herself drafted into service.

"But I have no *idea* how clothes are washed!" she protested plaintively.

"High time you did, then!" I told her firmly—and neglected to mention that *I* had no idea how they were washed, either. But, as I suspected, a little attention to how my own servants who were helping me carried out the operation was all that was necessary to show one what to do. By our united efforts the clothes were washed and dried and ironed with no casualties, and with Sandi and Niki considering it a tremendous lark.

The next day our washerwomen returned quite meekly, and I did not inquire whether this was because their consciences hurt them or because they had had time to reflect on what a possible report to the Party would do. They explained that they had come to finish the washing, and I replied calmly that the washing had been finished. There was silence while they thought this over. Then they inquired if they should come back next week as usual, and I said politely that I would be glad to have them, and that was the end of the trouble. (And I must admit that to encourage them in right doing I took the occasion of the next holidays to send extra food home with them.)

But that was the only time I had trouble in getting help for my hospital. In fact for a time it looked as if any trouble might lie in the other direction, for except for my secretary and the hospital orderly, all the household staff were women and girls. Since one of the great advantages of Sonnberg was the freedom the "walking wounded" had to move about, and since we had no "night staff," you can understand why one of the German medical staff who came to inspect the hospital was much disturbed. He gave me a serious lecture on the subject, ending with:

"And of course you must inspect all rooms at irregular intervals during the night!"

"Indeed not!" I told him. "For what would you expect me to do if I found something as it should not be? Say politely, 'Oh, I beg your pardon!' and withdraw? Or stay and try to deal with the matter? I feel I do not want to do either!"

Since the poor man could think of no other solution, he went off rather unhappily; but I tried to attack the problem in another way. We cleaned out a large room in the basement and made it into a recreation room; a pleasant lounge where properly supervised "parties" were held regularly. Since there was no need for furtive and sidelong glances when everyone knew there would be open social occasions, the atmosphere remained pleasant and wholesome; a fact which my close association with patients and staff made perfectly evident to me. In fact there were several romances such as that of my maid, who later married one of the soldiers who had lost an arm.

As the months went on we increased the variety of treatments we could offer at Sonnberg. We developed various kinds of occupational therapy: a favorite kind was the making of paper and fiber rope which could be woven into mats and sold, so that patients able to do this could earn a little money while they waited between operations. We also developed all sorts of exercises to re-educate muscles. There were many variations of simple equipment where arms and legs could work against the weight of sandbags of different sizes; there were finger and thumb rings attached to boards so that hands could be exercised; there were small "ladders" on the wall, up which partially paralyzed patients "walked" their fingers, hoping to get higher than their mark of yesterday.

For our patients were chiefly blinded soldiers, amputees, and soldiers who had been frozen. Some blinded soldiers, of course, were only waiting for the operation of transplanting a cornea, but many had been in explosions which had dreadfully injured their faces, and they were undergoing long and painful plastic operations. One soldier had thirty-six of these before he again looked human: another had had his chin blown off, and surgeons were working to rebuild one for him in successive operations. It is strange, now that I think of it, to reflect that only one of all these men ever betrayed a hating and hateful bitterness, but I feel that it was not his injuries which caused his attitude. It has been my experience that a hospital does not change one, but that instead it simply makes one *more* of what one is. In this case it was as the Romanian proverb says: *Isi da arama pe fatza*—"he brings his brass to the surface"—which is a way of saying that in times of stress gold plating wears off and the brass shows. The man was truly in a dreadful condition. His whole face had literally been blown away, so that he had no nose or cheeks. He had lost not only his sight, but also his senses of smell and taste; and the direct entrance of air into the holes between his eyes, without its being warmed and moistened through the nose passages, was both annoying and painful to him. Surgeons had begun the long process of rebuilding a face for him, and in time they produced a very normal appearance, but when he first came to Sonnberg I was grateful every time I walked with him that he could not know the full horribleness of his appearance. At first I was inclined to hope that his vicious behavior to his companions, his constant complaints, and his deliberate troublemaking were the result of his condition, but as I grew to know him better I felt that this was not so. His stories of his early life, his accounts of what he had done and thought and felt, were all colored by the same cruelty and hatred. In the end I came to feel that here was truly a poisoned soul, whose state had been accentuated, but not caused, by his misfortunes.

The soldiers who had had arms or legs amputated were in most cases waiting for stumps to heal so that they could be fitted with artificial limbs, and they too required not only occupational therapy but morale building. At times the greatest number, however, would be those who had suffered frostbite. They had lain too long untended on the battlefield, or at the improvised dressing stations back of the lines. Many, too, had come in unheated trains from the Russian front, and had been frozen on the way. There were whole hospitals in Vienna set up especially for these cases, and to enter them was to smell at once the sickening, sweetish odor of decay already familiar to me from my visits to the baths. A frozen spot on the body is like a burn: frozen flesh and bone will break as readily as do charred flesh and bone. I remember a soldier brought into one of these hospitals who was obviously in a dreadful state. Since his trousers were stiff with dried blood and dirt, the nurse and orderly began to take them off, but, to the horror of everyone around him, when the trousers came off both legs above the knee came off with them. The limbs had been completely frozen, and were so brittle that it required only a little pressure to break them away. Most cases that hopeless, of course, did not get as far as the hospitals, but many of the men had seen sights as bad or worse.

One officer had saved the lives of his men by getting from somewhere a whip and literally beating them, exhausted, sobbing, and cursing him, through the snow to a railroad. Many of his men suffered from frostbite, but they lived, and by the time they had reached the hospital they knew what gratitude they owed him. I would like to have met that officer, for when you realize he was no better off physically than his men, and yet found somewhere the strength of spirit that enabled him to save them, you know he must have been a remarkable person.

With many of the "frozen" wounded, only a part of a muscle had been destroyed, and in the leg or the arm there would remain a fragment which could be re-educated by carefully planned exercises and infinite effort and patience. We felt our greatest sense of triumph when a soldier learned to walk again, or to lift a sandbag with an arm which had been hanging helpless, or to manipulate his pencil and his knife and fork with the two or three fingers that had been saved after the others had dropped off, frozen.

During the spring and early summer of 1943, then, my time was divided between Sonnberg and Vienna, where the Romanian Student Club continued to work in the hospitals. A special group of about twenty, who had organized themselves as a chorus to sing for the wounded, was under the direction of my friend who died in Dachau. In spite of the difficulties of travel, and a three-mile walk to and from the station, this chorus made the trip to Sonnberg several times to entertain their wounded fellow countrymen at the castle, and I learned to appreciate the courage and ability of their young leader. I have thought of him many times since I received his dying message last spring in New York City.

My "road of the wounded" took a new turning that summer of 1943, and because of this fact I was in Romania when terms were made with the Allies in 1944. Had I not been there at that time, things might have been very different for me. There was Mafalda, daughter of the King of Italy and wife of Philip of Hesse. In 1943 Italy capitulated to the Allies while the Princess was making a journey home from the funeral of her brother-in-law, King Boris of Bulgaria. Since the train went through Romania, it happened that my sister-in-law, King Michael's mother, had a brief visit with her, and so became probably the last friend to see her. For in Germany Mafalda, who had not even heard of Italy's surrender, was removed from the train as an enemy of the Reich and sent to Dachau, where she died without ever having seen her husband or her children again.

So it might well have been with me, and there would have been no need for my friend to send his message in such a roundabout manner. I would have been in Dachau to receive it.

I. Pennock
1951

NINE

B ESIDES THE message from Dachau, my former life spoke to me
again on one evening in the spring of 1951 when I went with friends
to a showing of some adventure films. For among these films was one
taken of the bombing of the oil fields at Ploesti in Romania, on August
1, 1943. There on the screen was the long, straight road between the
dusty fields full of oil wells and storage tanks; the road from Ploesti to
Campina. Since it was a road I considered monotonous and uninteresting
to drive, I used to hurry over it, keeping my mind on something else to
make the time seem to pass more quickly. Yet when I last drove over that
road, one night in 1948, it lay in darkness and I strained my eyes to catch
a glimpse of the landscape, while I wished that time might slow and stop
altogether, for I was leaving Romania forever. It was, therefore, a shock
that evening three years later to see the familiar ribbon of road unroll
before me on a moving-picture screen in Massachusetts, and to realize

that those pictures had been taken in 1943, from the planes I did not recognize as American bombers.

I had taken the children to Romania for the summer, and while I was there I had a number of consultations with the military and Red Cross authorities in Bucarest. It had become evident to me that the work for the Romanian wounded must be extended, since not all of them were being sent to Vienna where our organization could reach them. On the first of August I had promised to open a training school for girls in Ploesti, with Madame Antonescu, and I drove out early from Bucarest to spend the morning with a friend who had just had a new baby. While we were talking, planes flew over the house, and I looked out to see what kind they were. Their insignia was a star, but—I said to my friend with relief—it is not a Russian star! And we went on talking about the baby. Then there were explosions. They must be doing practice runs, I said to her: but the noise continued. When it was time for me to leave for the school exercises she protested a little, but my secretary and I assured her that since the noise had stopped the practice must be over, and we drove across town to the school. Secretly both he and I had each begun to feel a little suspicious about this "practice," especially after we passed a wrecked plane, still burning. At several points a policeman stepped from the side of the road as if to stop us, but hesitated and stepped back when he saw the royal insignia on the car. It was not until we reached the school, however, that we confirmed our suspicions. There had been an American bombing raid on Ploesti: the war had for a moment been extended to the gates of Bucarest.

The school program went forward, although Madame Antonescu did not arrive because the officials in Bucarest had been warned of the raid. In the joy of finding among the school staff several young women who had been my Girl Scouts a dozen years before, I did not think too much about the raid until later, but when I did I realized that new dangers threatened my country. Could I be satisfied to remain in Austria if Romania needed me?

I went finally to talk with Prince Stirbey, an old and trusted friend of my family, who both before and during World War I had occupied the highest post at the court of my parents, a post to which he had been appointed by King Carol I. The high regard felt for him in Romania was again proved in 1944, when he was recalled from his retirement to try to help with the difficult problems I have mentioned in an earlier chapter. When I went to him for advice in 1943, he kindly and wisely, but very frankly, discussed the Romanian political situation and world conditions with me, until I could understand something of the tragic situation in which my country found herself. I put my problem before him. It had become increasingly difficult for me to live in Austria. My work with my own wounded countrymen had in many ways shielded me from direct contact with political events, but the increasing pressure of Nazi indoctrination was beginning to affect even Austria. It had been, I felt, my duty as the wife of an Austrian citizen to avoid any expression of an opinion which might make things difficult for him. Brought up as I had been, I could not avoid strong personal objections to the totalitarianism of the Nazi political philosophy, and to the methods used by the Party, but I expressed these only to Anton, and only in private. Up to this time, also, little was known—at least in Austria—about the atrocities that were later published to the world, and therefore my objections were to abstract ideas rather than to concrete examples, since few of these were known to me.

I had been secretly highly amused at the necessity of proving, before Anton could get his officer's commission, that for four generations (I believe it was) our parents and grandparents had been christened in Christian churches. It seemed particularly funny to write to England for proof that my great-grandmother, Queen Victoria, had been so christened, and I was quite sure that the official who solemnly replied shared my amusement. I also had been interested to find that I was descended from a much wider assortment of people than I had realized; the Emperor of Brazil, for example, and a niece of Napoleon's first wife, Josephine. It was some time, busy as I was with war work and with my own children, before I realized the full implications of such policies.

After the first few months of the German occupation there was no violence visible to the general public. News of political imprisonment or of concentration camps was, as you can understand, not published in the daily press. You in the United States can have no conception of how entirely the totalitarian governments control publications and communications. For example, now in Romania no private citizen may purchase pencil, paper, or ink without a petition to the Communist government, and the possession of a typewriter requires a permit such as the United States demands for the possession of firearms. Since the people in Austria were for a long time not aware of how complete this control of the press had become, for those who knew it had no way of telling it, it is literally true that a full knowledge of what had gone on during those years was later an appalling surprise to many people whom you might expect to know about it. (Even in the United States, we must remember, I have now and then heard intelligent citizens express an equally complete and sincere surprise when some investigation has exposed certain undesirable conditions in this country.)

Yet, as I explained to Prince Stirbey, I was beginning to know too much about affairs in Austria and Germany to remain detached from them. The position that had at first protected me from knowledge was now bringing me inside information. The Nazi philosophy was not one I wished my children to learn to accept. What should I do? He looked at me seriously as he answered:

"But you must decide what you feel yourself to be. Are you Austrian, German, or Romanian?"

There could be only one answer to this, and I made it from my very heart of hearts.

"I am a Romanian," I said.

His reply was sternly challenging. "Then stand by your choice! Be a Romanian!"

His words continued to echo in my ears as I went on with the responsibilities I had undertaken. Perhaps because of them I made a last-minute change in my plans for the children. The sixteen-hour train trip the two older children must make when they went to and from their school at Salem, and which now Alexandra, too, would have to share, had become steadily more of a worry to me because of the increasing bombing of the railroad lines. I decided to leave the three older children in Romania, where they could attend the Saxon schools and perfect their knowledge of Romanian gradually; but I took the three younger children back to Sonnberg with me in September, 1943.

I went back, however, with a plan to make the work with the Romanian wounded more widespread and efficient, and because of my talk with Prince Stirbey I also had a half-formulated determination to arrange it so that it would not depend on me personally. I took with me a letter which charged me with the care of all Romanian wounded within the Reich, Czechoslovakia, and Poland. All consulates were to give assistance as I required it. It was to be my duty to search out the wounded, and to decide, after learning their condition, which ones should remain in Austria or Germany for treatment and which should be sent to Romania.

The letter was signed by the Romanian Chief of Staff, General Steflea, a man who was more fortunate than many of his comrades. His fate in 1946 was to be the happy one of falling dead of a heart attack as he bent over his newly born first grandchild, before the Russians got around to punishing him. For the Russians took a very broad view of war responsibility, once they occupied Romania. Anyone who had in any way contributed to the war effort, they said, was a war criminal and deserved any penalty they liked to assign: imprisonment, forced labor, or death. Therefore, they had their choice not only of military but of civilian victims, for the road mender and the girl who sewed buttons on uniforms, the farmer who sold food which might find its way to a soldier's stomach, and the engineer whose plans made a factory more productive—all were contributors to the war effort and all were, therefore, war criminals. No one was safe, even after the first years of the occupation were past. The

Russian memory was long, and if a man himself could not be found for punishment, his family would do as well. There was, for instance, a White Russian who had escaped with his baby son in 1919 from the Bolshevik Revolution. In 1945 the unforgetting Russians looked for him in Bucarest, and since he had disappeared into hiding they arrested and killed the son, who did not even remember Russia. As Romanian Chief of Staff, General Steflea's fate could not have been anything but a horrible death from the Russians, which is why I consider him fortunate to have died a natural one.

In order to be more free to leave Sonnberg for the traveling I must do in setting up my new work, I installed at the castle in the fall of 1943 a resident doctor and a nurse. Besides the hospital in Vienna that was a clearinghouse for Romanian wounded, there were eleven other hospitals there which specialized in specific types of cases; and there were at least five such places for treatment in Berlin. Some dealt chiefly with blinded soldiers, some with amputees, some with bone tuberculosis victims, some with those needing plastic surgery, and so on. Perhaps the surgeons best known in the United States were the Drs. Lorenz, father and son, in Vienna, who were bone surgeons, and Dr. Sauerbruch in Berlin, who was one of the first men to operate on a lung, and who invented instruments still used in this type of operation. During the latter part of 1943 and the early part of 1944 about three thousand Romanian wounded passed through the bureau at Vienna, and were assigned to one of these hospitals or sent back to Romania for treatment. At the same time a real beginning in the training of blinded soldiers and of seeing-eye dogs was made in Romania at the Sibiu School of Equitation, which I shall tell you about later, and arrangements were made for technicians to go to Austria to learn how to make artificial limbs and eyes.

To "search out the wounded," as I was commissioned, I made many journeys, learning the techniques of wartime travel. Since stations and railway junctions were bombed regularly and were most vulnerable targets, one learned to travel with hand luggage only. At the warning of a raid, trains moved quickly away from stations whenever possible, and passengers got out and lay down in the fields, since the bomb shelters available at the stations themselves were only adequate for the railway employees and could not be used by the traveling public. Gasoline was so scarce that most of my travels began at five in the morning, when I left Sonnberg to drive three miles with a horse and carriage to the station at Hollabrun to catch the first train to Vienna. There were bright, pleasant mornings when I remembered with amusement my girlhood ambition to own and drive a horse and carriage, but there were other raw, cold mornings when I definitely regretted that my ambition had been achieved. Sometimes the children's governess—the lady who had had no idea how clothes were washed and ironed—went with me as far as Vienna, but I cannot actually say that we traveled *together*. She felt that her dignity demanded she go second class, which was always crowded, while I had discovered that the workmen traveling third class got on and off at the way stations in such numbers that I could be sure of getting a seat before too long. Therefore, when the train came in, the governess stood with dignity in a second-class carriage all the way to Vienna, while I sat down with thankfulness in a third-class one!

On these journeys I visited Freiburg, Leipzig, Breslau, Berlin, Linz, Salzburg, Prague, and other cities, besides making occasional short trips to Romania. While I found all the journeys strenuous, I remember especially the trip in December of 1943, when I went to bring the three older children home from school for the Christmas holidays. I had only four days to spend in Romania, and in connection with my work I had to keep many appointments with officials and to hold audiences myself. There were friends to see, a christening to attend, personal business to transact. In addition to this, I traveled with a long list of requests from wounded soldiers whom I had come to know particularly well, and whose families lived in or near Bucarest and Brasov. Would I not have a moment to telephone to a father or a mother that their son was really recovering? If it should happen that I was near this street, or went through that village,

My family: the girls and I in Romanian dress, 1945

could I not stop a moment to see a blind grandmother, or a sick little son, and tell them that grandson or father would be thinking of them at Christmas? It is difficult to refuse requests whispered through bandages or made by men bravely enduring the pain of complicated operations, and I tried hard to deliver my list of messages.

Because most of the cases held for treatment in Austria were serious ones, I could not always be entirely reassuring. The bravery of the soldiers' families in their efforts to conceal their anxiety and grief was very real and very moving, and my calls and visits were not easy ones to make. Only rarely was there a lighter moment, as when I telephoned a businessman at his office to deliver a message from his son, and said—as is the custom in making a telephone call—"*Aici Domnitza Ileana*"—"Here is the Princess Ileana." Obviously thinking he was the victim of a practical joke, he replied sharply, "And the Emperor of China here!" and hung up the receiver. It was not until the third attempt that he suddenly realized I was in earnest, and I was glad to have an encouraging message for him so that we could laugh together about my difficulty in delivering it.

What I had not foreseen was the response to the messages. The families of these soldiers, and of others in Sonnberg and Vienna, at once saw an opportunity to send a little gift back to the dear one who must spend Christmas in a foreign land. In no time at all I was the recipient of literally scores of packages, each one small, but the total amounting to an appalling pile. They were brought personally, each with an eager plea that son or brother or sweetheart or husband be given this special delicacy which he must be missing. How could I refuse? In the end an entire bed in our compartment on the train had to be sacrificed to take care of the incredible number of small parcels, which we had bundled together as well as we could.

As if this were not enough, it became evident that Minola was really ill. She had had her tenth-birthday tea the day before, so that when she complained of feeling sick before we left I had not taken it too seriously, but had got her to bed to rest until it was time to leave. However, once the journey began it was clear that it was no mere upset, but something more serious. From Budapest on we had only one compartment. With our own luggage and the soldiers' parcels, there was literally not room to move. The train got later and later, with Minola more fretful and clearly very ill, and eventually I felt certain that she had scarlet fever. Then I was terrified for fear the officials would discover it and put us off the train, miles from home. Since the compartment was already contaminated, I felt it would do no harm if we could get as far as Vienna, and fortunately it worked out that the difficulties of wartime travel kept anyone from observing us too closely.

I was so thankful to get to our apartment in Vienna that I could bear with fortitude the reaction of the railway officials when I warned them what I thought the child's illness was. Of course they regarded it as a last straw added to their already burdened existences, and I was as apologetic as possible! We spent a wakeful night in Vienna, trying to keep Minola comfortable and to find a doctor, who promptly verified my diagnosis but cheered us by saying that he thought it was going to be a light case. The next morning we proceeded to Sonnberg. Warned by telephone, they had made provisions to isolate Minola from the other children and from the soldiers, and my friend, Frau Ilse Koller, volunteered to nurse her through the quarantine so that I might be able to go on with my other responsibilities—which at the moment included overseeing the delivery of a quantity of packages from Romania! And that night, just as I finally managed to get thankfully to bed, the telephone rang. Anton, on his way home with Christmas leave, had had car trouble and was stuck thirty miles away. The fires had to be made up, water heated to start our car, and a rescue party dispatched. It was seven o'clock in the morning before everyone was safely back at Sonnberg, and the holidays really began.

They were good holidays, however, even though they had begun with such difficulty. We did not know they were to be our last in Austria. On the fifth of December St. Nicholas had been impersonated by a friend who was home on leave from the front. Robed magnificently in the ermine wrap I had given my mother, but with his military boots showing all too plainly beneath it, he had made his comments on the children's behavior in clever verse which amused everyone—even Niki, whose six-year-old conscience was a little tender on some points. Now, at Christmas-time, trees were set up in the hospitals, and the packages from Romania, along with parcels the rest of us had been making, were delivered to the wounded. There was a special tree for Minola, who was feeling only comfortably like an invalid. Changing my clothes and disinfecting my hands had enabled me to go to see her regularly, which kept me from worrying too much about her, and she was charmed with having her own special Christmas celebration. We had the large tree in the castle, and the village children and as many officers and soldiers as we could manage were invited to share it. To make the occasion as festive as possible we all dressed in our best, and I wore the lovely sapphire and diamond diadem because so much of the time my family and my household of soldiers saw me only in traveling clothes or nurse's uniform. There were carols, and gifts, and the joy of the children, which triumphed for a brief time over the thought of a world at war—and another year had come to a close.

Nineteen hundred and forty-four began in the shadows of growing anxiety in Austria over the progress of the war, and to this in my case was added my personal anxiety for my own country. Conditions of living and of travel became worse as the destruction from the Allied bombing increased. Everyone was irritable and tired. There were constant minor frictions everywhere, to a degree which no one can imagine who has not lived in a country which is a battleground. I remember, for example, a series of domestic squabbles between some of the maids and some of the refugees we had found room for, which resulted in the police being "informed" that the maids had more shoes than the rationing system allowed. When a thorough hausdurchsuchung was conducted to count our shoes, and some of the servants were indeed found to own more than the legal two pairs, nothing was done about it by the police, but much bad feeling remained in the household.

There were the more serious problems of the soldiers. Some of those with the most terrible wounds were unable to bear the pain, and managed sometimes in the confusion of wartime conditions in the cities to get extra morphine. They would become addicts, and before later treatments could be given them they would have to be broken of the habit. This was a long and agonizing process in which I tried to do my share of helping. Inevitably, too, we failed to save some lives for which we fought long and desperately, and each defeat of this kind was a personal sorrow because we came very close to the people we tried to help in their struggles to live.

There were the upsets and accidents that any household suffers where there are children. During one holiday when the children were all at Sonnberg, Sandi, turning a cartwheel, bumped into Stefan. To recover his balance he threw out his arm so quickly and vigorously that he put it through a glass window and cut himself badly. The nurse, seeing the blood spurt from a wound in his forearm, quickly put on a tourniquet and ran for a doctor without noticing that another cut above his elbow also was bleeding badly. Only the fact that a doctor happened to be in the castle and came at once prevented Stefan from bleeding to death, and he still carries the scars of the accident. Niki, almost seven in 1944, crushed his hand in the door of the motorcar, and one of Anton's short furloughs was spent largely in taking the poor child back and forth to Vienna until it was certain that the bones were set correctly and were healing. But my main concern for the three children who were with me in Austria was caused by the war news. More and more I felt that I wanted them to be in Romania, even though the Russians were steadily advancing and my Austrian friends felt that I was mad to think of going toward the enemy instead of staying where I was.

I had had little personal experience with Russians since my childhood days, when the Bolshevik Revolution brought a constant succession of desperate refugees fleeing to Romania for protection. Russians were associated in my mind with the cruel deaths of members of my mother's family in Russia, and especially with the murder of my little cousin, the Czarevitch Alexis, who had been my personal charge when the Czar and Czarina visited Romania with their children in 1914. I had seen the effects of the Revolution on the Russian armies in Jassy, and later there had been the stories of refugees who were helped by some of the charitable organizations with which I worked in my teens. In Austria, however, during these war years there had been actual Russians scattered through the country: some who were war prisoners and some who had run away from their own land by choice.

One I remember was a servant girl working for a Viennese woman who had come in distress to live at Sonnberg. I had insisted, over the protests of her mistress, that the Russian girl be invited to that last Christmas tree in the castle, where I wore the diadem. She had surprised everyone by suddenly bursting into tears, and when she could control herself she explained in broken German that her parents had—safely hidden away from the Communists—a picture of the Czarina wearing just such a diadem, and that I reminded her of it, and of her home. Another Russian girl worked for a lady who was very kind to her, and it was through this girl that I had my first inkling of what the Communists had made of their people. In this spring of 1944 the advance of the Russians seemed to bring them daily nearer, and this particular Russian was convinced that it was only a matter of time before they would enter Austria. But she was anxious to show her gratitude for the kind treatment she had received, so she reassured her mistress.

"When the Russians come," she said earnestly, "I will tell *them* how good you have been to me, and they will be good to you in return, you will see! For they will kill you quickly"—and she made a brisk and vivid gesture of throat-cutting—"and not torture you at all! This I promise I will do for you!" Her evident satisfaction with this generous intention was to me almost unbelievable at the time, but I lived to learn that she spoke matter-of-factly and out of a life which then people could hardly imagine existed.

It was perhaps incidents and experiences of this kind which made the Austrians feel it was insanity to think of taking my other three children to Romania, but for that I had only one answer. If there was to be worse danger, I wanted my children to be where every man was my friend. So in March I took them to Bran and made arrangements to leave them there, intending to return to Austria and continue as long as possible my work for the wounded. There was a joyous reunion when the three older children came from school for a weekend. Stefan had suddenly grown enormously, so that I felt small when he stood beside me. But on March 27, when I was to have left for Vienna, travel suddenly became impossible. The Russians were rumored to have entered Moldavia; refugees were crowding down into southern Romania; the Germans had set up defenses and were engaged in a quarrel with the Hungarians, and all civilian travel across Hungary was forbidden. For the time being, decision was out of my hands. I was in Romania, and there I must stay, even though I had brought only hand luggage with me.

I wrote letters to Austria, turning over the administration of the hospital at Sonnberg to Dr. Gligore and making arrangements for my other work there until I could return. During all this time I had a curious, unreasoning feeling that, in spite of my willingness to go on with the work in Austria, my place was now with my own people in my own country. And so it proved to be, for though I went back again in May for a week to check up on the hospital, I had by that time already been drawn into a work in Romania where I seemed to be needed badly. It was still my intention to travel between Austria and Romania often enough to keep in touch with my work with the wounded, but conditions made it impossible for me ever to return to Sonnberg again after that one hurried week in May, 1944. During the last days of April there was a lull in the work I had begun in Romania. I was anxious to see for myself how the hospital in the castle was getting along and how the other plans I had made by mail were working out. Even though travel through Hungary was still difficult and limited, I managed to get the necessary permissions to leave and to return, and I set off by train one evening with my secretary. The Commanding General of the Mountain Troops saw me off from the dark and ruined station of Brasov, so that the memory of destroyed trains was uncomfortably present through all our journey. I must confess that my experiences on trains during bombardments had made me unable to lay aside my dread of them, but we arrived in Vienna safely after only one alarm.

At Sonnberg we were given a heart-warming welcome by the wounded and by my household, but I found that because of the infinite difficulty of communications our telegrams had not been received, and we had missed Anton by a matter of hours. However, he was able to return for two days during that week; a week crowded by appointments and visits to hospitals, by interviews with the military officers and medical staffs, and by the usual personal messages from Romania for some of the wounded. I had hoped to be able to drive my car back to Romania, but when the permission came through it was only for train travel. I realized I was fortunate to have even that, for the intensive bombing was having an effect upon everything. At my last visit to Berlin, earlier in the spring, I had found many parts of the city so destroyed that I lost myself several times while going from the Legation to various hospitals, and this was true of many other cities. Much as I dreaded a train journey, since I always felt imprisoned in a vulnerable target for bombs, it was the only way I could get to Romania. I got my tickets, therefore, with thankfulness, still with no premonition that I was leaving Sonnberg for the last time.

There on a May afternoon, weary from all I had had to do in such a short space of time, I remember with what content I sat down in the garden of the castle. I looked at the flowers I had planted; I looked at the beautiful building that had been my happy home for eight years, and I loved it with all my heart. I am glad I had no warning that I would never see it again, or that its loveliness was to be so wantonly destroyed, for this last picture I carry in my mind is unspoiled. Gently and without my realizing it, as I sat there in the quiet garden, one door closed definitely behind me and another opened. *Nu aduce anul ce aduce ceasul,* we say in Romanian: A year does not bring what an hour brings.

Ileana
1951

TEN

HERE IN my New England bedroom, on the night table beside my Bible and prayer book, is a heavy silver cross. It is about four and a half inches long, and the crucifix is engraved upon it. Wherever I go it accompanies me. Whether I am in a friend's house or have made a journey to a strange town where I must lecture, it lies beside me; a continual token of the power of faith and sacrifice. It reminds me of my home and of my work, and of the trust that those whom I left behind have given me. It is a symbol of the Strength that enables me to "live again," for as I look at it the words spring to my mind: "In the world ye shall have tribulation, but be of good cheer; I have overcome the world." If He had not overcome the world, and in so doing left us His example, how could I ever have borne the day upon which I received this silver cross?

It was January 12 in 1948. My nephew, King Michael, had been forced by the Communists to abdicate on December 30, 1947, and we were being sent away from all we knew and loved to an unknown destination. The train that was carrying us out of Romania stopped in the station of Brasov, a place of ruin because it had suffered badly from bombardments. I looked out sadly upon the empty, cold platform where I had worked in the Red Cross canteen, but it was night and no one except the Red guards were permitted anywhere within sight. Here, as in all the rest of our sad journey, the people were forbidden a last farewell look.

Suddenly I saw a figure familiar and dear. In her canteen uniform, muffled in a heavy winter coat, stood a friend beside whom I had worked day after day. Indomitable as ever, fearless and headstrong, she had braved the authorities by daring to disobey orders, and had come to say good-bye to her departing comrade. I rushed to the compartment door and swung it open. Before the guards could intervene we were in each other's arms, and she pressed something into my hands while she whispered to me:

"God bless you! And carry on wherever you may be."

I could only nod my head. Words failed me, as did my tears. The train moved on. I stared, dry eyed, upon a countryside well known and well beloved, lying silent beneath the snow and the still, cold moonlight, and in my hands I clasped a silver cross.

When I hold this cross today, and look out my window in this country which is so far from my own, my eyes rest upon a silver fir tree, and for a moment I seem to be looking at the firs my mother planted around the little wooden church at Bran. How gratefully I used to take fleeting rests in my castle in the little valley of the Carpathians, where I had settled the younger children while I worked in the Red Cross canteen in the town of Brasov, about twenty-five miles away.

As I have said, the three older children had been attending day schools in Brasov since September, 1943. The problem of where they could stay had been solved by my secretary's sister, whose husband was captain of the fire brigade there. In Romania this was controlled by the army, and men might do their military service in the fire departments of the towns and cities if they wished. The Captain had a nice apartment in the barracks and by an arrangement with an unmarried officer also quartered there he was able to use extra rooms for Stefan, Minola, and Alexandra. Since the children were well acquainted with my secretary and his family, they felt satisfied to be there even when I was still in Austria. When I brought Niki, Magi, and Elisabeth to Romania in March, 1944, I settled them into a house in the village of Bran, since the castle there could not be used during the winter months. Frau Koller and their nurse, Gretl, were in charge of them, since at first I expected to be able to travel back and forth between Austria and Romania. Had I not thought so I would have sent some of my precious possessions from Austria to Bran, instead of leaving them in Sonnberg. As it was, because of the danger of bombing when one traveled by train, I stopped carrying with me on my journeys, and so I have forever lost, my two most cherished treasures: my Bible and my last letter from my mother.

The suddenly strained relationship between Germany and Hungary that stopped all civilian travel in March would, I thought, keep me in Brasov only temporarily. Nevertheless, I foresaw several weeks of inactivity, which I have never been able to bear, and I also saw the need of every available pair of hands. The Russians were pressing hard upon our northern and northeastern frontiers, and innumerable refugee trains which passed through Brasov were taking the threatened population to safer districts. I applied to the Brasov chapter of the Red Cross to give me work until I could return to Austria, and I was assigned to the station canteen there.

Brasov is a charming old Saxon town. It lies as if in a fold of the skirts of the Carpathians, just where the rich Transylvanian plateau begins. Like all medieval towns with any pretense to dignity, it boasts of a castle and a Gothic church. The castle, which stands on a hill in the middle of the town, is not particularly interesting from an architectural standpoint, and is used as a prison, but the church is a very beautiful one of its kind. It is called "the Black Church" because of the dark color of its stones, and it adds a great deal to the charm of the town's appearance. Viewed from the air, Brasov looks somewhat like an octopus, with its body lying on the plateau and its many arms winding up the valleys formed by the out-spread little foothills of the mountains towering above. The streets wind up and down and round about, and except for some taller buildings and the anachronism of a modern hotel in the center of town, the houses are almost all one and two stories, many with red-tiled roofs and ocher-tinted walls. The flower-filled gardens merge with the forest itself, and on market days peasants from the surrounding villages add the gay color of their costumes to the picture.

Romanians, Hungarians, and Saxons make up the citizens of the town, as these three distinct peoples make up almost the whole of Transylvania. Though the Romanians form the overwhelming majority, and trace their ancestry back to the days of the colonizing of Trajan's Dacia Felix, they have always been farmers. Their forebears were referred to in the old chronicles of invading nations as *pastores Romanorum,* and pastores their descendants remained during seven hundred years of oppression by the Austro-Hungarian Empire. Under the protection of the Teutonic Knights, Germans came to settle in Transylvania eight hundred years ago, and there is a legend that the original group were the children spirited away by the Pied Piper of Hamelin. The Hungarians who finally ruled this land "across the forests" as masters and conquerors were never able to destroy the Romanian language or culture, in spite of unbelievably drastic efforts to do this. The German settlers were always permitted their own schools and churches, even by the Hungarians, and as a result the three languages still exist, and many Transylvanians are as matter-of-factly trilin-gual as are the Swiss. With the establishment of Romania Mare in 1918, the learning of the Romanian language was required, but no attempt was made to eradicate any other language. For this reason I was able to place my older children in a Saxon school, where, in the German they already knew, their education could continue without interruption while they improved their knowledge of the Romanian language.

Brasov had kept its pleasing Old World look, as I have told you, but it had developed many and growing industries both within the town and in the surrounding villages. There were plants manufacturing a wide variety of products: textiles, hardware, munitions, airplanes, paper, and railway carriages, for example. There were extensive market gardens and green-houses, where both vegetables and flowers were raised, and the valleys were dotted with small but rich and well-cultivated farms. In addition to this, and making it a military objective as the war came ever closer, was the fact that Brasov was an important railway center.

It was a sunny, cold morning in March, 1944, when I presented myself, not without some trepidation, at the Red Cross canteen in the station. The station building itself was old but quite imposing, with a shabby dignity of its own. It was rather like a nice old lady who had known better days, and was now lost in the bustling, dirty, miscellaneous crowd that thronged the platforms and waiting rooms. Soldiers, officials, women, children, important-looking gentlemen, and stray dogs jostled one another. I shouldered my way through them to the door leading into what was then the canteen; a room much too small for all the activity it housed. In it there were two enormous caldrons for tea and soup, large tables, cupboards, a sink, and what seemed to me innumerable cups, baskets, bags, and cans.

I was met by a tall, fair-haired, strong-looking woman, who looked straight at me with steady blue eyes. This was Mrs. Podgoreanu, who for four years had been running the canteen tirelessly and efficiently. She had a direct and commanding manner, and she viewed me speculatively, with a sort of "So! What am I to do with *you?*" expression. There was something uncompromising in the way she shook hands. I felt there was no nonsense about her, and that she would tolerate none, and my usual desperate shyness came over me. Inside I felt small and incompetent, while outside I felt as though my hands and feet were suddenly abnor-mally large and completely awkward. This self-consciousness, combined with a desperate desire to please, has always been a great handicap to me, for though outwardly I have through a strong sense of duty overcome it, it still greatly disturbs me. When I was younger I sometimes actually fainted from the exertion it took to dominate it. I tried to smile naturally and easily at Mrs. Podgoreanu. "Please," I said, " could I wash up, or do something else, or shall I just wait?"

"A troop train is coming in. You can serve tea at that window over there," she replied, in a tone which seemed to imply that perhaps at least I would be doing no actual harm in that job, and she gave me some simple, specific directions which I hurriedly tried to follow. Soldiers came to the window, and the canteen suddenly hummed with activity. More Red Cross workers arrived and were introduced to me, and I was delighted to see from what very different social levels they came. There were wives and daughters of judges and apothecaries, soldiers and generals, factory directors and workmen, all evidently used to working together in an efficient team. The canteen was organized in two shifts: from 8:00 A.M. to 1:00 P.M. and from 1:00 P.M. to whatever late hour it happened to become! Not all could do as much as this but, on the other hand, there were a few who were able to work an incredible number of hours, and the chief of these workers was Mrs. Podgoreanu.

I arranged to work sometimes with one group and sometimes with the other, which seemed to please everyone, although my thought was that by working an afternoon shift and the following morning one, I could spend the next twenty-four hours in Bran with the younger children. In Brasov, of course, I stayed at the barracks with the older ones. However, I rarely got to Bran as often as I expected to, and often I worked a number of days continuously, for I felt this was the least I could do as the misery of those tragic days unfolded before my horrified eyes.

Even so, my record never approached that of Mrs. Podgoreanu. She seemed the one person to be there always; the first to arrive and the last to go. Her administrative ability was colossal, her strength a thing to be wondered at, and her leadership so positive and able that I obeyed her gladly even though at times her insistence on an unalterable method of doing some routine task seemed unreasonable. I remember, for example, that instead of weighing out sugar for the jars of tea, we had to count out *exactly* forty-seven pieces and tie them into little bags ready for use. There were times when an aching back made sitting for hours and counting forty-seven sugar lumps seem an unbearable operation, and her routine habit of picking out an occasional bag at random and recounting to be sure there were exactly forty-seven pieces made us all feel as if we were being treated like children—especially when her finding forty-eight or forty-six pieces meant that all bags must be counted over again. However, I realized even then that perhaps this insistence on a routine of simple, exact work for our hands furnished an outlet for the nervous tension of our other activities. At any rate, I learned to love and admire her unstintingly. Bearing a deep personal sorrow bravely, she was one of the grandest workers, the best leaders, and the most selfless women I have ever known.

The first morning my performance at the tea window apparently proved satisfactory, for I felt that Mrs. Podgoreanu looked at me less skeptically when the troop train pulled out and word came that the first refugee train of the day was arriving. I well remember that first train, for though it seemed terrible to me, it was nothing to compare with the misery I was to see later. In the first place, the morning was sunny and everyone was fairly cheerful, and in the second place, this train had come by a route well provided with canteens, and had not had too many long waits on the road. Still I found their plight unbelievably pathetic, and the condition of my wounded soldiers in Austria, tucked into clean beds and under expert care, seemed suddenly almost enviable in comparison. Women, children, and old men were crowded into cattle cars or third-class carriages, together with all the belongings they had been able to bring with them—and these belongings included livestock. Hens, geese, cows, dogs, and pigs added to the noise and dirt. I saw then for the first time what incongruous things people will take away with them. There were cows standing uneasily next to handsome bronze lamps; hens nesting in Louis XV chairs. The most moving things to me were the solemn-eyed children, tired, dirty, and hungry. How I longed to be able to take them and give them a good bath in warm water!

We of the canteen, loaded with great baskets and large cans, hurried as fast as possible down the rails to begin serving the train at the last carriage, begging the people as we went to remain in their carriages and come in turn to the windows to receive their portions. In our flat baskets we carried bread, smoked ham and bacon, apples, and cheese, and in the cans were milk for the children and hot tea and rum for the older people. Sometimes we had a few orderlies to help carry things, and then we could serve more quickly. It was not at all easy to control what one was giving, and to be sure not to give twice to the same family. It was especially difficult not to be carried away by pity into giving as much as one felt was necessary, for there were so many that we could not really *satisfy* hunger, we could only appease it. We fed from two to five thousand people daily, and most of the food came from donations. Over us hung always the dread of having a train come in when we had nothing to give.

In addition to distributing food and drink, I learned that one of the workers must always go through the carriages looking for illness or special need. This, too, had its difficulties, for some would complain in the hope of getting an extra portion of food, while others would dissemble for fear of being put off the train and separated from their families. In my first train I found one child ill, and an old woman who was obviously dying. Horrified, I rushed back to Mrs. Podgoreanu for instructions, but she accepted my news calmly and gave the necessary information to the doctor, a young man in uniform whom I had not seen before, and who seemed to me to have a rather careless and irresponsible manner. He left in the direction of the railway carriage, and I got a new load of food and drink and continued my work. I seemed to walk back and forth endlessly. Full baskets, empty baskets; full baskets, empty baskets. My arms seemed to grow longer and longer, while my legs grew shorter and shorter.

At last this train moved off, leaving us with the relieved feeling that we had been able to give a little comfort, but it was closely followed by another. This was a military school being evacuated; six or eight hundred boys, all in open railway trucks. They had food, but they were terribly cold, and their officers and instructors were much concerned about them. We gave them hot tea as well as generous portions of sweets, and everyone was pleased to help them because they were such a nice, gay crowd, determinedly making light of their miseries. When one of their officers recognized me and passed the word along, they were delighted, and as the train moved out they gave me a rousing cheer which did me good. I returned to the canteen with my heart a little lighter, and found there the young doctor fussing over the injured hand of a workman and grumbling because he had no help. I glanced at Mrs. Podgoreanu for permission, and then offered my services to him. He accepted them with a shrug, and ordered me about in a highhanded manner, interspersing his directions with condescending remarks of a rather personal kind.

"You should do it this way, madame—or should I say 'miss'?" he inquired, looking at me sidewise under his eyelashes in what I suppose he thought was an irresistible manner.

"You may say 'Madame,'" I replied severely. Then, as he grinned in an amused manner, I added, "I have six children."

"Nonsense!" he retorted. And he added a slangily rude remark which indicated that I must be confusing myself with my sister.

Inwardly amused but outwardly stiff I said solemnly that *she* had three children of her own, but that I *thought* the subject in which we were both interested was the injured hand I was bandaging. Before he could reply further, another train was announced, and I finished my job and hurried out, once more heavily laden with supplies.

The people in this train were much worse off than those in the first one had been. Some of them had come from Jassy, Moldavia's capital, where I myself had been a refugee in World War I, and I felt a special anxiety to help them on that account. In one cattle truck I found a woman in labor, an old woman attending her, and the two of them surrounded by the rest of the family as well as by a cow, a few pigs, and some annoyed and cackling hens. I rushed off to get the young doctor, hot water, towels, and other necessities; not an easy or quick job because the train had stopped on a far line and it was a long distance to the canteen and its medicine chest. Back again, and anxious because we had no way of knowing how long the train would stay, I found myself becoming extremely annoyed with the doctor's nonchalance, and I began giving him a few crisp suggestions. He looked a little surprised, and apparently revised his estimate of my age. "You seem to be accustomed to giving orders!" he said with some irritation at one point.

"I certainly can give them when people don't seem to know their duty!" I replied briskly, and continued to attend to the matter in hand.

All went well with the birth, and presently we had a nice little baby girl. The doctor left to take care of another call, and I helped the old woman to clear up and make the young mother as comfortable and safe as the circumstances permitted. During this process a girl who stopped to see the family recognized me, to the general delight, but no one was especially surprised. One pleasant Romanian characteristic is that they are never astonished at anything! However, when the family at once begged me to be godmother to the new baby, I agreed, and set out to find a priest.

As I was hurrying up the platform I met the Commanding General and his staff, and I stopped to greet him. He was General Nicolae Tataranu, an old friend of mine, and one of our best and bravest generals. In World War I he had been severely wounded and taken prisoner by the Germans, but he had managed to escape. I could remember well how as a little girl in Jassy I had sat at my mother's side when she received him, and had listened with her to the exciting tale of his adventures. In World War II he had commanded our troops at Stalingrad, but because he suffered from Parkinson's disease his increasing illness had obliged him to leave the front, and had saved him from the terrible fate of becoming a prisoner of the Russians. I shook him warmly by the hand, and embarked at once upon my tale of the new baby. Would he please send for a priest? He gave the order at once, and then, reminding me tactfully of my royal obligations, he formally presented his staff to me. Suddenly I noticed in the background my flighty young doctor, looking extremely uncomfortable. At the same moment General Tataranu's eye fell upon him.

"Does Your Royal Highness know the doctor on duty here?" he inquired. And when I replied that he had not been presented to me, the General said briskly, *"Prezinta-te!"*—"Present yourself!"

Stammering a little, the young doctor sheepishly began the proper formula. "I have the honor to present myself, Lieutenant Doctor—" but his alarmed expression as he evidently recalled his former remarks to me was finally too much for me, and I spoiled his presentation by bursting out laughing. It could have been the beginning of a good friendship, but I never quite got over my feeling that he was too careless in the performance of his job, which to me seemed much more important than caring for patients in the safer surroundings of their own homes or of a hospital. I was therefore not too much surprised to learn some time later of the final incident in his career at Brasov. Mrs. Podgoreanu, making a surprise visit to the infirmary on a night when he was on duty, found him definitely *off* duty, and not alone. He tried to brazen it out by offering to present the lady, but Mrs. Podgoreanu refused to co-operate.

"I do not need to be told *what* she is," said Mrs. Podgoreanu icily, "and I do not wish to be told *who* she is." And almost immediately we had a new doctor assigned to the canteen.

On my first day at the station, however, the doctor faded quite quickly and unobtrusively into the background as soon as his "presentation" was over. While we waited for the priest to appear, General Tataranu informed me that he had come to make a general inspection of the work and to designate a room for the dispensary. He asked me if I would be willing to take over its organization, working with the head of the military hospital in Brasov, and of course I was delighted to accept the job. Then with Mrs. Podgoreanu we inspected a restaurant just outside the station. Because it had acquired what was apparently a well-deserved reputation for various shady activities, it was possible for the army to requisition it for Red Cross uses. It could be used as a rest house for the needy when trains were delayed for long periods, and—as I realized with joy—it would give me a place to bathe the children!

With this settled, I returned to the baby and found that the priest had arrived. We hoisted him with some difficulty into the truck, since he was both old and portly, and there, with the cow in uncomfortable and unaccustomed proximity, he performed the sacred rite. I held the baby over an improvised font while hens scuttled about and pigs grunted, but the mother smiled contentedly, the grandmamma wiped away a tear, the other children giggled shyly, and for a moment everyone was happy. The only real interruption occurred because of a stout orderly, who had heard of the baptism and had somehow found a candle which he felt would add to the solemnity of the occasion. There was no room for him in the crowded railway truck, but he brought from somewhere a small, rickety stepladder upon which he stood just at the door, his candle held high in one hand. Suddenly there was a splintering crash. The ladder had collapsed under his weight, and candle and candleholder together landed in a pile of kindling wood. After a moment, while we made sure he was not seriously hurt, the service continued, hurried a little at the last moment because the train was leaving. As it pulled out everyone waved and smiled for all the world as if there were no misery or heartbreak at all.

I managed to keep track of my goddaughter. She returned later to Jassy, but of course after I myself left Romania I never heard any more about her. Let us hope that others do not remember how she was born and christened, since in the Communist world it could bring her only harm, but I believe that she and those who love her have not forgotten.

On the heels of this train came another, and then another, and another. Finally it was after midday. The other group of workers arrived, and I felt I had earned my rest. But what pleased me most was that I knew from the way Mrs. Podgoreanu spoke to me that I had won my spurs.

From that day until the day I left the canteen we worked together in perfect harmony and in devotion to the Red Cross and each other—I and my friend and comrade, who one night so gallantly defied all rules to put into my hands a silver cross.

In my nurse's uniform

Ireland
1951.

ELEVEN

NOT ALL my days at the station canteen left me with the feeling that we had been able to alleviate the misery of the thousands of people who had been driven from their homes. For some we could do nothing, and then my feeling of frustration added to the depression always lurking in the background of my mind as I worked. What, after all, was a little bread and hot soup to someone who had lost everything?

I remember especially one bleak Sunday afternoon. A cold, cutting wind was blowing, and a merciless sleet added to the discomfort of the weather. The mixture of rain and snow froze on our coats until we walked in armor plate, and the bitter cold everywhere made our aching and swollen hands clumsy in handling the icy slices of raw bacon we were working with in the canteen. There were three trains to be dealt with at once. The people were hungry, cold, and unreasonable in their misery and despair, while the space between the lines was all too narrow for the seething mass of distraught humanity that surged out of the trains in a desperate attempt to get food. The air was full of the cries of frightened children, the pleas of frantic mothers, and the noises of hungry beasts who had also gone a long time without food or water.

We of the canteen, even with the extra help of soldiers sent for in the emergency, had a hard time to distribute food impartially and efficiently, and even to keep our tempers: for there comes a point when one's pity is unbearable, and it takes much self-control to avoid expressing one's helpless anger at conditions one cannot relieve. At one moment I found myself alone in the crowd, trying to save my two big cans of precious milk from being overturned in the desperate scramble from all sides to reach it. Suddenly, as I was forced against the outer platform of one of the railway cars, an officer standing above me on the platform reached down and lifted my two cans and then me to a position beside him.

"Domnitza Ileana?" he asked in a quick aside. And, when I nodded, out of breath from the last strenuous minutes in the crowd, "I thought so! We have worked together before!"

With his bulk between me and the crowd, I was able to serve the milk over his shoulder without spilling any of it; and the orderly assigned to me, with his uniform and broad shoulders to carry him through the milling people, was able to bring us fresh supplies. Never shall I forget those hungry and exhausted faces looking up at me. Their expression of patient acceptance of an awful fate was in many ways harder to bear than resentment would have been. At long last the immediate needs of the crowd were satisfied. The train pulled out with no chance for me to exchange more than brief expressions of thanks and good will with my officer friend, but as always I had been deeply moved by his recognition of me. Such things seemed to link my present with those years of my girlhood in Romania, and to make me feel that I had indeed come home. Perhaps I needed those moments to strengthen me for my later bitter experiences.

That Sunday evening all of us in the canteen were glad to sit down for a little and try to soothe our hands, which had become more bruised and aching, and to warm our feet. We hoped that no more trains would come, since our supplies were low and we were exhausted, but Mrs. Podgoreanu had no illusions. Eying her little army expertly, she put us to work. The boiling of tea started again; the counting out of sugar; the cutting of bacon—but there was no more milk or bread. When the coming of another train was announced, I for one felt tears of exhaustion and anxiety coming to my eyes. Outwardly I tried to work even more quickly, and inwardly I prayed both for strength and for supplies. I felt that to face hungry children with no milk and no bread would be something I could not bear, and glancing at Mrs. Podgoreanu I realized that she shared my fears. *Dear God, let not Thy children go hungry! Give us this day our daily bread!* ran my thoughts, while my hands measured out tea and emptied bags of exactly forty-seven lumps of sugar into the cans. It was growing dark. We worked in silence, bracing ourselves for the noise that would tell us the train was coming into the station.

Suddenly the outer door of the canteen opened, and through the storm and rush of bitter air we saw women muffled in shawls, their arms full of bundles. Some carried cans of ready-boiled milk or of coffee, and others had great baskets of freshly baked cozonac, the Romanian holiday brioche. We could have hugged the good women, bundles and all, but instead we hastened to help unload the supplies they had brought.

"Ah!" they sighed. "The bad roads! The men taking it easy on a Sunday! Everything seemed to keep us back! Are we too late?"

"Dumnezeu dragutzu v'a trimes!" we told them, using the familiar local expression which literally means "God, the Dear One, sent you!" and I know that we all felt we had received a prompt answer to the prayers in our hearts.

"The train is in!" Off we went down the line to the very end of the train, my faithful orderly and I carrying as much as we could between us. We were by this time doing good teamwork, so that the moment I emptied the first half of the cans and baskets he left for a refill, and the task went more quickly. There was little light because of the blackout, but enough to show us carriage after carriage of unfortunates, as we moved along the line. Sleepy and exhausted, many of these refugees stayed within the cars and let us serve them through the windows, and so it was that near the end of the train I came to a window where a woman stood in the shadows, holding a little bundle in her arms.

"Milk! Milk for the child!" I called to her.

"What for?" came her bitter answer. "It is no good now! Here! Take him and bury him if you have a heart; my heart is dead!" And out through the window she handed me the frozen little creature, blue and cold in death. I took him, and for a moment I felt my heart stand still—he was so cold and light. But I had to go on with my duty. There were other children in the car who were alive and wanted the milk, so I put the pathetic little bundle between my feet so that it would not be trampled, and served out the last of my supplies. The train moved on. With the empty cans and baskets on one arm, and the dead child on the other, I walked back to the canteen, and never was the way so long, so weary.

There were many of these tragedies, and they were deepened by the fact that they must be handled so quickly, in the little space of time while a train waited in the station. On another afternoon I went into the dispensary to find our new doctor arguing with a desperate mother about a baby who had pneumonia. She had six other children, this youngest child was obviously almost dying, and the refugee train was about to leave. We pleaded with her to leave the baby with us, since that offered it the only possible chance to live. Finally she agreed, if I would swear to care for it as if it were my own. Everything else was put aside for the moment while I found a proper nursing home, a doctor, and a nurse. That afternoon we won our race with death, and for six long weeks we battled, but death won in the end. It was a bitter sorrow for me, for it is always hard to learn to accept the mercy of God in taking to Himself those too weak for living in this world we have so mismanaged. My only consolation was that the mother felt we had done all we could, and more than she could have done herself.

This matter of death on the trains always added anxiety and strain to the sorrow that comes at such a time. Families anxious to get as far as possible from the battle lines, and afraid that inspection at a station would result in separation, or in the whole carful of people being held in quarantine, would go to incredible lengths to conceal sickness. And when someone died on the train, many times the body would be pushed out a window as the train moved through the darkness, and found along the railway lines the next day. In the crowded confusion of the evacuation no real check on families was possible, and there was no one to notice at the point of arrival whether or not a family was the same size it had been when leaving home. If a mother had died, and the children were divided among other families in the car, who would report it? And if a family had a child or two less, who was to know that somewhere little dead bodies had been abandoned in a flight to save the living? Yet because of the ever-present danger of plague the authorities tried to be watchful, and there were severe penalties for concealing death or illness.

I remember one evening walking from the canteen to the dispensary, and suddenly noticing a man with a suitcase dodging furtively through the crowd. Something in his manner made me watch him, and almost at once a man following him burst through a group of people, crying desperately:

"Stop him! He's stolen my bag!"

With a bravado I did not feel was honest, the first man tried to brush him aside and deny the charge, but the second man was almost hysterically insistent. The gathering knot of people interested in what was going on brought a gendarme to the spot almost at once, and he was none too gentle as he shouted at the crowd to disperse, while he angrily ordered both men to walk ahead of him to the station police office. I followed them, anxious to see if I could help. It seemed to me that there had been more than anxiety, there had been stark terror in the second man's expression as he tried to snatch the bag from the fugitive.

When we were all in the police office and shut away from the crowd, the officer in charge brusquely asked what the trouble was. The second man, obviously making a heroic effort to control himself, repeated his accusation that his suitcase had been stolen. The first man, evidently sensing as I had the insecurity of his accuser, stoutly denied the charge again. The officer shrugged his shoulders.

"But this is simple," he said. "Tell what is in the suitcase, and we will open it. If you are right—" He shrugged again.

Once more I saw an unaccountable terror in the man's expression.

"No! I—I c-c-can't tell you!" he stammered hoarsely.

The first man was quick to seize his advantage. "You see!" he said triumphantly to the officer. "He's lying!"

I tried to think of a possible explanation. Could it be that because the suitcase belonged to some other member of his family the second man was afraid he could not identify what was in it? Or, what was more likely, was he carrying contraband? I talked with the police officer, who also began to feel that there was something out of the ordinary here. Then I talked to the second man, trying to persuade him gently that we would do all we could to help him, but that the suitcase *must* be opened to support his charge that it had been stolen. With a final gesture of desperation he surrendered and gave us the key. We opened the bag. Inside was the body of a little boy in a ragged gray suit: his two-year-old son, who had died on the train, and whom he was trying to take with him so that he and his wife could bury the child where they might visit his grave.

We looked at one another—the police officer, the thief who had stolen the suitcase, the gendarme, and I. Almost without words we came to an agreement. If Her Royal Highness would assume responsibility, the concealment of a body need not be reported officially. Her Royal Highness did, so that the sorrowing father could continue the journey with his wife: both parents a little comforted by the promise I later fulfilled, that there would be a Christian burial, and a picture of the little grave for them.

They were little worlds of tragedy, those refugee trains; yet because they were truly little worlds of their own, there were gallant deeds done, and glimpses of romance, and even moments of something like gaiety. In the canteen as well there were many sunny days when we found we could laugh again, and there were days when no trains came and we grumbled as we counted sugar lumps, or wrestled with the problem of food storage as the donations came in and the refugees did not. There were less tragic but ever-present problems: how to feed the assorted livestock on the trains; how to install baths and the unglamorous but essential sanitary facilities; how to arrange for overnight lodgings where stranded soldiers and passengers might get a few hours' restful sleep; how to prepare and store stretchers and arrange for quick transport of emergency cases to the hospitals when Brasov had only four ambulances for the whole community. And for me, in addition to the hard work, the feeling of being useful, and the moments of drama and high tragedy, there were also occasional embarrassing incidents.

One day while I worked in the dispensary there appeared a retired colonel who was being evacuated on one of the refugee trains. He was a pompous little man, who quite evidently considered himself not only important but irresistibly charming. Since I was alone, he greeted me with a profusion of compliments, and proceeded to confide in me about madame his wife. Madame his wife, the train journey having been long and the facilities inconvenient, had—amusing, was it not?—developed a little difficulty. She was, in short, although he confessed he hesitated to discuss such a thing with so charming a young lady as myself, she was, in short, a trifle constipated! Was there such a thing as a little pill or two which would relieve her discomfort?

As matter-of-factly as possible I assured him that such a condition was common under these difficult travel conditions, and I got out the little pills and put them into a bottle for him in a businesslike manner, hoping to end his unnecessarily familiar and personal remarks. But it was no use. He persisted in his little compliments, as well as in his somewhat snickering observations on life in general, and *nothing* seemed to discourage him. I busied myself in getting out the record book, and I politely inquired his name, since it was necessary to make a list of those receiving drugs. He was most happy to give me his name, with full military titles and a little boasting thrown in. And then he wished to know my name, since so charming a young lady must have a charming name, he was sure!

I realized a little desperately that he would be far better off if he left without knowing my name, and I wished with all my heart that the departure of the train would suddenly be announced or that someone else would come into the dispensary, but nothing happened. I hesitated, and he became yet more condescending and leaned yet farther over the counter. But he *must* insist on knowing my name; he must be able to treasure in his memory our delightful little encounter; I need not be shy with *him*; he had always been a ladies' man, able to encourage the most bashful of girls. So! What was my name? Trying to make the best of the situation, and regretting that the royal family of Romania had no surname I could have used casually, I mumbled it under my breath. "Domnitza Ileana." But he could not hear it; I must say it a little louder! I said it a little louder, and without really listening at all he beamed happily—and chucked me under the chin in a most encouraging and patronizing manner. But what a pretty name it was, indeed! Nothing to be shy about, after all!

And then there was a blank moment when his face suddenly froze and his eyes grew large and horrified. But—but—had I really said—? Was I—was I *really*—Domnitza—the Princess—? Annoyed with myself for feeling so embarrassed when really I had nothing to be embarrassed about, I felt myself turning slowly scarlet. Yes, I admitted in a low voice, I had really said—I really was— And then, to the everlasting gratitude of both of us, the train was at last called, my little colonel faded quickly out of the dispensary, and I saw him no more. But he contributed to the war effort by furnishing a great deal of amusement to Mrs. Podgoreanu, when I told her about him, and we were both quite certain that madame the Colonel's wife would never be told the full story of her little pills.

Mrs. Podgoreanu and I spent little time in being amused, however, since we had plenty to do. Relief and hospital trains had to be served, as well as refugees and military transports, and we were constantly trying to improve our services. The dispensary had to be equipped and kept supplied and the resthouse which General Tataranu had obtained for us had to be at least partially furnished. The Red Cross was by this time extremely low in funds, and it was necessary to appeal constantly to the general public, especially to the merchants who could give articles we were not always able to buy with money. I found people extraordinarily generous and ready to help. One factory director, besides giving us two enormous cooking kettles, gave me his own children's portable bathtub. I was overjoyed by this, and I had a grand time, whenever a train stopover permitted it, washing as many of the tired, dirty children as possible.

It was of course necessary to solicit food continuously, as well as to beg from the farmers a supply of forage for the livestock on the trains. After these things were procured they had to be stored, and distributed as wisely as possible. Soon it was evident also that the dispensary required a permanent medical and nursing service, and that our problems were touching many authorities, both military and civilian. Since the coordination of all this was in the hands of the Governor of the region, and he had also been asked to provide for the establishment of a new Red Cross hospital in Brasov, he decided to call together a big meeting for reports and suggestions. A harmless enough occasion, one would think, but it led me into serious trouble.

The meeting took place in the city hall and was well attended. Many useful suggestions and valuable offers of goods and services were made. General Tataranu, Colonel Franz Josef of the military hospital, Mrs. Podgoreanu, and the Prefect, as well as the Mayor, were all present. I had been asked to sit at the speakers' table, and at the end of the meeting I was called on to make whatever suggestions I thought necessary.

By this time I had worked long enough in the canteen to feel deeply the value of the work done there, and to realize how very shorthanded Mrs. Podgoreanu was most of the time. The dirt and confusion, the risk of contagion, the actual squalor and misery of many of the refugees, discouraged many workers from returning after one difficult day. I had not only given up most of the "free time" I had hoped to spend with the younger children in Bran, but I had actually brought the older children down to the station to help out now and then when we were desperate. I felt that if the women in Brasov could only understand the great need of these helpless victims of war they would respond in greater numbers, and I knew also that more help would be essential when the new hospital was opened. So, carried away by my enthusiasm, I made a strong appeal to the women present to do volunteer work for the Red Cross. I called on them to give an unstinted contribution of their time and strength in the many places they were so badly needed, and asked them to remember that the place of honor was where one was needed most. This place was seldom decorative or romantic, I told them, but instead was liable to be most tiresome and unpleasant, yet it offered a glorious chance to demonstrate their patriotism.

I do not remember what words I used, but I do remember that it was one of those rare occasions when I felt that what I had to say had gone directly from my heart to the hearts of others and had been received with perfect understanding. Since speaking in public is something I never do easily, I was pleased with the storm of applause that seemed to confirm my feeling of success. But alas for pride! It always comes to a fall!

More than a week later General Zwiedineck came to see me with a serious face. Since he had been my mother's aide-de-camp and trusted friend, and also looked after my business affairs in Romania, I knew him well, and I realized from his expression that something unpleasant was brewing. He did not keep me in suspense long, but spoke in stern accusation.

"You have addressed an appeal to the Romanian women! Both the Marshal and the court are very angry indeed!"

"But what nonsense!" I replied. "I never wrote a word or gave an interview to anyone! I have been working here at the canteen ever since I came from Austria!"

"Well, but what have you to say to this?" he insisted, and he opened a copy of *Universul*, the largest newspaper in Bucarest, so that I could see the black headline splashed across the page:

PRINCESS ILEANA MAKES AN APPEAL
TO THE ROMANIAN WOMEN

I stared in horror. At first I was completely at a loss to understand what had happened, but as I looked at the article more closely I realized that it was a more or less accurate account of what I had said at the meeting in Brasov a week earlier, and had already nearly forgotten about. Only a modest article had appeared in the Brasov paper, but some reporter in the capital city—perhaps honestly intending to do good—had seen an opportunity for a feature story. He could hardly have done anything worse to me, for I was now in an unpleasant and difficult situation.

At this time Romania was under the military dictatorship of Marshal Antonescu, and the Marshal's wife was undisputed head of all relief activities. Both were good friends of mine, but I knew they could quite readily become most exasperated if things went wrong. Besides, power seems to go to the heads of even the best of people, and certainly theirs was no easy position. At this same time my nephew, the young King Michael, and his mother were living in dignified disapproval of the dictatorship, although wholeheartedly concerned with the problems of our country. In a momentary bit of harmony, the Queen and the Marshal's distant cousin, Premier Mihai Antonescu, had decided that she should write an appeal for aid to the refugees, and this was to appear in the newspapers the following day. It was at this unfortunate moment, General Zwiedineck told me coldly, that my own "appeal" had been headlined, completely stealing the thunder from the Queen's article.

I realized the seriousness of the situation even while I felt I had done nothing wrong. I immediately telephoned the Queen (my sister-in-law, Helen, who had divorced my brother Carol shortly after he first gave up his rights to the throne, in 1925) and explained the situation. She was so kind and understanding that I feared what later proved to have been the case; she had seen only the Brasov article, and not the Bucarest head-lines. Then I called Mihai Antonescu, who *had* seen the headlines and who did not mince his words. It took some time for me to be heard at all, but after he had thoroughly expressed his feelings I finally managed to state authoritatively that I had written no word, and had addressed only the local women at the Governor's meeting. I reminded him that his own organization was to blame for an article quoting a member of the royal family having appeared in a newspaper without verification, and he finally admitted it. But none of this really helped the situation any, even though there were no further consequences. The Queen's appeal appeared a little limply; I felt guilty and unhappy when I was innocently congratulated by friends and officials on my own speech; and I was hurt by the reproaches I felt I had not deserved, and which had been heaped on me so quickly. I resolved once more to hold my tongue and to avoid all public appearances.

The whole experience had indicated freshly to me how difficult my sit-uation in Romania might be. As the youngest of my family, and—because both my sisters had married—the only girl at home after World War I, I had been active in work for my country, as I have told you. I had gone everywhere, and ever since my own refugee experience as a little girl in Jassy I had been treated as a loved child of the people. Even after I mar-ried a Habsburg and went to live in Austria, the Romanians, who have a fine disregard for form, continued to consider me theirs, and this had annoyed some people very much. The law of Romania has a loophole for her departing daughters: they can petition to keep their citizenship if they marry foreigners. I had availed myself of this privilege, of course, but my bond with the people was much deeper than this, and both they and I knew it. That this warmed my heart was natural, as was the temp-tation to me to bask in this affection. Natural also, I suppose, was the resentment of this affection that was felt by others. My mother and I had suffered bitterly from this resentment during her lifetime. I had learned to try to stay out of the limelight, to keep in the shadow; but this was not always easy to manage with a people so enthusiastically demonstrative as the Romanians. They were often hurt by my evasions of them, and would reproach me for what they thought was my "change of heart." Now I realized that a resentment still existed, and at first I felt it would be a serious impediment to the work I hoped to accomplish.

With time, however, I came to understand that this also was a form of temptation. The wish to succeed the easy way, to take the road that lies open and clear before us, often makes our work superficial. Besides, an outward success is not an adequate measure of the depth and durability of what we accomplish. Worldly success did not crown even our Lord's life when He was on earth, though that work was divine and far above our own human efforts. If One as great and pure as He evaded popularity as a temptation, who was I—limited by human weakness, shortsighted and imperfect as I knew myself to be—to shirk this little cross? And good can be accomplished in a small and intimate way even better than in the larger and more impersonal ways. This I came to understand more and more. What greater honor can we ask than to be permitted to save a life? And this honor was to be vouchsafed me often.

But on that day in Brasov I did not foresee what lay before me. I found the reproaches I had received difficult to bear, although I was grateful that I felt only hurt and sorrowful, and not resentful. I have always prayed to avoid feeling bitter toward anyone, and my prayer has been answered. I reminded myself how often I had proved that when I went up what seemed to be a blind alley, if I could wholeheartedly give up and bow my head, if I could truly say, "Thy Will, not mine, be done!" a new and marvelous road would open before me. But it is so hard to give up! Deeply hurt, I left for a few days the work I loved, and went back to Bran and the younger children.

And as I went I felt a sorrowful longing to be a child again, and to be going to my father for comfort. Over and over again I remembered something that had happened to me when I was about sixteen. A cousin of mine had got us both into difficulties, and had laid the blame on me when I did not deserve it at all. Since the cousin was the daughter of my mother's favorite sister, and our guest, my mother hesitated to pass judgment on the matter. It was one of those completely unhappy moments the young experience. I felt that the whole world had turned against me unjustly; there was no hope or joy anywhere.

That night my father came home and heard the story. He was a quiet and reserved man, who never expressed himself without careful thought, and for that reason his words had special weight with everyone. You can imagine, then, how suddenly radiant my world became when I heard what he said.

"But I know my daughter very well, and I know she could not possibly have done this, whatever others may say about it."

And, although it was rare for him to express his affection for us, he came to the room where I lay crying bitterly and told me what he had said, and stayed with me quietly and comfortingly until I had fallen asleep.

Thinking of this as I rode to Bran, I felt desperately lonely for my father. I felt I needed his strength and his kindness, his deep understanding of life. But most of all, I felt, I needed someone to say of me:

"But I know my daughter very well, and I know she could not possibly have done this."

TWELVE

THEN IN my room in Bran, as now in my New England bedroom, a photograph of my father stood on a table where I could see it as I entered the doorway. It is the last photograph taken of him, and it shows his beautiful, clear-cut profile, with his hair and his beard turned slightly gray. I remember thinking when I was little that all kings had beards, and being very astonished when I was presented to the old King of Sweden, who was clean shaven. According to my ideas, also, kings always wore uniforms. My father wore mufti only in the country, and even then only on days when he felt especially gay and in a holiday mood. Secretly I wonder now if he ever felt really quite at home in civilian clothes.

Always my thoughts seek him out most easily in Sinaia, because there his royal duties were a little less exacting, and we could see more of him. We migrated to Sinaia for the summer at the end of June, and remained there until fall, when the opening of Parliament called my father back, and my studies summoned me also to the city. But do not imagine that life was ever simple, or lacking in duties and in calls from ministers, even at Sinaia! Once we were playing a game of writing epitaphs, and my sister Mignon wrote her epitaph for a king: "Rest him, O Lord, far from his ministers!" That is how she who was the daughter of a king and the wife of a king felt about it. Always things were spoiled for us children by some minister coming to hold consultations with our parents. I realize now that the lives of the ministers also were interrupted, but in those early years I had small sympathy for them, and only felt sorry for us.

My father was at heart a quiet, gentle scholar, who all his life kept a lively interest in the science of botany. But above all else he was what the Germans call *pflichttreu*, which means literally "duty-faithful." It was this innate sense of duty that made him overcome his personal shyness and gave him an air of royal dignity which made him stand out among other men, in spite of his retiring nature. One of his greatest personal pleasures was to go for long rambles with his dogs through the Sinaia forests, looking for rare plants for his rock garden. Deep satisfaction he also found among his books. I can see him now, his spectacles on his nose, one eye half shut because of the smoke of his cigar, one eyebrow a little raised, as with his beautifully shaped hands he selected a favorite volume, his long fingers lovingly turning the pages as he looked for a well-loved passage. He read with ease the old Greek and Latin classics in their original tongues, and he knew the ancient Romanian Cyrillic alphabet.

His knowledge of Latin stood him in good stead when he visited the villages in Transylvania, where language would have been a barrier between him and those speaking only Hungarian if he could not have talked in Latin with the Catholic priests, and so have had translators the people would trust. He read widely also in modern languages, and in addition to his thirst for knowledge and his love of beautiful literature he enjoyed a good detective story. He and I were great admirers of Bulldog Drummond, and used to carry on long fanciful conversations, pretending we had met one or another of the characters in the series. Later, when

I met certain Communists who reminded me of people Bulldog Drummond had encountered, I used to long to have someone like my father, who might share with me what seemed almost a recognition of people I had not really believed could exist.

Although his outward reserve with his children was great, my father had a deep inner comprehension and understanding upon which I unconsciously relied always, even in little matters. When I was about ten or twelve years old I developed a passion for dressing up, and I loved to arrange a costumed dinner party. My father joined in cheerfully when his duties permitted, and I remember one most successful evening when he put on an old dressing gown made of an Indian blanket which had been given him by the Red Cross during the war. Binding a few feathers around his head, he took the part of a red Indian chief to my entire satisfaction.

He was quite extraordinarily modest, and rarely wanted anything for himself. Once on his return from a journey to Paris he gave each of us a lovely and thoughtfully selected gift. Then, almost shyly, he showed us a beautiful jade vase. "This," he said firmly, "is for myself! I will not give this one away." We admired the vase and encouraged his intention, but in only a few days he brought it down from his study. "I really don't know just where to put it," he said apologetically. "I think you'd better have it down here somewhere." And he handed it to my mother, who solved the problem by placing it where we could all enjoy looking at it.

It seems strange that Fate sought out this quiet and self-contained scholar to guide a nation to the realization of all its dreams. His life demanded of him great and terrible decisions on every level; the sacrifice of the loyalties of his youth; the sacrifice of his relationship to his oldest son when this son did not measure up to his responsibilities. He was so modest that I think he never quite grasped his personal contribution to his accomplishments. He did not accept it as a tribute to himself when a whole people were swept with joy and gratitude, adoring him as a victorious liberator. After World War I, when he returned to Bucarest and when he entered Transylvania people literally knelt in the streets as he went by. I myself saw an old man step out of the kneeling mass of people and hold up a child, saying to him:

"Look at him well! Remember his every feature, that when you are old like me you may remember and tell your grandchildren what our Liberator looked like!"

After the war, because of his great love and understanding for his people, he set about the agrarian reform, aided by Ion I. C. Bratianu—son of the Bratianu who had persuaded King Carol I to come down the Danube to Romania. Thus the soil at last became the possession of those who tilled it, and because this social reform was headed by the King, for whose vast acres no exception was made, everyone had to follow suit. And, to do them justice, most of the landed proprietors did not protest: a Romanian's love of the soil is well understood by all other Romanians. When at the end of his last illness he closed his weary eyes, it was as quietly and unassumingly as he had always lived.

"I am very tired," he murmured as he rested his head against my mother's shoulder. "I must once just rest a little."

The whole nation wept as for the death of a dear parent. And with the unfailing perspicacity of the people they called him not "the Liberator"; not "the Victorious." For the title that should live in their hearts they gave him a dearer one: "Ferdinand the Loyal, King of the Peasants."

The Sinaia that he loved stands in the valley of the Prahova River, which cuts the principal pass through the Carpathians. It is a narrow valley, but very beautiful. The great forest comes down to the very edge of the turbulent river and the rocky peaks stand grandly outlined against a Mediterranean-blue sky. It is indescribable, that marvelous blue of the Romanian sky; a deep, intense blue where often no cloud will be in sight for many weeks. As a result, rain for us is always a blessing, and we can enjoy its cool silver-gray falling with a grateful heart.

The town of Sinaia is formed by old-fashioned villas of the last century, when society, following the example of King Carol I, built their summer residences in the beautiful valley. They grouped their houses around a park, a casino, and a shopping center, but the King built his magnificent castle up in the forest where it was peaceful and secluded. When my father became king in 1914 he did not move into this Castle of Peles, but preferred to remain in the Castle of Pelisor, which had been built for my parents just before the birth of their fourth child, and which was full of charm. It resembled a comfortable English country house more than anything else, and it was a home we all adored. As a child I was greatly chagrined by my brother Nicholas's boast that *he* had been born up in the mountains, while I was born in a mere suburb of Bucarest!

Dear, comfortable Pelisor! Always there was the sound of rushing waters about and through it, so that visitors on their first night thought it was pouring rain outside, and were startled to awaken to an azure sky and see that the ground was stone dry. Our mornings started with breakfast taken in the long dining room. Following a Romanian custom, my mother sat at the head of the table with my father on her right; then, in succession, came all the members of the court that had followed us, any visitors there might be, and we children. All meals except the evening one were taken with the whole court, even to the officer of the guard. Everyone was included in "the family"; everyone seemed to belong together; conversation and jokes flowed freely around the table. On Sundays at the changing of the guard, which was housed in a building of its own, the band would play and the people on their way home from church would wander up and listen to the music and walk about the beautifully laid-out terraces of the palace. My parents used to saunter down and mix with the crowd freely; they needed no guards to protect them. That is the Sinaia I cherish in my memory: the beautiful mountains; the sunshine, flowers, and music; the smiling holiday crowd; my father and mother, gracious and dear to everyone; a feeling of good will and contentment everywhere.

But in later years when I went to Sinaia I felt my heart contract a little. After my mother's death the Pelisor was closed. My brother Carol, returning to Romania in 1930 as King Carol II, used the Castle of Peles for official entertaining, and he had other conceptions of how life should be lived. He built a wall around the terraces, and the guard was no longer there for show but to keep people out. The life of his court was much more orderly, formal, and correct, but it was also less happy and congenial.

When my nephew, young King Michael, came to the throne after his father's abdication in 1940, he inherited a troubled situation. The country was bitterly resentful because of the lands that had been taken from it by the combined threats of Germany and Russia, then allies. In less than a year Romania was at war with Soviet Russia. The government—as I have said—was a military dictatorship under Marshal Ion Antonescu. Michael decided to go on living in the Foisor, a house that had been rebuilt and used by his father after the original dwelling of that name had burned down, and that lacked the charm of the others for those of us who had known the old days. Though his court was full of sober dignity, and his beautiful, gentle mother lent it charm, there was an atmosphere of sadness about it, and it lacked the vigor and zest of former times. But Michael had been too young to remember the sunny days of his grand-parents. His youth had been a sad one. His father had left his family and his country when Michael was hardly more than a baby, and had not returned until Michael was seven. Then, because Carol's wife had divorced him, Michael was unhappily without a mother most of the time until, at eighteen, his father's abdication made him king. He is said to have remarked sadly on one occasion:

"When I needed a mother, I had a father; and when I needed a father, I had a mother."

All these things were in my thoughts during those few days at Bran with the younger children, when I had left Brasov temporarily after the newspaper accounts of my speech. I realized after a day or two that, in addition to having been badly hurt by being blamed for something I had not done, I had also been really exhausted by the long hours of work I had been doing and by the misery and despair I had so constantly witnessed. A little rested, I knew that I must not let my personal feelings keep me from working where there was so much need. The best thing would be to see Michael and his mother, Queen Helen, whom the family had always called Sitta. Then, too, I had been thinking so much about my father that I felt a great longing to see his favorite home again, so I motored to Sinaia over the magnificent pass, of which I never tired no matter how often I crossed and recrossed it.

Michael, unlike the three kings of his family who had ruled before him, preferred the comfort of civilian clothes to a uniform. He is a tall, blond young man, somewhat broad and solid. His hair has a wave in it, his eyes are blue, and he has a most enchanting smile. It brings with it deep dimples that are almost disconcerting in the face of a man so serious and given to so few words. To me, of course, there will always be in him things which remind me of the sunny-haired child who brought so much happiness to us all by his birth, and whose carefree baby ignorance of what had happened added to the stunned grief of the whole family when Carol renounced the throne and left Romania in 1925. At Sinaia I found him always followed by a German police dog. Before that it had been a great Dane—I can never think of Michael without a dog at his heels.

Sitta, his mother, is a slim, tall woman, with the greatest charm and sweetness about her. Her appearance is always exquisitely neat and dainty; I have only once seen her ruffled. It is from her that Michael inherits his dimples and his sudden, entrancing smile. She is a little shortsighted, which gives her a slight air of hesitation, and which has added to her natural shyness. When she came to meet me, she in her turn was surrounded by a crowd of Pekinese dogs, barking and gamboling around her feet. As always, it was with a sigh of contentment that I glided into the atmosphere of her well-run house; the perfect service at a beautifully laid table; the simple but excellently cooked food. The conversation was easy and often amusing, since both mother and son have a strong sense of humor and an incomparable talent for describing an amusing situation. Yet lurking in the background there seemed to be the shadow of tragedy past and to come. Intangible and ignored, it was nevertheless present, and I had the feeling of fighting against time and an overwhelming fate.

As I had thought, Sitta and Michael were both interested in hearing of what was being done in Brasov for the refugees, and of the plans for the Red Cross hospital soon to be opened. The hospital had of course been one of the reasons for the luckless meeting I had attended, which I explained and described fully. Once they understood what had happened, and how really innocent I had been in the matter, they were most kind. We discussed my situation, and they came to the conclusion that I could go on working as long as I accepted no leading position. In the Red Cross hospital I was to be simply one of the nurses, and to have nothing to do with the official side. I told them of the class for nurses' aides which Colonel Franz Josef of the military hospital thought was needed, and which he had spoken to me about organizing. They felt that if I joined it as a pupil, so that I should not seem to be assuming any leadership, it would be satisfactory for me to help with it.

Although at first thought these restrictions seemed somewhat hampering, I found in actual practice that they were most advantageous. I was at first much freer of responsibility, and yet my work in Austria had actually given me so much valuable experience that I was able to be of considerable service. When I was later asked for help and advice, I had the satisfying feeling that it was because I had proved myself to be a thorough and efficient worker, and not because I had, as it were, come in at the top on my title. Therefore, as time went on I saw that a blessing had come out of the experience.

I left Michael and Sitta with a lighter heart than I had brought. The woods of Sinaia, too, had worked their old magic. Yet one small anxious question remained in my mind. Did Marshal Antonescu and his wife also understand by this time that I had been the victim of circumstances? There was one way to find out: I would go and ask them.

THIRTEEN

O N MY way back to Bran I stopped in Predeal to see the Antones-cus. Predeal is the highest point of the pass, and it was for many years the frontier between Old Romania and a part of the country which had been occupied by Austria-Hungary for seven hundred years. I well remember as a child driving up to the pass by horse and carriage, and looking down into the unbelievably beautiful valley of the Timis; down upon Transylvania, the land where brother Romanians dwelt under a foreign rule. On both sides of the pass lived the dream that one day Transylvania would be liberated, free to join the mother country. It is still wonderful to me to think that I lived to see that dream come true; to see the barrier of the frontier destroyed. Later, as a young girl in the company of fellow students from the School of Physical Education, I went skiing on those slopes, always with a conscious thrill of joy in passing freely across what had once been a boundary, and entering the country into which as a child I had only been able to gaze hopefully. A dream came true, and then the nightmare of slavery again descended, but I know my country. From the passes of the Carpathians, no matter in what direction he looks, our enemy keeps watch over a country where the dream still lives!

In the spring of 1944 one still crossed the old boundary freely, and so I came at last to the home of the Antonescus. It was a simple and charming villa, built of whole logs and furnished in keeping with the surroundings, and it commanded one of the most magnificent views I know. From the sunny glass veranda one had the feeling of overlooking the world: the panorama of mountains and forest unrolled farther and farther away until it reached an incredibly distant blue horizon. I could readily understand Marshal Antonescu's love for his villa, and why he found it a place of rest and refreshment.

I, too, found it such a place that day. For a moment I had a feeling of timelessness which lifted me out of the difficult present in which I was living. It was a timelessness infinitely far removed, also, from the future that was two years in front of us, when I was to come by accident into the square in Bucarest where a small unhappy crowd were being forced under the guns of the Russian soldiers to produce a "spontaneous" demand for the Marshal's death—a "spontaneous" demand picked up and magnified by radio. It was infinitely far removed from a day in 1947, when a little haunted ghost, home from the Russian prisons, a ghost who had been the wife of the Marshal, was to beg of me as a parting favor that I try to get for her a poison which she could hide, and so save herself from further torture.

Much criticized Marshal Antonescu! His political actions may be condemned, his self-assurance deplored, but no one ever doubted his deep patriotism. He was the implacable enemy of communism, and to the Communists he was given for punishment. His death was ignominious and brutal, yet in it he achieved a greatness which had not been his in the days of his power. This is not a political history, although in order to supplement my own observations of what occurred in my country I have read much that has been written, both published and unpublished accounts and analyses. Therefore, when I speak of the Marshal I do not speak of him as a politician, as perhaps someday I may do. I speak now of him as a personal friend, and to me friendship means loving one's friends, faults and all, even though one does not love their faults.

In World War I, Antonescu was aide-de-camp to Marshal Prezan, who was Romanian high commander, and an intimate friend of my family. At Jassy during the retreat we lived in a house in town, but the Prezans had a small villa outside the city. It stood on the edge of a wood overlooking gentle hills, and quite often "Papa Prezan" and his wife would invite me to spend a day there and enjoy the country. Antonescu was then a captain, young, good tempered, and with a very real love for children. He would enter enthusiastically into my games of imagination, and he did a great deal to help a child forget the unchildlike scenes among which she was living. I remember that I enjoyed pretending to take his picture, using as a "camera" a pencil that an American of the Red Cross had given me. He would pose in all seriousness, and be properly astonished at the unflattering sketches I produced as the finished "photographs." When I was at school in England and he was military attaché at the Legation in London, he would come to visit me on Saturdays, greatly amused at my invariable requests that he bring me some ginger beer. His standards for everything were always high, and I can never remember a time when I did not have the feeling that I would hate it very much if my friend Antonescu should hear I had done something wrong. No matter how powerful and autocratic he became in his public life during the years after my marriage, to me he was always the same. I had remarked on this to him once, and he had laughed.

"It is my own youth that I find when you are with me," he said.

Therefore, I was not wholly surprised, when I made my visit to him and his wife, to find that even if he had been angry and had stormed at General Zwiedineck, he softened when he saw me. He was a short, well-proportioned man, with ruddy complexion and reddish hair which—together with his severity—had gained for him the nickname of *Cainele Rosu*—The Red Dog. He had kept a youthful figure and appearance, and was still fond of skiing. This fact also set him apart from other Romanian generals, who somehow usually seem to acquire rotundity along with the dignity of high rank. His wife, whom he adored, and who could in his eyes do no wrong, was a small neat person with an orderly brain. She was a marvelous organizer, and I have never known her to forget a promise or to fail to carry out what she had promised. She was somewhat handicapped by the fact that she often did not properly evaluate the flattery given her because of her high position, and she consequently was too apt to think of herself as infallible. This meant that she often annoyed people, or unnecessarily hurt or offended them, but her intentions were of the best, and I know that she was truly kind.

Since I have always found it best to be honest, I proceeded to bring up the reason for my visit immediately. I found my old friend not difficult to appease, if indeed he had ever been as angry as I had been told he was. That is another thing I have discovered: things always become exaggerated in the telling, because few people can resist the temptation to enlarge upon a story, especially if it is at the expense of someone else. Then, too, many people prefer repeating unkind remarks to telling the kind ones, although often in the heat of anger more has been said than is really meant. Romanians have sometimes been said to be much given to this sport, which is dignified by the name of intrigue, but I have never felt that it was from real malice so much as from the pleasure of letting their imaginations run away with them, and the fun of seeing the results. I do not share this particular enjoyment, perhaps because my position made me so often a victim of it, and I finally learned that it was best stopped by pinning people down to the facts as soon as possible. Then they smilingly and deprecatingly got out of it, and it all boiled down to nothing—although sometimes one was burned by the steam just the same!

Marshal and Madame Antonescu accepted my explanation, which relieved me very much, although I realized, as I told them, that they wanted to believe well of me rather than the opposite—which, unfortunately, was not always the case with others. We talked of the general situation in Romania. Antonescu was decidedly anxious and unhappy, but he still believed in the German military machine.

"I know," he told me, "that many think I should turn around and capitulate to the Allies; but if this were done without warning I should be a traitor to the pledged word of my country. There is also the fact that Germany is still strong, and could crush us in a day. But more than all this, it shall never be my hand that signs a document agreeing to the entry of Russian troops upon Romanian soil. We learned in the last war what it was like to have them as friends! What would it be like to have them enter as victorious enemies? They have always wanted to annex us, and in the past they were prevented only because the Turks got here first."

What would have been the result if Antonescu had acted differently? What would have happened to our country if he had joined in the plans to make terms with the Allies, instead of opposing this plan until he was arrested by his own people and turned over to the Communists? If this tough, realistic soldier had been free to warn and to protest against the treatment he foresaw Romania would receive from Russia, would it have made any difference? No one can say. The "ifs" of history have always fascinated me, but we can only speculate about them. At any rate, the visit had ended my immediate apprehensions about my own difficulties, and I felt I could return to Brasov and begin work again.

FOURTEEN

IN BRASOV once more, I found an order for the establishment of the
Red Cross hospital there. These hospitals in Romania were considered as being under the orders of the army, which provided the doctors,
orderlies, and all the staff except the nurses, who were Red Cross. The
linen, beds, and general equipment also belonged to the Red Cross, and
the medical supplies came from both sources. The Bucarest Red Cross
headquarters sent two excellent nurses to organize and begin this new
unit—two sisters who had both had considerable hospital experience. The
elder, Mrs. Simone Cantacuzino Pascanu, was a charming and gentle but
energetic person, who for two years had nursed the incurable cases. She
was to be head nurse, while her assistant would be her sister, Mrs. Nadeje
Soutzo; a vivacious and enterprising young woman who had been with a
field unit as far as Rostov-on-the-Don, nearly four hundred miles east of
the Romanian-Russian border.

From the very first moment our understanding was perfect, and the three of us worked in harmony through good days and bad. I confess I had been a little anxious about the women who would be appointed to head the unit. When one is dealing with the horrible effects of war it may seem that matters of precedence and protocol are slight things to think of, but an awkwardness in the small relationships of life often becomes far more important than it should, if everyone is working under a great deal of nervous tension. I knew perfectly well that there could be embarrassing incidents. High-ranking officers of the military staff, together with government officials, visited hospitals at various times on trips of inspection of one sort or another. Even though, in accordance with the wish of Sitta and Michael, I joined the staff simply as one of the nurses, to the visiting officials I would always be the daughter of King Ferdinand and Queen Marie, and the aunt of the reigning king. They would have felt it contrary to their habits of courtesy, as well as to all rules of etiquette, if they failed to treat me according to my rank. Fortunately both Simone and her sister had sufficient social experience and sufficient sense of humor to appreciate the situation. Such small matters as who received whom, who was presented to whom, and who went through a doorway first, were all handled to the satisfaction of our visitors without the administration of the hospital being disturbed in any way!

The two sisters faced the dangers of bombardment and of Russian occupation with the same harmony and good humor they were able to muster for the small, everyday worries of getting a new hospital in running order. Naturally it took courage, as well, to face many of these things, but a depressed or a bad-tempered courage does not carry you far, and we have all suffered from martyrs to duty who are continually pointing out the greatness of their devotion! I felt that the hospital was fortunate to be organized under such direction.

The first and most important problem was to find a suitable building for our three hundred fifty beds. General Tataranu and the Mayor were anxious to give us all possible help, but they had no jurisdiction over the one building that really pleased us, which was a high school belonging to the church. It was a beautiful and modern red brick building, named after one of the Orthodox Church's greatest Transylvanian prelates, Archbishop Saguna, who had been head of the church in that province about 1880. To use the building we would have to have the permission of the Metropolitan, who lived in Sibiu. This was a drive of only an hour or an hour and a half from Brasov, and I was happy to ask for an audience with him because he and I were old friends. This prince of our church had been one of Transylvania's greatest fighters for Romanian freedom from the rule of the Hungarians, and because he had much administrative capacity as well, the church in Transylvania had made great progress after its long years of repression. During my Y.W.C.A. activities I had often come in contact with him. In fact, it was under his sponsorship that the Y.W.C.A. had held its first rally in Sibiu in 1924, where at fifteen I made my first public address. Therefore, it was not difficult for me to approach him and explain our need of the high school building, and I returned to Brasov with the desired permission. Knowing as I do his devotion to the cause of our freedom, I cannot help wondering today what has happened to him to make him co-operate with the Russians, as I hear he has.

Now my work fell into a regular pattern, although I still expected that I would be returning to Austria in a few weeks at most—as soon as the difficulties between Germany and Hungary were finally settled. In the meantime I spent three mornings a week on bringing up to date the courses in nursing at the military hospital, and four mornings at the station canteen. The afternoons I spent in helping to organize the new Red Cross hospital, and often in the evenings I would return to the canteen to give Mrs. Podgoreanu a helping hand. Terrible sights still passed before my eyes, and there were days when I felt that even the burden of witnessing it all was too much to endure. Now, today, I still feel that of all the sorrows of war, those of the fleeing and of the refugee are the worst. Bombardments are destructive and terrible, but they are swift cataclysms that leave you either alive or dead. You know where you are, so to speak.

But to the fugitive and the refugee there is one long-continued misery for which there can be no end, either happy or unhappy.

The days of March and early April passed. Catholic Easter was celebrated, and I took that day to go to Bran and attend service with all my children. Spring advanced, with all its hopes of returning life in nature. Lent for the Orthodox Church ended, and our Easter, which has to be after the Passover, was about to dawn. Once more I returned to Bran to be with the children for the service.

In the Eastern Orthodox Church we celebrate the resurrection at midnight on Saturday. At first one enters a still darkened church, in which prayers are being read in a low monotonous chant. There are no lights, and the church is shrouded in the mourning used on Good Friday, when the service is really a funeral service in memory of the funeral of Christ. At midnight, the dawn of Easter Sunday, the altar doors are flung open and the officiating priest comes out in golden vestments, carrying a lighted taper, and saying:

"Take light from me!"

The congregation, each holding an individual taper, light theirs from his and follow him out of the church, where the service is read out of doors. At the words "Christ is risen!" the choir bursts into triumphant song, and the whole congregation, joining in the hymn, follows them back into the church, which is now full of light and flowers, with every sign of mourning taken away. There the Mass is celebrated. Whether it is performed in a cathedral with all pomp and ceremony or in a small village shrine, the service never fails to be beautiful and moving. Now, because of the war and the necessity for the blackout, the services all over Romania were postponed to the early morning. It was at the very earliest dawn that we gathered in our humble but beautiful wooden sanctuary in Bran, and that service remains ever present in my mind. There was something not of this earth in the half-light; something that made one feel nearer to the women who went to the grave in sorrow, to have it turned into joy on that first Easter morning.

This feeling of peace and beauty was still with me when, later in the morning, I left my children in Bran and went to celebrate Easter Sunday also with the ill and wounded of the military hospital in Brasov. It was April 16, one of those perfect spring days with the wonderful promise of greenness seeming to hover over the woods and fields. The air was crystal clear and the sun shone warmly from the intensely blue sky. For once I laid aside my nurse's uniform and put on the Romanian peasant dress: the overskirt, the wide belt, the embroidered white blouse with its full sleeves, and the long head veil that is worn by married women. This, I thought, would make the soldiers feel that I was making the day one of festival.

I was joined by General Tataranu and other officials in the large hall of the hospital, where the gifts, the red Easter eggs, the cozonac, and the wine were set out. The army priest read the prayers of blessing, with those of the patients who could leave their beds sitting around him. There was an atmosphere of peace and brotherly love which triumphed over the small troubles and irritations of those who are wounded and those who are tired, who must live together day after day and night after night.

The service over, I went to take a share of the eggs and gifts to the men who could not leave their beds. It was at this moment that the General's aide-de-camp came and told me enemy planes were heading for Brasov. Quick orders were given for the evacuation to the shelters of patients who could go by themselves, but to my horror I learned that the dugout for the stretcher cases was not ready and that there was no shelter for them. They were brought into the central hall, which was considered the safest place inside the hospital, and I prepared to remain with them, but the General refused his consent. When I insisted, he spoke sternly.

"Must I remind you," he said, "that I am in command? This is no moment and there is no need for you to demonstrate your courage. Just now you are a liability, for which I would be held responsible, and you must be protected. Remember also that I will need your help when it is over."

That seemed to settle it, although I felt that inward protest one always feels when a spontaneous impulse is suddenly thwarted. I stepped out into the courtyard to make my way to the dugouts on the hillside just as the first wave of planes was overhead. They were silver and beautiful against the blue sky, so that for an instant they seemed no part of war and destruction. Then suddenly the air was rent by a tremendous sound, and engulfing dust and acrid fumes seemed to surround us from all sides. It was as if a huge, impersonal hand pushed me down flat on my face. Stunned and deafened for a moment, I was roused by the terrified shrieks of a woman whom I saw running downhill and away from safety, carrying a child in her arms. I scrambled to my feet and caught up with her. There was no time to argue even if she could have heard me, so I chose an easier way to stop her. I snatched the child from her arms and turned and ran up the hill, while she followed me, still screaming. We reached the dugouts and jumped into a trench just as the second wave of bombs fell. When the dust cleared a little for the second time I found myself surrounded by weeping women and terrified young girls. I was a little surprised to find that I felt no fear and that I could repeat the 91st Psalm. Slowly it calmed the others, and they quieted. It was then that my own self-control was most threatened, for I saw when I opened my eyes that on each side of me they had taken hold of my long head veil, and had spread it over their heads as if for protection, as if they were indeed my children.

How much time passed before the raid ended is no longer clear to me: there were to be so many raids! I remember that when it was over I went at first to the station, the bomb holes in the roads making it difficult to get through the city, for I knew help might be needed more there than at the hospital with its regular staff. I found the station with its walls still standing, but otherwise a complete ruin. The railway lines themselves were a mass of twisted iron, with destroyed and burning carriages strewn about the yards and oil fires springing up in great tongues of flame. To my relief and joy, there was Mrs. Podgoreanu, calmly attacking the heaps of ashes and burning refuse. Since happily the dispensary, though windowless, was still partly standing, I was able, with what I could salvage quickly and with what I had in a first-aid kit I always carried, to treat several of the wounded before the ambulances arrived.

Once they had got through and rescue work was begun, General Tataranu came to tell me that all hands were badly needed at the military hospital. How we wished that the Red Cross hospital was finished and also functioning! Changing quickly into uniform, I went with him and found a truly dreadful scene of confusion. The wailing cries, the deep anguished groans, and the horrible sights where it was impossible to distinguish man from woman, or the living from the dead, were enough to appall anyone; yet the urgent need, the absolute *must* with which we were faced, made even the horror insignificant.

Only once did my knees give way under me. A man who had not seemed very badly hurt suddenly struggled wildly for breath, and in his paroxysms tried to jump off the table. A doctor called me to help hold him down, and as I bent over him a jet of blood from a small wound in his chest suddenly spurted out and hit me in a warm sticky stream on my neck, and gushed down my chest. Instantly I put my fist over the hole, pressing hard, but one of the principal arteries was pierced, and my efforts were vain. It was then that my knees buckled, but the cry of a child close by forced me to forget my deep-seated horror of blood, and to look for it. The poor little thing lay unhurt on a stretcher beside its dead and mangled mother. I picked it up, still feeling dizzy and a little vague, and finally deposited it temporarily in the bed of a willing and kindly soldier, where it stayed until later that night, when I found a proper place for it.

In such ways all of us who were able to do so continued to work until a little order and comfort had been brought out of the confusion, but by that time wounded from the neighboring villager were being brought in. The General appeared again, tired and drawn with strain and fatigue, to ask me to accompany him to other hospitals. He said that in one there were wounded men back from the front who had not suffered actual hurt from the bombardment but were badly shaken in nerves. Could I possibly clean myself up and go with him to give them their delayed Easter gifts? He felt that such an informal visit would calm them, and stop the harm their present nervous and disturbed condition was doing them.

For a moment, as I looked about me and thought of what I had been doing, the idea of giving Easter eggs and holiday bread to men lying in clean, unbloodied sheets seemed so incredible as to be madness. Was it only this morning that our holiday gifts had been spread in this hall? But obediently I found a clean apron. The source of the water supply had been damaged, and water was scarce, so I used only enough to get rid of the blood that showed before going with the General to carry an Easter greeting.

I continued to have this dreamlike feeling during our other visits of inspection, and it was not until after we had finished that I realized suddenly I had had nothing to eat since the early morning breakfast after the Resurrection Service in Bran that morning. I stopped for some food, and then took the baby from his guardian soldier and found a nursing home for him. After that I was free to go back to Bran and to my family, where there would be water enough finally to wash away the blood that had dried on me and on my clothing.

As I drove I thought back over the incredible hours that had passed since I went over the same road on my way to Brasov that morning. It was of course not the first bombardment I had witnessed. As a child I had lived through many in World War I, and in World War II, I had been through more than a dozen in Berlin. Yet these later ones had always happened to be in another section of town, and unless one is in the thick of it one does not realize how terrible it can be. I remembered that I myself, hearing descriptions of a raid which had not come very near me, had thought, *After all, it can't be so bad as all that!* It is a sad truth that we seldom really understand the pain of others and are rarely deeply moved by what does not happen to ourselves. Until we somehow overcome this, there is little hope that the world will improve, for obviously no one of us can experience everything in one lifetime. I feel that we should try harder to develop our understanding of evil things we have not experienced, and so be better able to sympathize and help others.

"After all, it can't be so bad as all that!"

It is a comforting thought, but the comfort is false. Somewhere that evening there was a radio news commentator who must have had that comforting thought, for otherwise he would not have described any bombardment in quite the terms he did. I had been welcomed by my relieved family and had cleaned myself thoroughly. Alone in my bedroom I was realizing that the air raid had brought keenly home the fact, so regretted in Romania, that overwhelming circumstances had made the United States our enemy. It seemed to me a tragic thing that on the crowds of families going home from church on Easter Sunday it had been American bombers that dropped bloody death and suffering. The things I had seen that day rose before my eyes again, and I prayed earnestly for peace. Surely, I thought, surely in America they also pray for an end to something so dreadful, even though in their homes and in their churches the families of their soldiers are safe from death from the skies. And then Stefan and Minola burst into my room, pale and horrified. They had already seen enough of war to imagine what Brasov had been like on this Easter, and they had been listening to the short-wave radio with its comments on the news of the day. Clearly and cheerfully—almost gaily—the voice of the commentator had come to them:

"The city of Brasov in Romania today received its Easter eggs!"

FIFTEEN

THE VILLAGE of Bran lies in the very narrow valley of the Turcu River. Where the river curves there is a rocky promontory, and on this the Teutonic Knights built in the twelfth century a castle to defend the fertile high plateau, Tzara Barsei, against the hordes of Eastern invaders. They built the Castle of Bran out of rock and brick and rubble, and planned it according to the shape of the rocky outcropping. In places the lower walls are nine feet thick, but nearer the top of the castle the thickness decreases to four feet and finally to two.

There are three kinds of openings in these walls. On the lower levels there are the apertures that begin on the inner side of the wall as windowlike spaces large enough for a man to stand in, but narrow toward the center so that only long slits, just wide enough for the use of a bow and arrow, are left in the outer wall; and there are the oblong openings, near the floor, which can be closed by great beams of oak that swivel around on a central pivot, so that when the "window" is "open" the beam sticks out into the room on the inside, and beyond the castle wall on the outside. On higher levels of the castle, where the missiles of any attacking forces could not reach them, are windows of ordinary size, but all are set into walls so thick that window seats have been built, not below the window sills, but along both sides of the window embrasures. Besides these openings there are two in the tower room over the entrance which resemble nothing so much as the magnified ventilating "hoods" sometimes put over kitchen stoves. These are built into the wall at a convenient height so that the castle defenders could remain comfortably protected within the room, while a curved, masonry "hood" formed a sort of small bay, open at the bottom. Through this opening melted lead, boiling oil, and other oddments could be dropped on the heads of the besiegers storming the entrance.

Since the castle was not built for comfort, but for defense, no regard was given to the regularity of rooms. These cling to the rock wherever the natural formation made it easier to locate them, so that they meander up and down at various levels, connected by steps, by long, crooked passages, by archways and balconies, and by frequent irregular stairways, some built inside the very walls themselves. One side of the castle is a thick wall enclosing a small, oddly shaped courtyard in which my mother planted a little, perfect garden, upon which one comes unexpectedly. The towers are built where the rock itself is highest, and the views are magnificent. One side looks down upon the narrow valley of the Turcu and upon most of the village, while the opposite side overlooks the plateau, the Tzara Barsei, with the long, dusty road leading to Brasov, and the eastern Carpathians standing on the far horizon. I used to love to sit in one of the tower windows, watching for the dust cloud on the road that would announce the approach of some awaited guest, and feeling like Sister Anne in the Bluebeard story watching to see her brothers come. As a girl sometimes, waiting for my mother, I took delight in the fact that from the cloud announcing her arrival there came now and then dazzling flashes of light, where the sun touched the bright metal work on the bonnet of the specially designed Rolls-Royce she liked so much.

The town of Brasov presented the castle of Bran to my mother shortly after World War I. She took delight in restoring it, and in her hands it became an enchanting, fairy-tale castle, full of flowers, standing "on the rock where the four winds meet." Because I loved it as she did, she left it to me when she died, and it had for me an importance which had nothing to do with the actual days I was able to spend there physically. As a matter of fact, because of the difficulty of heating it and of keeping the water from freezing, we considered it habitable for only about four months of the year. It took the Russian occupation to teach us that actually a man might live there the year around—if he was sufficiently in desperate fear for his life; but that story comes later.

In the spring of 1944, because the weather was still cold, I had installed the younger children in a pleasant building at the foot of the castle hill. This had once been a customhouse, because Bran was almost on what had been the old frontier between Romania and Austria-Hungary. It was actually two old, one-story houses, joined together by a wide passageway which we used as a dining room. The walls were thick, the ceilings low, the floors made of wide, dark boards, and the whole interior was whitewashed, as are the walls of most Romanian houses. All the windows had flower boxes full of nasturtiums, and the whole place was very pleasant for what we thought of as entirely temporary headquarters.

At each end, this "house" which was really two houses was continued by tall walls. On one end these enclosed a farmlike courtyard, in which we kept a few hens and geese as well as the children's pets—rabbits, including one white Angora rabbit, lambs, a red Angora kitten, and a tiny, orphaned fawn. At the other end the walls enclosed the garage and a guardhouse, for as in all royal residences there was always a small guard for us, with a sentry at each gate. In my mother's days this whole building had been the quarters for the entourage—aide-de-camp, secretary, post officer, etc.—that came with her, and it also provided guest rooms for people who were not intimate friends, but to whom she wished to offer a vacation in the good mountain air. Now, although we did not know it, it was to be our home for nearly four years, except for the short periods when the summer permitted us to move up into the castle.

After the week in May that I spent in Austria, and which I have already described (the week which I did not then know would be my last in Sonnberg), the Red Cross hospital in Brasov had to be made ready with a rush. I had to give up my work at the station canteen almost entirely except for emergency calls, but my collaboration with Mrs. Podgoreanu never came to an end as long as I was in Romania. She often had cases from the trains which needed hospital care, and which I could follow up for her, and I frequently went to her for help and advice in regard to my problems. During the second bombardment of Brasov, on May 6, enough damage was done to make the military hospital inadequate. We had to take an overflow of cases to the Red Cross hospital, even though it was not officially open and we still lacked a number of supplies. However, on May Tenth—our National Day, which is like your Fourth of July—it was officially opened with the traditional service of blessing and with all due ceremony, and given the designation "Z.I. 161." (The "Z.I." indicated that it was in the "zone interior," and the number showed that it was the one hundred sixty-first emergency hospital to be established. Field hospitals, which were set up back of the lines and designed to be as mobile as possible, were designated only by numbers.) The local authorities, both military and civilian, took part in the exercises, everything went well, and we were all truly proud of our combined efforts. To add to the joy of the occasion for the whole community, the King's mother attended the opening and afterwards made a tour of inspection and spoke personally to each patient. She also consented to go with me to the station canteen, which gave Mrs. Podgoreanu and the staff there a real and well-deserved pleasure.

May 21, my saint's day and Alexandra's ninth birthday, brought me another new experience. We were having a quiet family celebration of the occasion at Bran when word came that a transport of over two hundred wounded soldiers straight from the front were arriving in Brasov, and all hands were needed. I drove to the Red Cross hospital as quickly as possible, anxious not only to help but to learn how such a problem was taken care of. Simone Cantacuzino, the head nurse I have mentioned, was a wonderful leader. She not only quietly and efficiently set up her organization, but deftly instructed the rest of us as we went along, for few of her staff had had this particular experience.

The men were first put in the charge of an officer, who took their papers and filed them. Their clothes were then taken off and marked, and their personal possessions were put into separate bags, each tagged with the number that had been put on the clothing. In groups the men were brought to the big shower room just below the former high school gymnasium, which was now our largest ward, and here they were washed, shaved, and disinfected. It was a damp and messy job. We had to be most careful of their wounds, which we protected with oiled silk, pieces of plastic, and every bit of waterproof material we had. Some of the men had to be carried, others could stand, but only a few were able to wash themselves. The odors of hot water and soap, steam, dirty humanity, and festering wounds soon made the atmosphere unbelievably difficult to breathe. We ourselves became sodden. Our starched caps went soft and sloppy, our backs ached, our feet swelled—and still the men came, naked and dirty and miserable. It was an indescribable satisfaction to send them, clean and robed, first to the dispensary for bandaging and treatment, and finally to bed, where they were fed. This was my first, but by no means my last, experience of *deparasitare*, or delousing.

Except for special work of this kind, the regular hospital routine was soon well established, and the round of bandaging, operations, and treatments continued. I worked in the wards because, in spite of the experience I had had thrust upon me after every bombing raid, I still could not endure the sight of blood during operations. It took me a long time to overcome this feeling, and I assure you that in 1944 no one could have made me believe that in later emergencies I would assist with the surgery itself. I did not, however, feel that I was shirking by remaining in the wards, because that was where our greatest need was at this time. Wardroom nursing is unromantic and exacting, having to do largely with basins and bedpans, with endless miles of steps to be taken, and with the resentful aching of a back which bends and lifts and strains during much of the time spent on duty. Such jobs did not please those members of the volunteer group who had pictured themselves as white ministering angels floating between the beds of heroes and dispensing flowers and smiles to men who miraculously never vomited into basins or called for bedpans—or who sometimes were not able to call for either one in time. These women were much happier helping in the dispensary or in the operating theater, where there was less monotony and uniforms could be kept much neater.

I do not mean here to belittle any of the volunteers who gave time and energy unstintingly, but I confess that I formed certain prejudices against women who would not accept humble jobs because they thought that "a lady" was above an "ordinary nurse." No hospital, military or civilian, can be run without a great deal of work which is in itself highly disagreeable, and which can be happily performed only if one looks firmly not only at what is under one's nose but also at the object for which one is working—the comfort and healing of mankind. Our *real* "ladies" accepted tasks as they came, and among such true aristocracy there were women from many classes. I remember especially one girl who sold tickets in a movie theater to earn her living, and who spent all her free time helping cheerfully with the most menial jobs, even the difficult one of carrying stretcher cases down into the cellars and up again when bombardments made this necessary.

The two sisters at the head of the hospital were delightful to work with, as well as truly efficient, and our head doctor, Dr. Dogariu, was an able man and one easy to get on with. Our greatest problem continued to be that of alarms and bombardments, since we had no really safe bomb shelter and since there were always cases who could not be moved in any event. These last we put all together in one ward, and we took it in turns to sit with them during the hours of danger. It was a most harrowing experience, because there was nothing to do except to wait. Whether or not bombs fell near us, these hours were hard for helpless men to endure. I cannot properly describe how cheerful and pleasant they were; how they joked the hours away, telling stories from the front or anecdotes of their homes and childhood. It was only

In my nurse's uniform

by the drawn expression of their faces and by the occasional unguarded and haunted look in their eyes that they betrayed the fear in all our hearts. We nurses were very proud of the fact that the feminine members of the hospital staff were quicker to volunteer for the duty of "waiting it out" than were the men; but these gentlemen assured us that prudence was the better part of valor. The medical staff also took the lofty position that it was their *duty* to go to safety, for what would we do when the "All clear" sounded if there was no one to care for our wounds! That, of course, was one way of looking at it, but their philosophy did them little good when one day a surprise inspection was made during a raid, and the visiting General found not a single man on duty anywhere.

Alarms and air raids came with such frequency that finally we received an order to prepare in a more sheltered locality an annex to the hospital, where at least part of the more seriously wounded cases could be moved for convalescence. This meant that we were again out searching high and low, far and wide, for available space, but all big buildings had long since been requisitioned by other institutions. Whether they were actually using it at the time or not, the "owners" of such space were most unwilling to surrender it, and they were often so extremely disagreeable about our request that I became furiously indignant on one or two occasions. When we were refused the use of a village hospital which was almost empty, I remember saying bitterly to the doctor, "I suppose you are waiting for the Russians to come and teach you to appreciate Romanian soldiers!" It is terrible now to think how very right I was.

Once more I was to learn that every apparently blind alley can actually lead to new possibilities, for it was then that I first thought desperately to myself, *If no one will give us help, I'll get on without it! I'll build my own hospital!*

I owned one piece of ground at Bran which was suitable, but it had been lent to others for raising a potato crop. Nevertheless, I began thinking of ways and means for a project which at first seemed madness, but at the same time I did not cease my efforts to locate space for immediate use. I suddenly remembered the Orthodox priest in Bran Poarta, a part of the village of Bran which lay in a little gorge branching out of the main valley. He had once offered me for refugees the use of a schoolhouse belonging to the village church, but I had not then needed it. Now when I went to him he readily agreed that we might use it for a hospital annex.

Spitalul Inima Reginei—the Hospital of the Queen's Heart

The building was not very big, but it could house about forty wounded. It was low, one-storied and whitewashed, built in an L shape. It had a gushing mountain brook on one side, and the lovely old village church on the other, while as a background stood the Bucegi, one of the loveliest of the Carpathian ranges. Nearly eight thousand feet above us these mountains seemed to stand as a protection and a promise of peace and of things eternal. Often as I looked up to them I felt how small and unimportant before eternity were our troubles, no matter how great they seemed to me at the time. Again and again I found comfort in gazing at them, for to me God's smile is reflected by mountains as it is by the sea, and I felt that here was a lovely place for suffering and frightened men to come.

It happened that among the refugees from Moldavia was a friend of mine with her children. Since her father had been court physician and a friend of my father's, and she and I were only twelve days apart in age, we had been friends as long as we could remember. She had always been called Noelle because her birthday was on Christmas Day. The few possessions she had been able to bring from her lovely home had been standing in one of the freight cars in the railroad yard at Brasov during the first bombardment, on Easter Sunday. Fortunately that car had not been hit, and she had been able to set up housekeeping with her children in a little garden house of mine. Since I knew how capable and active she had always been in her own estates, and how interested in looking after the welfare of the peasants and their children, I asked her to take over the organization of our hospital annex.

Perhaps it would be of interest to you to know that later, to help Noelle and her husband make a new life after they had lost everything in the war, I "sold" them—at the lowest price that would make the title a legal document—a piece of land. Actually, of course, no money passed between us. She and her husband, by putting together everything they had and by incredible efforts of their own, built there a house where they could live, and where they could also take summer boarders in the season and run a skiing school in the winter. Through others I have learned that after

I was forced to leave Romania in 1948 the Communists passed another new and convenient law which decreed that any contract made by any member of the royal family during the past ten years was invalid. Noelle was among those who suffered from this. Her house was confiscated, with no compensation, and she was again stripped of everything she had worked for. One of the most bitter things in the world is to discover that one's friendship is a danger to those one loves.

To help the hospital in its emergency, Noelle found among the other refugees in Bran women who were willing and capable, including two trained nurses; and the "staff" she assembled proved to be excellent. They began by thoroughly cleaning and freshly whitewashing the former schoolhouse, doing all the work themselves and putting in long hours to get it ready as soon as possible. We rounded up beds, mattresses, and cooking utensils that could be spared from the big hospital or were donated, and in an astonishingly short time we were ready to move in.

This, too, proved to be quite an achievement, since transport difficulties were great. We had no ambulance of our own, and before I had rounded up transportation for our forty wounded I had fairly exhausted the telephone operators and had thoroughly annoyed a great many people. Romania had no lack of gasoline and oil, although it was rationed, but automobile parts and tires were in short supply. No one wanted to make the fifty-mile round trip over the bad roads between Brasov and Bran if he could possibly avoid it. A few people in Brasov even suggested that I had gone as far away as Bran in setting up an annex only because I wanted to be nearer home myself, but I was happy to ask them at once to find us a place we could use in Brasov. Naturally they could not. Their attitude was really only a reflection of the extreme nervous strain under which one lives when one's community is a target for frequent and unexpected bombing raids, but I do not want you to think that what we were doing was simple or easy, or went along as quickly as you can read about it. I have never found that anything worth doing can be accomplished without considerable effort, and transporting forty wounded was no exception. In the end I had to go as far as Bucarest, and even to beg the use of the Queen's private ambulance, before all our soldiers were installed in their new quarters.

Since we had only two orderlies, who unfortunately did not arrive until after most of the wounded had come, we carried many of the stretchers ourselves. The peasants, encouraged by the good priest, had brought in provisions of fresh eggs, vegetables, and fruit, and had made the hospital rooms gay with marigolds from the cottage gardens. It was an excellent and a happy beginning, and the little annex kept that feeling of being set apart and safe even during the most terrible times. Yet it was too small to be adequate, and very primitive in its arrangements; all water, for example, had to be carried in by hand. It could be used only after the patients were operated on, since it had no facilities for surgery, so that in Brasov our "Ward of Terror" still existed during raids, even though there were fewer men who must "wait it out" there.

This realization of how much more we actually needed intensified my thought of trying to build a hospital myself, and I returned to the thought of my potato field. Perhaps I could buy off the people who had planted the crop, but when it came to a building—and then I suddenly thought of the wooden barracks buildings occasionally dismantled and sold by the army. I began making inquiries, and finally located one which could be bought, but I did not have the money. A part of my property from which I received the greatest income had been in the section of Romania taken by the Russians, and other holdings had been seriously damaged by the war. While I did not know how great my loss in Austria was to be, I had already realized that in the future I must plan on receiving very little of my former income. I got out a bracelet I thought I might be able to sell to start the needed fund, but here my friend, General Tataranu, heard what I was doing and appeared on the scene.

"What are you thinking of?" he said. "Have you not six children to support? And if you can save a jewel to leave to them, so much the better. Why not consult me? This is nothing you are doing for yourself! I will let you have an army barracks—not a very grand one, but not so bad! In fact, you can have two of them!"

I could hardly believe it. Then, to my delight those who had planted potatoes on the chosen plot refused to take money for their crop loss, saying that they also wished to make an offering. The next thing was the matter of furniture, utensils, and such things, and for the furniture I appealed to Colonel Serbu, the director of an ammunition factory in Tohan, one of the neighboring villages. He was a former army officer, and at first sight not a very prepossessing man. His manners were gruff, and I felt he was decidedly annoyed at having to obey my summons, but still I liked him: he looked capable and enterprising. I told him that it had been suggested we might get cupboards, tables, and benches at cost from his workshop, but instead of leaving it at that, I surprised myself by going on to explain all I really wanted to do. My dreams got the better of me, and I shared with him what I had confided to no one else: my whole vision of what could be done also in a time of peace with a hospital out here in the mountains, where a whole countryside lacked the medical services they should have. I was astounded to hear myself talking so freely of all I inwardly hoped for, but I was still more astonished to see his eaglelike glance soften, as he looked with me at the accomplishments my words were striving to picture. He caught fire, and his enthusiasm outstripped mine. He made suggestions. We must make it permanent, of course.

"*But*," he suddenly said, "you can't do that if you begin with a horrible old army barracks!"

"Oh, but I can!" I told him. "Why, at first I had only a piece of ground, and even the crop that grew on it was not mine!"

He still objected. "But I will give you an almost new barracks if you can arrange for the General to give me one of his old horrors instead," he finally offered.

This seemed too good to be true, but it was true, and it began a chapter in my life which continued to seem too wonderful to believe. When I look back at that time and at the four years that followed, when I think of the wonderful way the hospital was established, of how it never ran out of provisions, how it was protected in moments of greatest danger, how it grew when all else failed, I feel truly that I lived in a continual miracle. I would like one day to tell the whole story, but here I want to spend most of the time on the events that led to my country's loss of freedom; on the resistance put up by my people; on their great suffering and their great courage. Yet since it was the hospital that gave me an insight into what was happening, that broke down many barriers, that provided a common meeting ground for such an unlikely and antagonistic combination as a princess and the Communists, it must come to some extent into this story as well. Dearly beloved hospital, how precious you are to me, and how grateful I am to you!

The excitement of feeling that my dreams could come true had only one consideration that sobered it. How could I possibly manage to spend the time in Romania which the hospital and my other work would require if I continued my work with the wounded in Austria? This question was solved for me quite quickly and finally. I had been expecting Anton to come for a furlough when I suddenly received word that he was leaving the army and coming to Romania to stay. Hitler had decreed that the "propaganda" of princes dying for their country must cease!

This may sound an odd rule to you, but it was made in all seriousness. During the war many of the descendants of former royal families and of former nobility had played a gallant part, and many had been killed or seriously wounded. To the funerals of these young officers, whose family names were deeply engraved in the history of their countries, came large numbers of all classes of people. Hitler apparently began to feel uneasily that an undue emphasis was being put upon paying respect to men whose friends and families represented a threat to the continued existence of his regime. He therefore decreed that commissions must be surrendered by all officers descended from families who had formerly reigned, and by all officers married to foreigners. In this way, Hitler decided, the "propaganda dying" of princes would be stopped.

The decree had been announced some months before, but it had been protested against strongly by Goering, who did not want to lose his "princes" who were officers in the air force. In any case it could not be accomplished overnight, since the commissioned officers had to be replaced before they could resign, and we had come to feel that perhaps no more would be heard from it, and that Anton would be allowed to remain. Quite suddenly, however, he also had been forced to give up his commission, and must make plans for a new life. He decided to come to Romania first, but he too left Sonnberg with no warning that it would be more than two years before we had even a message from our home there, and that it would be four years before he could get permission to return to Austria even to look at the empty shell it had become.

Anton arrived in Bran on a beautiful morning in July, 1944, after we had moved up to the castle for the summer months. The hospital construction was proceeding well. Some of Colonel Serbu's engineers were in charge of building a pontoon bridge across the river and making plans for the installation of water and electricity, and soldiers from General Tataranu's command were working with Russian prisoners of war in putting up the dismantled barracks, which had arrived by wagon and lorry. The work in the Brasov hospital and in the annex at Bran Poarta was going wonderfully well, the station canteen had been rebuilt after the last bombardment, and the work there was for the moment less strenuous because of a lull in the influx of refugees. In honor of Anton's arrival I had laid aside my uniform and decided to take a holiday, and he and I and the children were all laughing and talking at once with excitement when suddenly the hated sound of the alarm cut in upon our laughter, and was followed by the droning of planes and the dreaded noise of explosions.

As quickly as possible I rushed to change into my uniform, get my first-aid kit, take a hurried leave of the family, and start for Brasov. I made such haste that I arrived before the raid was over, and therefore spent some time lying in a gravel pit at the edge of town, regretting that I could not have foreseen I would be able to spend another hour with Anton and the children. Finally the planes were gone, and thanks to the royal flag on my car I did not have to wait until the "All clear" was given before going to the Red Cross hospital.

There I found everything in good order, since no bombs had fallen on the immediate surroundings, so with Nadeje Soutzo, assistant to the head nurse at the Red Cross hospital, I went to the station. Once more it had been leveled to the ground, once more the canteen had gone up in blue smoke, and for the first and last time I saw Mrs. Podgoreanu with her calm shattered. The small air-raid shelter, which had been so crowded that it was finally difficult to breathe in it, had received three direct hits. They had not penetrated, but they had left all who were inside badly shaken. By a miracle the dispensary had again been spared, so that Nadeje and I could set to work at once with the injured.

The condition of many of them was so serious that I felt a mounting irritation because the station doctor was quite evidently not at his post. Since there was a shortage of army doctors, a new system had put local civilian doctors on a sort of "limited draft." Theoretically one or another of these doctors was assigned to the station at all times, so that someone would be there in case of need, but actually not all of them were con- scientious enough about keeping their assignments. They felt they had neglected their own patients and lost money for no good purpose when they had to sit long hours in the station without being called on, and as a result there had been times when a sudden need developed and no doctor was available. In the case of a raid it was the duty of the doctor stationed at the canteen to take shelter at once, so that he would be safe and ready to help the injured, which made the breach of regulations obvious in this case. I allowed myself to relieve some of the pressure of my own horror and pity by nursing anger against the absent doctor, and for doing so I received a lesson I hope I have never forgotten.

When Nadeje and I had done all we could we packed some of the injured into the car and drove to the military hospital, where a scene of even greater tragedy met us. I will not try to describe in detail things which cannot possibly be imagined. Perhaps it will be enough to say that we helped to dig out sixty-two dead and injured from the very trench where I had taken shelter during the first bombardment. No one can tell what this is like who has not been forced to handle torn and bleeding arms and legs with tender care, in order to discover almost by touch in the mass of mangled flesh whether they are still attached to a living body or not. We were, of course, soaked in blood ourselves almost immediately, and while in some miraculous way I always seemed able in these emergencies to overcome my sick faintness at the sight or touch of blood, it was never easy for me. That is my only excuse for my thoughtless and cruel answer to the elderly man who approached me as I worked, and asked me if anything was known of the doctor at the station.

"No! He left his post of duty!" I replied curtly—only to see him draw himself erect with a pitiful expression of mingled grief and pride.

"My son would never do that!" was all he said, but it made my cheeks flush with shame, as they do today when I remember my angry and inconsiderate remark. It has made me try humbly ever since not to speak quickly any words which may hurt someone unnecessarily. Nothing was ever found of the young doctor except his cap on a hill not far away from the station, where a direct hit killed nearly a dozen people and left literally nothing except shreds of unidentifiable flesh. No one will ever know what happened; whether his nerves failed him, or whether he rushed to help someone. But no good was accomplished by my sharp answer, which could not be wiped out by all my explanations to the father.

The only bright spot in that unhappy afternoon and evening was a sudden, brief, informal visit made by King Michael, who drove into Brasov accompanied only by his aide-de-camp and his big police dog. His appearing so soon after the disaster did much to encourage the people, and to strengthen the bonds between him and them, and it did my heart good to hear them cheer him as he drove away.

King Michael (Mihai), 1947

SIXTEEN

NOW FOLLOWED a period of the curious calm that precedes a storm. The hospital continued to take shape before my admiring and still astonished eyes. Colonel Serbu came nearly every morning and evening to watch the growth of the building and he grew ever more enthusiastic over it. We had visions of what we might do after the war to enlarge and strengthen it; we even thought that we might then be able to add a school of nursing.

One day he said, to my surprise, "By the way, I have a whole operating theater over at the factory. Never used, you know. Put in when we added the dispensary. You can have it for your hospital."

In a day or two a lorry arrived with the big lamp, the operating table, a few instruments, and the essential and invaluable sterilizer. To me it was as if a gift had dropped from the skies, and I felt humbly grateful for the miraculous help I was being given.

On another day I went farther afield to get the pots and pans and all the other supplies of that sort that were needed. I drove to Medias, the birthplace of the little Romanian pony we had at Sonnberg, and at a factory there I received for half the factory price nearly all I needed, while at the same time I received from a glass factory the glasses and medicine bottles as a gift. On this trip I was able to take the children, and to make an excursion of it.

I was glad of every opportunity to have them with me, and also glad to contrive for them a little freedom and fun. It was not always easy to give them a fair amount of my time. Since the three older ones were in school during the spring, and Frau Koller was teaching the three younger ones while their nurse, Gretl, cared for them, I had felt satisfied about them then. The summer brought them more free time and also the joy of being together in the castle, which they loved. Frau Koller and Gretl were still constantly with them, so that I knew they were being well cared for during my absences, and all of them except Magi and Elisabeth were old enough to understand what work I was doing, and how much it was needed. Yet I was delighted with every chance to be with them, especially when I could try to re-create for them the Romania of my own childhood.

One of our most pleasant excursions had been to Sinaia in June. The Queen had come to lunch with us, and had visited the hospital annex at Bran Poarta, which she said she liked very much. Then, to the delight of the children, she had invited us all for lunch two days later, and we had driven over the mountains with a great deal of pleasant anticipation. A room at the Peles had been prepared for us, and until Sitta was ready I showed the children and Gretl over the palace. Then there was lunch at the Foisor, where Michael and Sitta were living, and more explorations by the children afterwards.

Michael was away just then, but his mother spoke quite frankly of many of their worries and difficulties, and I was pleased to find her feeling so pleasant and friendly. She ended by giving me a generous gift for my hospital, which made the day as completely happy for me as it had been for the children.

But it was after Anton's return that we had a special day of real and perfect enjoyment which I think each of us will always remember. It grew out of my need to visit Sibiu to inspect the beginning of the school for "seeing eye" dogs, which I had been instrumental in encouraging while I was still at Sonnberg. I was sure the trip would interest the children, and therefore we planned to make it a family party.

The training school for dogs was attached to the famous Sibiu Military School of Equitation, at the head of which was an acquaintance of my youth, Colonel Chirculescu. As a young sublieutenant he had suddenly come into prominence at the annual Military Horse Show because of his exceptional talent for training horses. With his own none-too-good army horse he had won the first prize, which was an Anglo-Arab from the state studs. Training his prize horse, he won with it another horse as first prize the following year; and with this second horse he won a third at the next show! At this point he retired from that particular competition himself, although he still trained horses for others. He himself, however, took many prizes in high jumping, and was the captain of our Romanian Military Team at the Olympic Games in Berlin in 1936—the team that won second place.

That had been an exciting event in my life in Austria, for after the Olympics were over the Romanian Military Team participated in another international competition in Vienna, and there they won first place. Anton and I were in a box a little to one side of the box where the President of the Republic sat, and I was of course full of joy at the triumph of my friends and countrymen. The fact that when the events were over the team came directly to our box and saluted me with full formality seemed perfectly natural to me—until they left us and went to the President's box for another military salute! It was then I suddenly realized that I was, after all, in Austria, and should not be given precedence over the head of the state. Anton and I walked over to meet the team as they dismounted, and

I told them that they must not come again to my box, but must go to the President's box and be introduced to the dignitaries there, instructions which they protested about but finally accepted. I confess that I really did not much regret the honor they had done me: it would, I think, have been more than human not to love sharing in the triumph won by my small country over many larger than she. My greatest pleasure, however, came later; for we entertained the team at Sonnberg, where they enjoyed rides in Anton's plane, played with our three babies, and joined with me in reminiscences of Romania.

It was, therefore, with happy anticipation that I told the children about Colonel Chirculescu and his career, for he had been no less outstanding on the battlefield. Now at Sibiu he had succeeded in forming an outstanding school of riding, where the old traditions of formal horsemanship, as well as the most modern methods, were both wonderfully taught. One of his staff, who had lost his leg at the hip and could no longer ride, had found consolation in undertaking the work of training dogs for his blind comrades, which made Sibiu the center for this new project.

The day was glorious, and from beginning to end was free of air raids and even of warnings. The high grass in the fields through which we drove was full of flowers of every color, and the feeling of joy reminded me of days when I had joined in my parents' visits to all parts of Romania. At Sibiu, too, we were received with full honors—trumpet, a guard of honor, and formal presentation—just as in the old days, and the children, who had never seen this, were of course enchanted.

Such a reception began when the royal party was sighted, and the trumpeter blew the call that was the signal of the arrival or departure of any member of the royal family. In cities trumpeters were sometimes placed at intervals along the route, and each would blow the signal as the royal party approached him, so that the lovely succession of musical notes seemed to be traveling with us as we rode. At Sibiu, of course, there was only one trumpeter at the gates, but he flung the call out like a banner on the sparkling air. The guard of honor stood at attention, and Colonel Chirculescu waited for us with about twenty officers lined up behind him.

The formal pattern for the occasion was pronounced impressively: "I have the honor to present myself—" and then his rank and name, the number and title of the regiment he commanded, the fact that it had "an effective force" of so many officers, noncommissioned officers, men, and horses; all ending with the information that they were ready for inspection and awaiting my orders. It was a formula I had been familiar with since I was so small that, as I stood waiting to offer my hand, my head was at the level of the officers' belts. I had the double feeling now of hearing it myself and of hearing it through the ears of my own children. It brought back memories of my years of young womanhood; of my feeling of pride in representing the royal family, of anxiety that the affair, whatever it was, should go well, and also (I must confess) of an occasional mischievous wonder as to just what would happen on such a formal occasion if I actually gave an order to the regiment that was, theoretically, awaiting just such an event! However, on this occasion as on those in the past, I did not yield to such a temptation, but bowed, smiled, and thanked the Colonel, and then walked down the line of officers so that each could present himself individually.

With a small force such as was stationed at Sibiu this did not take long, even though Anton and the children followed me through the presentations. I well remembered military receptions where we spent several hours going through these formalities! Here it was soon over, but to the delight of the children they discovered that part of the formal visit of inspection included assigning an officer to each of them. They quickly made friends with their escorts, and thought it was wonderful to have a special person able to answer all of their innumerable questions about the school.

After we had visited the new kennels to see the dogs and had talked with the instructors and seen the plans for the whole installation (which was one of the many projects the Russians destroyed in 1946), we were invited to see a demonstration of riding. The men wore the old blue cavalry uniform that had been used before World War I; the horses were unbelievably handsome; the sun shone; the mountains made a perfect background. It was a holiday being made in our honor, and the very spirit of joy seemed to permeate everyone. The men performed all the intricate maneuvers of the carousels—the complicated drills with horses and riders moving in the spoke-and-wheel patterns that require such perfect training. Exhibitions of the different schools of training and jumping were given, even those of the Somur and of the Vienna Hochschule. There was high jumping, and then a display of cavalry military tactics. For the children's especial delight, the old post chaises and coaches were brought out of the museum, horses were harnessed to them, and the children were permitted to ride in them and even to hold the reins! Finally Colonel Chirculescu himself rode on one of his famous horses, and was just as wonderful as he should have been. The entertainment ended with an excellent meal served in high style while the military band played for us. It had been a perfect holiday; an excursion into the past and into "charmingness." For one day we forgot the war and all our troubles.

It was with redoubled energy that I returned to my daily work and the hospital rounds in Brasov and Bran. I had already decided to call the new hospital *Spitalul Inima Reginei*—the Hospital of the Queen's Heart. When my mother died in 1938 she left, besides her will, a letter to her people, and in this she explained a wish she had expressed to her family many years before. She asked that her heart should not be buried in the church at Curtea de Arges, where the bodies of the royal family were laid, but that it should be removed from her body and placed in the humble little church she herself had built on the shores of the Black Sea. She said that there it would be more accessible than in the royal burying place; that always during her lifetime her people had been able to bring their sorrows and their wishes to her heart, and that she wanted it to be so even after her death. So her heart had been taken to Balcic, her beloved home on the seashore; but the cruel decision at Vienna in 1940 had given that part of Romania to the Bulgarians. A few hours before they took possession of the land that Romania had been so unjustly blackmailed into giving up, my mother's faithful aide-de-camp, General Zwiedineck, had taken the casket containing the heart from the chapel and had carried it to Bran, where it was deposited in our small wooden church. Later I had had a little chapel carved out of the rock of the hill just behind the church, with a winding path and steps mounting up to it, and there I placed the casket containing the heart. There it stood apart and alone, a shrine easily accessible to all.

Ever since her death I had wanted to build a memorial for my mother, and because I have always been interested in sculpting I had sometimes thought I might be able myself to create something which would express what she was. Now I realized that, instead, a place where those in pain could find comfort and healing was the most fitting memorial for one who had lived only to give and to comfort. Although the hospital would not be entirely finished on the twenty-second of July, I decided to have it blessed then because that was her name day. We made a great occasion of it. The Metropolitan Nicolae Balan of Transylvania came to officiate, and the entire service was held out of doors. Only for the actual blessing of the walls, with its symbolical sprinkling of water from the altar, did the priest go inside. The local authorities, our many benefactors, and as many of the hospital staffs as could come were invited. The weather smiled on us, the purpose and plan of the new hospital were appreciated and approved of, and many new offers of help were given. The Metropolitan made a most moving address, and I took this occasion to thank all those who had so generously helped to create this new center of healing.

There was in my mind that day only one question, but I was trying to think of it without too much anxiety. I had seemed able to get everything for the hospital except the sheets. All kinds of materials were difficult to buy as a result of the war, and when they could be obtained at all the prices made it almost prohibitive to think of getting enough linens to supply a whole hospital. I had begun to feel a little desperately that because of this lack we would be unable to use the hospital as soon as it

The crypt containing the heart of Queen Marie

was ready, badly needed as it was, when a friend said to me, perhaps not entirely seriously:

"But you who have so much faith—do you limit the power of God when it comes to sheets?"

I felt reproached by this, and from that time I tried to feel confident that this problem also could be solved, although I did not see how. This was the situation when one morning I woke up and had the curious feeling that there was a film over my left eye. I tried to rub and then to wash it away, but it remained the same. When I tried to focus my other eye to look in the mirror, that was difficult, too; so I went to Anton and asked him if he could see anything the matter. He told me that the pupil of the left eye was enormous, almost hiding the iris. My secretary drove me to Brasov, where the doctor tried to find out if I could possibly have got any solution splashed into my eye, perhaps in the hospitals, which could have had this effect, but I was sure I had not. He finally decided that it was simply a matter of general fatigue and overstrain, and that I must rest; this diagnosis was confirmed by a specialist in Bucarest whom Sitta highly recommended.

A little resentfully, therefore, I agreed to go to bed for a week. I have never been very strong, and it has sometimes seemed to me that my work has always been made harder by the fact that I so often feel ill or exhausted while I am doing it; a condition I have always found humiliating, for I had before me the example of my mother's health, always superb until her last illness. One day, while I was still "resting" unwillingly, I was told that a gentleman wished to see me, but of course he realized this was impossible if I was ill in bed. When I heard, however, that he was the proprietor of a big cotton mill on the south side of the mountain, and an acquaintance of Noelie's, I was alert at once. Waving convention aside, I had him shown up into my room, where I lay almost unseeing, and after I had excused myself I began to tell him all about the hospital. He seemed much interested, and said he would like to help. He felt the least he could do was to give me what I needed at cost, but he would have to talk with his brothers, who were partners in the business.

Two weeks later, when my eyes were once more functioning, a truck arrived with much more than I had ordered, and when I looked at the bills they were marked "Paid in full." With great joy Frau Koller sat herself down to do the necessary sewing, and I resolved to try harder not to let doubt cripple my work. It is actually a kind of conceit to do so, a feeling that it is our own work we are doing. If we acknowledge it to be God's work, certainly He is capable of bringing together men of good will who can be His instruments. Mr. Rizescu, the factory owner, and his family became great friends of ours. The children especially loved visiting them in their large log "block house" on the mountains above us; about six hours' climb from Bran. Just as I had in the past, so now my children loved climbing. Sometimes I regretted that I no longer had the time or the strength to join them.

August came, with the news from the front ever more frightening. In a sudden incomprehensible move the Germans took their best troops away from the Moldavian front, leaving our flank unprotected, and every available soldier was sent in a hurry to stop the gaps. General Tataranu was called back to the front, even though his Parkinson's disease was becoming worse, but before he left he brought his wife, his daughter, and his grandchildren to Bran. Our parting was a sad one. We had few illusions, but we would not give up hope for our country. It gave me a strange, lost feeling to part from him; he had been such a rock of efficiency and dependability. I wondered if we would ever meet again, and how.

Then we heard that the Russian offensive had started like a tidal wave. Wild rumors were everywhere; there were hints that Antonescu was losing his fight to avoid surrendering to the Russians without definite guarantees of Romanian independence; there were stories of German threats; of Russian threats; of threats of revolution; of vain appeals to Great Britain and the United States to say definitely what protection Romania would be given if she accepted the offer to "work her passage home," which Churchill had suggested. The soldiers in the wards followed me with pleading looks as I worked among them. What did the future hold for them? I could only tell them that whatever happened I would not leave them.

This seemed to comfort them, but I shuddered to think how little it might mean in reality. In spite of having kept my Romanian citizenship, I was also listed as a German citizen. Because of my frequent trips across the border during the past two years of working with the Romanian wounded in Austria, I had fallen into the habit of using my German passport. Using the Romanian one took a great deal of time because for every separate permission it had to be sent, with all the papers, to the Legation in Berlin, with the risk of its being lost or delayed on the way there and back. The authorities in Vienna, familiar with my work, gave me travel permission without delay. Therefore I myself was in Bran on a German passport, and my husband and children, as well as Frau Koller and Gretl, were listed as German citizens because Austria no longer existed as a separate nation. They had begun to urge recently that we get out of Romania while it was still possible, but I could not seriously consider deserting my country in time of danger. If the Russians came . . . But I firmly turned my mind away from this thought. It was little good wasting any energy in useless surmise. Everyone was suffering from weariness and war nerves; there was work to be done. If things grew worse, I knew I would need every bit of strength I had—and so I did. There were to be four years of continuous, unending strain, but happily I could not foresee this.

SEVENTEEN

THE TWENTY-THIRD of August, 1944, dawned and passed as did the days immediately before it, with no more uneasiness than usual. I was getting ready for bed when the telephone in my room rang, and the excited voice of the operator said:

"Domnitza! They have made peace! There is no more war—it is over!"

I could not grasp what she said at first. No what? "Listen to the radio!" she insisted.

I ran to Anton and we turned the radio on, to hear an announcement that the King had informed the people an armistice had been agreed upon. Soon we heard his own quiet voice giving the news, in an official message which I have translated informally into English for you:

Romanians! In the hardest hour of our duty, I have counted on the absolute unity of my people in the only way for the salvation of our country from a total catastrophe; to break away from the alliance with the

Axis powers, and to cease immediately hostilities with the Allies. A new national coalition government has been entrusted with the carrying out of the unanimous decision of the country to make peace with the Allies.

Romania has accepted the armistice offered to her by the Soviet Union, Great Britain, and the United States of America. From this moment cease all fighting and any act of hostility against the Soviet army, as well as the state of war with Great Britain and the United States.

Receive the soldiers of these armies with confidence. The Allies have guaranteed the independence of the country, and nonintervention in our internal affairs. They have recognized the injustice of the Vienna agreement through which Transylvania has been taken from us. Romanians, our people are understood to be masters and arbiters of their own fate. Whoever should stand against our free decisions, whoever should attack our rights, whoever this may be is an enemy of the nation.

I order the army and I call citizens to gather around the throne and the government for the salvation of the country. The one who will not obey the orders of the government is opposing the will of the people and is a traitor to the country. Dictatorship is at an end, and with it is ended all oppression. The new government means the beginning of a new era! an era in which justice and liberty are guaranteed to all the citizens of the country.

Romanians! On the courage with which we will defend our independence against any attempt to take away our right of self-determination, depends the fate of our country.

With absolute faith in the future of the Romanian nation, let us step forth on the new road of accomplishment for the Romania of tomorrow—a Romania free, powerful, and happy.

I listened with mixed feelings. It was something I could not actually believe in. Why was the injustice of taking Transylvania from us mentioned, while no word was said of Bessarabia and Bucovina, which had been torn away with equal ruthlessness? Receive the soldiers of the Russian army with confidence? I remembered what they had been like in World War I, when they had been our "comrades-in-arms" and had not had thirty years of Bolshevik training. I remembered the uninterrupted flow of fleeing refugees from Russia to Romania, and what they had had to say of the Communist regime. "With confidence?" *In what?* I wondered.

But the fighting at least was over—I thought. Thank God for that! And of course it would not only be the Russians who were to be received; the other Allies would soon be here too, to see that even in her humiliation Romania would receive a fair trial. How had Michael done it? Where was he? Was he safe? What of the Germans? Had they capitulated? Where did Romania stand? Everyone in the house was soon around us, each taking the news in his own way, with his own private doubts, fears, and hopes.

I decided to try to call Michael or Sitta. I was anxious about them, and I wanted to feel nearer them at this extraordinary moment. I asked for the Sinaia Palace, but the operator told me neither the King nor the Queen was there. I tried Bucarest, but I was unable to reach them there either. A cold fear entered my heart, but I pushed it away. Of course, at a moment like this they would not feel they could talk or communicate even with their own family. It had been stupid of me to try.

I could not know then that Michael, alone with his aide-de-camp, was driving across the country to the comparative safety of the western provinces, uncertain of what either the Russians or the Germans would do. Or that his mother drove also through that night with a friend, not knowing whether or not she would find her son at the appointed place; ignorant of how things had gone with him after the arrest of Antonescu and the declaration of the Armistice. What was in their hearts? I never asked. I feel a certain awe before the emotions of others, and I have never wanted to intrude. In fact, I have always avoided knowing more of such hours than I was forced to; this was not from any lack of sympathy or from cowardice, but from the respect for another's privacy.

I was not a witness to what happened in Bucarest. That is today a matter of official history, and can be found in books treating of this subject, one of which I have already mentioned. Since even now I cannot understand why certain decisions were taken, I can only state the facts themselves, as I have been able to discover them. From my own knowledge I can relate what happened to us—a handful of people in a mountain valley; but so that you may understand these experiences I will list only the barest outline of certain facts which are a matter of record.

On the afternoon of August 23, Marshal Antonescu was arrested at the Palace in Bucarest and turned over to guards who were members of the Communist Party, a party at that time numbering less than one thousand members in all of Romania, according to figures later announced by Ana Pauker. From that moment he disappeared from view until his trial, two years later. At the time of his arrest a new government was announced, which stood from August 23 to November 4, and which was headed by General Sanatescu. It was a military rule, but included as ministers of state without portfolio the heads of the four political parties: Iuliu Maniu, of the National Peasant Party; Dinu Bratianu, of the Liberals; C. Titel Petrescu, of the Social Democrats; and Lucretsiu Patrascanu, of the Communists. Patrascanu was also named minister of justice. When the second government, which lasted from November 4 to December 7, was formed, it was still headed by General Sanatescu, but it was a political government. Three-fifths of its members represented the National Peasant Party and the Liberals, and two-fifths represented the so-called National Democratic Front, which was a union of Communists, Socialists, and others. The "Front" retained the Department of Justice, while the former group of three-fifths of the members was given the Department of the Interior.

In the meantime, on the night of August 23, General Gerstenberg and General Hansen of the German army signed at the palace in Bucarest an "Accord" which provided for the peaceful evacuation of the German troops in Romania. On the next morning, August 24, acting on orders received directly from Hitler's headquarters in Berlin, the German army began to attack Romanian forces at various points, and bombarded Bucarest itself at frequent intervals, using the German-held airfields at the very gates of the city. At 4:00 P.M. that day, therefore, the Romanian government issued a proclamation stating that the Germans had violated the Accord signed barely twenty-four hours earlier, and had therefore put themselves into a state of war with Romania.

This created terrible individual situations, for here stood comrades who had fought side by side a terrible common enemy, and were now ordered to turn and kill one another. There were heartrending scenes and farewells before each turned away to do his duty by his country. In many places, wherever it was possible, a battle was avoided, and as usual the men themselves often did not understand for a long time what had gone on in the higher echelons to bring about this state of affairs.

In the same way we did not immediately hear what was happening as the Russian army crossed our borders, to be received "with confidence." As our army met them peacefully, ceasing "all fighting and any act of hostility against the Soviet army," according to instructions, the Russians imprisoned each regiment and sent it to Russia. Town after town the Russians announced triumphantly they had "captured"; and they continued to "capture" unresisting, bewildered towns, and to take as prisoners of war unresisting, bewildered regiments until the armistice was finally signed—in Moscow, with only Malinovsky signing for the Allies, and the Soviet High Command designated to "represent" the Allies—on September 12. Eventually a part of the Romanian army, hearing what was happening and yet unable to disobey our own government and turn and fight the Russians, itself was forced to flee from our advancing Russian "friends," to avoid being made prisoners of war after hostilities had officially ceased. Meanwhile other Romanian soldiers had driven the Germans out of Bucarest, as they were in a brief time to drive all German troops from Romania, and then to join battle with the Allies against the Hungarians.

The first Americans to arrive in Bucarest were a small group of journalists, who came in on August 25 with a group of Americans prepared to evacuate American war prisoners—the air crews who had been shot down in the bombing of the oil fields. As I have heard at first hand several times since my arrival in the United States, these prisoners had been exceptionally well treated, and they were now promptly flown out by their comrades, assisted by Romanian pilots. Apparently the American airmen felt no particular "confidence" in the advancing Russian army. There were friends of mine in Bucarest who saw the planes fly off, and expected confidently that the same planes would return at once, bringing American officials empowered to assist in carrying out arrangements; but no officials except Russians arrived until after the armistice was signed, on September 12, and then they were given no power in the Soviet High Command.

In the meantime, between August 23 and September 12, the Russian "friends" of Romania, received "with confidence," had captured and sent to Russia as prisoners of war *one hundred thirty thousand* Romanian soldiers.

This made, according to figures in the possession of the Romanian General Staff, a total of approximately 320,000 Romanian prisoners taken by the Russian army (the Russians claimed to have taken 500,000) besides 100,000 Romanian prisoners who had been serving in the Hungarian army. Of these 420,000 prisoners of war, the Soviet authorities have declared that 50,000 are dead. No names were listed for these. Approximately 190,000 were repatriated, at various times, leaving 180,000 still in captivity. In 1948 the so-called "Romanian People's Republic" issued a decree announcing that all inhabitants of Romania who had disappeared outside the national territory during the war "are presumed to be dead." This means that the puppet Romanian government can no longer ask the Soviet Union any embarrassing questions about its prisoners of war. Political prisoners, which include other hundreds of thousands of Romanian civilians deported to slave labor in Russia, are of course beyond the pale. No Communist-controlled government would ever dream of inquiring about them!

So much for a bare outline of events on the national level which occurred during the fall of 1944. My present knowledge of most of them came much later. Some facts I did not learn for several years, some I learned only after I had left Romania. In a small, partially isolated part of the country I had my family and my hospital work to take care of, which fully occupied my time. Furthermore, this work was for a time doubly hard and dangerous, and I was less free to ask questions, because I discovered to my sorrow and dismay what my "official" status was, so far as many of those highly placed were concerned.

The morning of August 24 dawned clear and peaceful, after a night when I imagine few people slept much. It seemed strange and incongruous that everything looked just the same. I suddenly thought of the Russian prisoners who were helping to construct the hospital, but I found them at work as usual, with no change of expression. I would have expected elation, but I was so grateful they were willing to go on that I did not think much about their reasons. Later, I was to understand.

I went up to the annex of Bran Poarta and found everyone at his post, although full of excitement and questioning. Noelle and I decided it might be good to cut down on rations, and to store up whatever food we could. There might be upheavals ahead, even at the best, and we were responsible for feeding men unable to care for themselves. I telephoned to Brasov, and since all was quiet there I decided not to leave Bran. I was anxious about my husband and children, as well as Frau Koller and Gretl, for, as I have said, they were all considered legally Germans. By this time we had heard that the Germans were being given time to leave peaceably, and therefore we knew they had not capitulated to the Allies, or joined in the armistice announced by the King.

The following days were a continual torture of uncertainty and wild rumors. We heard that the Germans had received orders to fight; that Bucarest was being bombed. We heard that Romanians were now to fight the Germans. We heard that our army was running for its life before the Russians, because Russian "friends" were imprisoning them.

In our own small valley these rumors were reflected in no end of pain and worry. The first of the Germans left Brasov without a fight, but in the Buzau Pass, not many miles from Brasov, a battle was raging. Since all available regular soldiers had been sent to Moldavia, men had to be gathered quickly from everywhere. Even the boys from the infantry school in Targoviste, about thirty-five difficult, mountain miles from Bran, were sent by forced marches to join the battle. One morning these untrained boys—some of them almost children—began struggling into Bran, footsore and completely exhausted. We mobilized every car and truck and driver; even Stefan, then barely twelve, was drafted into service. We picked up the boys from as far along the road as possible, and loaded in the knapsacks of those who seemed least footsore and could be left to walk. Meanwhile the Y.W.C.A., who had a lovely camp in Bran in a house given them by my mother, hastily prepared food for them, and water to wash their feet. We collected bandages from everywhere we could, and since by this time more drivers had volunteered, I could leave my car and help attend to the boys' feet. I must here confess that if there is anything that turns my stomach it is feet. I understood that day what Christ's example meant, and I did my best in a Christian spirit to overcome my weakness. At least I overcame it so that I could go on with the job, but it is one of the things that still takes all my will to overcome. Why? It is foolish, but there it is. It is so!

Just when I felt my back would break, and that I must somehow take a little rest, I looked up to see Nadeje in the doorway, looking worn and harassed.

"The Germans have started fighting in Brasov," she said. "People are losing their heads; all the patients who can move themselves, and part of the staff, are on their way here by whatever means they can manage. I hurried ahead to give you a little warning, but I must get back as soon as possible to my daughter and her baby. Where on earth can you put them up?"

Where indeed! I thought. Again the Y.W.C.A. secretaries volunteered to help by taking some. I went to Bran Poarta and got Noelle, who rounded up the other women on her "staff." To say that the work they did was a marvel is to say little, for by that night they had found food and lodging for more than two hundred people who managed somehow to cover the twenty miles between Brasov and Bran. It is extraordinary what people can do under pressure of fear and desperation.

Patients I had thought could hardly walk down a corridor had got to us.

While I had been working during that strenuous day I had also been concerned with no slight upheaval in my own house, since with the declaration that a state of war existed between Romania and Germany there had come an order that all Germans should be arrested. All my efforts to get in contact with the palace had been vain; I still did not know where the King was, which added greatly to my worries about him. I had telegraphed to the head of the gendarmerie for protection, since most of our own house guard had been sent to Brasov to help there. This all made the situation at home very difficult, and I was met, whenever I returned, by worn nerves and endless discussions and reproaches. So many different proposals were made that I felt torn in pieces. It took all my strength and courage to stick to what I knew was the only right course, as well as the only safe one: to stand by my wounded, and to trust the love and loyalty of the people. The end result was to prove me right, but at the moment I had only my own faith, and that to others was no proof.

Finally, feeling half dead with mental and physical weariness, I was about to crawl into bed when shots resounded at our very gate. My first thought was for Noelle's children because the house they slept in was near the gate. I quickly took our elevator, which descended through the rock and into the garden by way of the old well shaft, grabbed the poor frightened children, and took them into the castle, hoping Noelle was safe. The shooting did not last long, but hardly had I got the children settled when a terrified maid came to tell me that a dying officer lay in the hall.

Down the twisting stairs I rushed, to find Simone Cantacuzino's husband, not wounded but suffering from a heart attack. He had hurried from Bucarest in his anxiety to be with his wife and daughter. With Anton's help we put him on the only remaining unoccupied couch, and found that fortunately he had his own medicine with him. Anton volunteered to sit up with him, though he, too, was exhausted from transporting the cadets earlier in the day, as well as from his own anxieties.

The shooting we had heard, it then developed, had been because a group of German military cars had driven through and had not seen the sign to halt, and the Romanian guard had fired. It was one of those unavoidable, horrible things that happen. The German cars were unarmed and on their way to report as prisoners to the authorities in Brasov, but now two, who happened to be Austrians, were badly wounded. We took them to our already overcrowded hospital in Poarta, where room was quickly and willingly made for them. Once they were settled, I was able to see Noelle, who had been on her way back to see about her children, and to reassure her. She decided to remain at the hospital annex for the night, and I returned to the castle—this time beyond feeling, and convinced that whatever new disaster awaited me I did not care any more. Any further effort or feeling was beyond me. Even now as I write this I have the same feeling of exhaustion beyond belief. I do not remember when I got to bed that night, nor do I remember sleeping, though I suppose I must have.

Next day Simone Cantacuzino arrived, and I was more than relieved to let her take over the care of her ailing husband, while I tried to face the difficulties of too many people, too little to eat, and tempers not always in good condition. A telegram from the head of the gendarmerie informed me that a solution would be found, and that I should be confident. It was not completely reassuring, but it was a help.

When I had seen to the immediate needs of those at home I went up to Bran Poarta, where I found one of the Austrians dead and the other in a serious condition. I refused to give him up to the guard that had come to fetch him, since I knew that the journey would kill him. I pointed out that the annex was a military hospital; that the man could not possibly run away; and that taking prisoners was one thing and murder another. This may not have been solid military logic, but it did work for the time being.

The dead Austrian did not interest the guard, and they were happy to leave him with us. We decided to give him a proper Christian burial, and when we found by his papers that he was a Lutheran we managed with great difficulty to get a minister from a village about ten miles away. The soldier's coffin was borne by those of the wounded who were in a condition to do it, wearing their hospital garments, which were all the clothes they had. Anton and I, the children, the nurses, and some others of the wounded followed in a procession to the lovely flower-filled cemetery near by, and the Lutheran minister intoned the prayers in the soldier's own language and according to his faith. None of us were members of his church, and he was of an alien army now actively our enemy, but in that hour he was not alone. When Anton finally managed to get back to Austria in 1948 he was able to take to the man's parents his watch and a photograph of his grave in the faraway Carpathians.

More days passed in continual doubt as to what would happen next. The radio gave conflicting news, depending on which station you happened to be listening to. When people met, their greeting was "What have you heard?" "What do you know?" We heard that the Russians had entered Bucarest. Our only hope of accurate news was Mrs. Tataranu, who was self-controlled but worried because she had not heard from her husband. Suddenly one day all the Russians left off working at the hospital and never came again. Orders had come for them, but the thing that made me anxious was that they were all unenthusiastic about leaving, and that some even tried to escape their liberating brothers.

At last one day, after what seemed endless waiting, Mrs. Tataranu came to me to say that the General had written her he was safe, and had sent a letter for me also. It was a sad letter, saying that he was well and would be returning for a brief time, but that perhaps those who were dead were better off.

A day later, which as nearly as I can remember must have been at the very end of August, a colonel of the gendarmerie appeared in full uniform, complete with sword. He presented himself formally and then conveyed the message that to safeguard the Archduke and the other German members of my household, they were to consider themselves prisoners under arrest in the castle, the grounds of which they were not to leave. I felt sorry for him because he had to convey such a message to me, and I thanked him and told him I was grateful.

I was sincere in saying this, for it could have been much worse, but I did not know until later how much worse it had almost actually been. At first Anton was to be taken to a concentration camp, and the children and I were to be imprisoned in a monastery in the mountains, but the Romanian government had refused to carry this out as the Russians at first demanded. However, the order as it came through to Brasov had been that I, too, was to be confined to Bran. My friends of the gendarmerie in Brasov had flatly refused to carry out this order, and had begun at once working to have it reversed, but since they did not tell me about it until the order for my release came a short time later, I never knew I had been arrested until after I was freed! Anton's order for release did not come until late in 1946 but, as it was, he was safer at first, and later the restrictions were not carried out too severely as long as he did not go far afield, but the idea was not a pleasant one.

During these last days of August, Romanian troops from Moldavia who had managed to escape their "friends" the Russians began passing through Bran on their way to fight the Hungarians in the cause of the Allies. They were received with a love and a joy that reminded me of my angry words to the village doctor who had denied us the use of his empty hospital. Russian soldiers had already taught many lessons, and were to teach more.

There were two incidents of those days which I remember vividly. An artillery regiment was passing, and a friend asked me to join her in waiting for her son. She chose a place where the road was so narrow that we were obliged to stand in the ditch, because it was just past a sharp bend where the trucks must slow down, and she was sure that she and her son could not miss each other there. She watched each car and truck with eager expectation. One after another they passed, until at last a car stopped and a young officer jumped out.

"A friend of my son's!" cried the excited woman, and rushed toward him, but the expression on the boy's face sent a tremor of fear through me.

"Alas, madame! Your son is not with us," he said. "At the moment the retreat sounded he jumped out of his trench toward the enemy and cried,

'Forward!' No one has heard of him since. Perhaps later the Russians will send him back, or perhaps he is in hiding . . ."

My poor friend clasped her hands together and fought visibly for control. "Thank you, dear boy! God bless you! I understand. Go now: the others are moving on!" The young man jumped back into the car and drove on. I stood speechless, for what words are there in such a moment? I could only hold her in my arms there in the ditch until she felt she could face again the light of day, from which all joy was gone for her.

"Will you get me one of the doctors, please?" she said at last. "You know the state of my husband's heart. This might kill him." So I saw her safely to her door, and then went in search of the doctor.

On another day when I was returning from Brasov I saw the baggage van of a regiment, and to my joy I saw painted on one of the carts my mother's monogram. It was her own regiment, the one of which she had been made honorary colonel: the 4th Rosiori. I stopped my car and ran across the road to an officer, whom I stopped by holding on to his horse's bridle. He was at first astonished, but when he recognized me a great grin spread over his face. Alas, they were not coming through Bran! But the next day the commander and a delegation of officers and men came to place a wreath where my mother's heart lay buried.

By this time all the wounded and the staff that had run away to Bran had returned to the Brasov hospital, where I visited them whenever I could. Thanks largely to Colonel Serbu, the construction of the new hospital went on, and was nearing completion. I spent as much time as possible there, attending to the details, and it seemed as if a special benediction lay upon it. On the eighth of September, by dint of an enormous effort in which everyone joined, Spitalul Inima Reginei opened its doors to the first forty wounded. We had a small but moving ceremony to bless this beginning of its service; the men were delighted to be the first patients, and Noelle and her "staff" and I were proud indeed. Our only regret was that Colonel Serbu could not be present; he had been called to Bucarest for work there. He was a great loss to all of us.

I was happy about my hospital, but still concerned with family problems. All the Saxon schools were now closed, forbidden, and confiscated. The question of where to send the children for the coming year arose, especially in regard to Stefan, who was beyond the work of the village schools. During the summer he had become great friends with a fine boy from Bucarest, whose mother had worked in the Poarta annex. She proposed to take Stefan to live with them and to send him to the school her son attended, and I was delighted.

Just as this arrangement was made I received a message from a friend, asking me to come to Bucarest. Mrs. X, as I must call her, lived near the house of General Aldea, Minister of the Interior in General Sanatescu's first government. He wished to see me as unobtrusively as possible, and she therefore invited me to spend a few days with her.

She was most wonderful then and afterwards in going to everyone she could think of who might be of help to me, although this I did not know until later. For example, it was she who told Prince Stirbey, on his return from the vain and unhappy appeals made by Romania at Cairo and at Moscow, that I was at Bran. He had not known I was in Romania, and when he went to Maniu about my difficulties I was proud when I learned that Maniu had said:

"But how it is possible that anyone could think of doing harm to Domnitza Ileana?"

All this I was told several months later, and by that time I knew how to appreciate it. On this first trip to Bucarest I had no idea how people felt about me, and I did not realize what true and brave friendship Mrs. X was showing in her invitation, but I soon learned.

With more innocence than wisdom I set out by car with Stefan and Bittermann, my secretary. The four-hour drive was uneventful, and since as we entered Bucarest we passed my sister Elisabeta's house, I decided to go in and see if she was there, so in at the entrance we drove. There were rather a lot of police about, and I thought, *Certainly she is being well guarded!* I walked in, and I noticed that the servant at the door looked frightened, although he said "Yes" to my inquiry if my sister was at home. He went ahead and I followed him down the corridor, when suddenly I was met by one of the King's aides-de-camp. We were, I think, equally astonished to see each other.

"Is the King here?" I asked.

"Yes, we came yesterday. The Queen is upstairs."

"Where is Elisabeta?"

"In Sinaia."

I continued to follow the servant, who ushered me upstairs and into Sitta's room. If she had seen a ghost, Sitta could not have looked more horrified. She told me I could not have done anything more dangerous than to come to them; that no one knew what would come next; that the Russians were howling for our blood. When I told her of Stefan and his school, she became even more upset and reproachful, and told me in no uncertain terms that such a thing would add a great deal to their danger. Of course, the horror of finding the country left in the hands of the Russians and not in those of the united Allies, the terrible uncertainty, the total disregard by the Russians of all the promises of freedom and noninterference they had given—all these were reasons enough for her fears and her distraught condition. She told me that she felt the less we saw of each other the better. She and Michael had no power to protect me, and I was technically an enemy.

I suppose I should have realized this before but, strangely enough, such a thought had never occurred to me. It was not easy to face the fact, but there it was. If Sitta felt so strongly that I was a danger to her and Michael, others would feel so still more deeply. I would have to make the best of it, and find out what I could do to save my own family without endangering others. So Sitta and I said good-bye sadly and fondly, and in fact it was well over a year before I saw her again, although at Christmas she sent us lovely presents.

Saddened and still a little dazed, I went to my friend's home. It was small, but the welcome I got was large, and I appreciated now the real courage Mrs. X was showing. Stefan went to his friend and Bittermann went to relatives of Mrs. X, and I waited patiently until General Aldea came. He was a big, round-faced man, full of cheer and confidence, and we made friends on the spot. It was a friendship that withstood political storms and prisons, and though once I was told that when caught in his underground activities he had betrayed my part in them, I know that if it was true only the worst torture could have made him do it. In the next world we shall be friends still, if I may enter the place where heroes have gone ahead of us.

Even at this first meeting he proved himself a rock. He encouraged me about my situation, and he promised to take up the question of Stefan and his school at once. Unfortunately he was not able to do much about this, for others did not have his courage or his convictions. Word came that Stefan was not permitted to go to any state school whatsoever. My children were "Germans" and had no right to any education at all. This was a terrible blow, and one that at first I could hardly believe. General Aldea was able, however, to have the arrests and confinement in Bran of Anton, Frau Koller, and Gretl confirmed by the ruling powers, which then were entirely mysterious ones to me. Otherwise the constant threat of the arrests having been "provisional," and of the orders being changed to confinement in a concentration camp, would have hung over us all the time.

I was grateful for this contact with the General, and for the feeling it gave me that there was at least someone to appeal to in what had become a nightmare. Of course General Aldea did not last long in power, for when Sanatescu's short-lived first government collapsed, the General with his uncompromising insistence on what he felt was right was the first to go.

A friend of mine in Bucarest later told me about a "demonstration" against the General which occurred a short time before the breakup of the government on November 4. It was one of those staged by the Communists, with luckless Romanian workers forced to carry banners and shout slogans as they "marched" unwillingly along the street. The slogan in this case was supposed to be "Down with Aldea!" but since most of the workmen had no idea who Aldea was, and were only anxious to get through with it and get home to supper, they had misunderstood the word and assumed it was one more familiar to them. They were therefore shouting perfunctorily but distinctly "Down with Anglia!" (England) when a shocked Russian heard them; and since at the time Russia had no wish to express her real opinions of the other Allies quite so openly as she has since, the Romanians were stopped and sent hastily home—which probably only added to their complete and annoyed mystification over the whole exercise!

My short stay in Bucarest was long enough to show me who was my friend and who was not. Or at least it showed me those who were not strong enough to stand up for their friends, although perhaps these people were simply more realistic than I am ever able to be. I thought on my way home that I would like to see Elisabeta in Sinaia, but I had learned prudence. I telephoned her first, and she also thought it safer not to see me. Again I forced myself to try to realize that I was a public danger, an "enemy" in my own country. It was obvious that I could not hope to recover any of my property in Austria, for it was certain that the Germans would have no friendly feeling toward a Romanian, and I doubted if it would even occur to *them* to consider me a "German." I was responsible for my family and household, with no one to turn to. I thanked God in my heart that my mother had not lived to see this.

The return to Bran was in itself not easy, for the Russians had nearly reached Brasov and the roads were not supposed to be safe. With the help of the guard General Aldea had sent with me we got through; but I had not minded the thought of danger as much as I had minded breaking the news to Stefan and his friend that he could not remain in Bucarest at school, but that we must find another solution. I could not bear just then to tell him the whole humiliating truth.

It was not easy to return unsuccessful to my family at home. I put as good a face on it as I could, and I began to realize that in reality, considering the turmoil everything was in and the complete power of the

Russians, as well as the helpless fear felt by so many, I had really not done so badly, after all, in assuring the safety of those in the castle. One great comfort was the usual loving reception of the children, to whom the only thing that mattered was that I was safely back. In a way the wounded were the same in their welcome, since they had a simple faith that I was, after all, Domnitza Ileana, capable of solving problems and difficulties by some magic power that no man, not even a Russian, could change. This was both touching and at the same time infuriating, because they attributed any failure I had to my not *really* having put my heart into it. They never blamed me, but there it was. Had I *really* wanted to? For if I had, of course, then I could have accomplished it.

More than ever now I had to fall back on my own inner strength. God had indeed given me a great gift when He gave me that simple and absolute faith that has never failed me. But there were many days when I had to go away alone and battle it out; days when I would walk along the flower-edged path and up the steps that led to the little chapel where lay my mother's heart. . . .

EIGHTEEN

IN NEED of comfort, I would sit quiet at the little chapel door, looking down upon the church of Bran or up toward the mountain back of the castle and often a great peace would come upon me. "Be still, and know that I am God."

I remember especially one day a year later, in July, 1945, when a great sorrow had come to me in the form of what seemed to me a terrible injustice. I had been excluded from being present in Curtea de Arges, where the seven years' memorial service was being held for my mother, an important service to us in the Orthodox Church. It was one of those needlessly cruel things which hurt beyond words. I felt, *This I cannot endure. This is too much. I cannot bear it.*

So I sought refuge again at the little chapel, seeking for strength to bear the unbearable; for even physically I felt that I could not endure the pain. Then my eyes fell upon the eternal unmoved perfection of the mountain. So long had it stood there just like that—so very long: even before history began. It had been unchanged and unhurt by human strife and endeavor, by humiliations, hopes, and despairs. How small I and my pain were! And suddenly I understood that such things did not matter; that they were of no importance at all. Such things were there simply to be overcome; they were put in our way for us to use in building the staircase of life. On each one we could mount one step higher until finally we attained the Mountain, the eternal reality of living.

I mention this moment because it was such a deep and real experience that it was one of the greatest events of my life: a day of revelation when I definitely opened another door and stepped forward. It was then also that I better knew and understood my mother, and how she had been able to build from anguish and sorrow a stairway to attainment.

We had always stood close together: our understanding had been extraordinarily complete. Apart from being mother and daughter, in our relationship we were friends, and something still more nearly perfect; companions in our tastes and ideas, as well as in our aims and ideals. I can see her so clearly now, wandering among the flowers she understood and loved, and which she planted with such extraordinary knowledge. They always looked perfect where she put them. They stood as if they had always grown in their beds in the garden, or in the vases in her room, or on the dining table. Their beauty was enhanced by the background she had provided for them. In her paintings, too, they were perfect. It was one of her great gifts that she knew her limitations: she painted only flowers, which she did beautifully; she never attempted landscapes, for which she had no talent.

This enabled her to grow old gracefully; she stepped aside simply and naturally from things she could no longer do. She did not try to compete, but found new outlets in sympathy and understanding, so that the young loved to have her with them. No party of mine would have been complete without her. She would start us off and then leave us, but we would seek her out. Even at the end of one of my rare balls we would stream into her bedroom and wake her up, just to have her know we loved her and to feel she had participated in our fun.

To the very last of her life she was genuine and near, understanding and simple. No one was too humble or too exalted for her not to see the human being first. Kind and long-suffering, her every thought was for others. Royal to the backbone, she had no false modesty as she had no false pride. She knew her worth and the part she had to play; she was sure of herself; her very walk was regal. Once when I protested at her crossing a Vienna street in total disregard of the traffic, she answered, "But who would run over me?" And of course no one ever did. Her pride lay in the fact that as both the symbol of an ideal and the implement of an accomplishment she served her people well. As a private individual she regarded herself humbly and modestly. When her favorite sister lay dying, of all those who were there and who claimed to be most wanted and essential my mother alone stood aside, conscious of her lack of medical knowledge and unconscious that of all the hands outstretched to help, hers alone gave the dying woman peace.

Brave and wise, she was as guileless as a child. She loved riding, and was a consummate horsewoman. Romantic, as her novels prove, she beautified life, even though at the same time she was practical in planning and efficient in carrying out her plans. A great organizer, she had little love for detail, but her need for harmony drove her to create order even in small things.

Her strength was fabulous, her health marvelous. When in the end a cruel illness fell upon her, she could not believe that she—Regina Maria, who had walked the plague-ridden hospitals with impunity, who had driven endless hours over impassable roads in midwinter to reach some distressed village, who had been tirelessly at need's beck and call, endlessly giving ear to the complaints, hopes, and joys of her people—that *she* could possibly be ill. Yet her stupendous strength finally failed, and for nearly two years she fought her sapping illness, remaining always the same—busy, cheerful, and thoughtful of others. Her face ever became more beautiful and harmonious. When in the end the doctor's efforts proved useless, she sighed, "Poor doctor! I am so sorry for him. He is so disappointed!" The last time I spoke to her it was by telephone when she was at Dresden, and we discussed her having received a person who had hurt her deeply. "I received her with open arms," she said, and I could almost see her perfect smile that made her startlingly blue eyes so extraordinarily tender. "You see, there is little left to me except to be kind." Yes, to be kind. That was, I think, the purpose of her being.

Death had never parted us. Even as no shadow came between us when we walked together in this life, so death cast no shadow between us either. Why, then, should it matter that I could not kneel at her grave on the anniversary of her death? So near did I often feel her that when I rearranged things in the Castle of Bran I almost felt it was she and not I who did so, in a strange, momentary union of personalities which brought us together and yet left us distinct and two. Even here in New England, as I place some belonging of hers on a table or wonder what she would say to this or that, she is so near me that I am as conscious of her as I am of myself, yet without ever losing the feeling of my own personality. Curiously enough, at such times I have heard people remark suddenly, "Oh, how you did remind me of the Queen just then!" although actually I do not at all resemble my mother.

Once this happened to me when I was visiting one of her favorite convents in Romania. As I stood in the courtyard I had that strange, double feeling, and was awakened out of my reverie by a peasant woman exclaiming, "Oh, I almost thought you were the Queen standing there!" Another time it happened was in the New York Town Hall, after one of my lectures, when I had had that especially conscious feeling of my mother's presence. An old friend of hers—no fanciful person, but a poised woman of the world—who had loved her well, came up to me and curtsied and kissed my hand with tears in her eyes. "You are so like your mother," she said.

What is "now" and what is "then"? There are moments when things merge and time is not. I live again—both the past and the present.

Someone once said to me, "All your mistakes come from loneliness for your mother"; and a psychiatrist once told me, "You must get rid of your mother complex and stand on your own feet." Each had put things in the wrong order. It was my mistakes that made me lonely for my mother, not the loneliness that made me make the mistakes. It was after my feet stumbled that I had the "mother complex"; not the complex that made my feet stumble. No, the memory of my mother, the spirit she instilled into me, the knowledge of her deathlessness—all of this is, next to my Christian faith, one of the greatest factors in my life.

These pages may not seem to you to belong here, but to me they do because of the merging of time and of the thread that binds life into a whole. Let me therefore pause a moment, and return to the house in Newton to take a deep breath and rest awhile, and to explain how it is that I can bear to write and to tell all this.

I do not know if you can imagine what it is like to part from all you have loved and known, and to start again without being able to share memories of the past with any one of those you live with. There are those with whom I can share this or that fragment of the past, but the whole I carry alone. It is sad not to be able to turn around and say to someone, "Do you remember . . . ?" But because wonders never cease I have found a friend who has come so close to me that she understands. What I tell her becomes real as if we had shared it in very truth as sisters. It is thanks to her love, appreciation, and intelligence that all these stories I have lived can be put together; that I can say to you, my reader, "Come and see these two rooms which hold my present and my past."

God's mercies come to us in devious ways. We go through sore travail; we lose all; we suffer all. But if we do not lose hope, even when we have lost faith in ourselves, if we still cling to what God is, to what the death and resurrection of our Lord are for each individual, then "All these things shall be added unto you." But first we must realize that there is only one Power that does not fail; one Love that is eternal; one Friend who never leaves us, however imperfect and sorrowful we may be: God.

Until we learn this, disappointment after disappointment will meet us. We must not seek for human comfort, but rely upon our Father to give us our desire. And in due time, in the moment when our hearts are still and ready to receive in full understanding, and not merely in blind hunger, then only do we receive what we most need. Thus I found a mother and a sister.

Perhaps to you this does not fit in here, but to me it does. I am writing in these chapters of the fullest and most creative period of my life; of the years when I was, I believe, giving the utmost of myself spiritually, intellectually, and physically—and all of that was wiped off the face of the earth as a sponge washes off a blackboard. It was not easy to find my balance again; to live again; and when I did I was bitterly lonely. It was only when I had turned entirely to God and forgotten myself and my pain that I found I was neither lost nor alone.

There is in Louisburg Square, in one of those lovely old Boston houses so full of dignity and of the tranquil atmosphere of an undisturbed past, a house of prayer, where the quiet, gentle nuns of St. Margaret receive those weary and lost souls who are seeking a surer footing. A co-worker out from Romania led me there one September morning, and I knew that I had found my spiritual home. And as with time I went there more often, I felt less and less a lost and wandering spirit, but more as one who returns. One evening, when more tired than usual I knelt in the chapel, not praying with words but seeking to enter the communion of peace, I felt a hand on my shoulder and a kiss on my forehead, "Just to welcome you home, my child!" and I knew that in my home I had also found a mother.

Later, in the world of work and striving, in the course of giving one of my first talks about Romania—an activity which now seems to be developing to an extent I never dreamed of—I met Dorothy; though then I did not know her name, nor that she would be as a true sister to me, nor that her home would be mine. For when one is a mother one's own home is especially the home of the children; the place in which one carries the burden and is responsible. That life would be empty and meaningless without this responsibility for the children does not change the fact that to be at home somewhere where one carries *no* responsibility is unbelievably wonderful, and restful beyond words.

I do not feel I would be telling my story truthfully if I did not mention these two other homes that I have been blessed with, that give me the strength, the courage, and also the wisdom to keep the home of my children happy, harmonious, and on solid foundations.

Lecture on Communism and Christianity, Chicago, 1952

What is the connection between Jassy, Sinaia, Sonnberg, Brasov, Bran, and today in Massachusetts? There is a golden thread that binds them and makes them one, in time that is past, present, and future only to our imperfect, human conceptions. They are together and one in me, in the object for which I am striving: the achievement of a better, higher concept of events and of actions as mounting by slow and painful steps toward a final goal which is beyond home, country, and race; a goal which is the development of an understanding of the reasons for the happenings in a world where joy and sorrow seem so inextricably mixed. I have not yet found my answer—not wholly, because my road has not yet ended. One thing I know: the golden thread that binds a life together is love in its many and wondrous forms; love of beauty, love of children and of mankind, love of home and of country, and ultimately love of God—whose perfect Love includes all others.

NINETEEN

WHEN I had returned to Bran from Bucarest in the fall of 1944 I gathered strength as quickly as possible to face the difficulties that pressed in on every side. As is so often the case, once I had overcome my own fears and depressions, help proved to be at hand. The headmaster of the village school said that he had received no order against accepting my children as pupils, and as long as he knew nothing of the situation officially, why not let him have them? This took care of Niki, and of Minola, Alexandra, and Magi, for of course Elisabeth was not yet of school age. Since Stefan was too far advanced for the village school, a solution was found for him by enrolling him unofficially in the Saguna, the school in whose building the Brasov Red Cross hospital was lodged. Teachers from there were scattered about in Bran, and one of the local priests was an ex-schoolmaster, so that Stefan could study at home and take his exams in the summer when the other boys did. This was a great weight off my mind, and it confirmed my trust in the love of the people themselves.

We had heard that the Russians would not take the road through Bran, because the bridges along that route were bad, but suddenly parts of their army began arriving. Word ran before them of the way they "lived on the country" as they advanced; of their raping and stealing. Women, livestock, cars, and watches seemed to have the most attraction for them, we heard. The peasants drove their animals into the mountains, hid their wives and daughters, and waited. There was no protection to be obtained anywhere. Since our garage stood directly on the highroad itself, it offered no hiding for the cars that were so necessary to us. We had not only those used for our family—for transporting farm produce, getting supplies, and doing necessary business in a village without public transportation— but we also had the truck and station wagon that were necessary for the hospital work. Finally we took the best cars into the garden and covered them with branches and straw to make them look like piles of compost, and to our relief they escaped the Russian eye. For the hospital no concealment was possible. It was reached from the main road by crossing the river on a bridge that ended in the courtyard of the hospital itself. We therefore trusted in the invaders' respect for wounded, but it was not until later we realized how wrong we were to believe this existed. It was nothing short of a miracle that saved the situation: the Russians simply never crossed the bridge.

Can you think what it is like to sit waiting for brigands, knowing that you are at their mercy, that there is no law or order to which you can appeal? It is a condition which American civilization has forgotten about since the days of its frontier. The Soviet army was not like anything which had been seen since the days of Genghis Khan's Tartar hordes. Soldiers arrived on foot, in carts, on horseback, in haphazard groups. Sometimes there were many, sometimes few, but they were all armed to the teeth with the most modern weapons. They did not worry about food or anything else. With frightening and unhuman simplicity they took what they wanted at the point of a gun, and they shot at people with that complete lack of feeling which a normal man has when he shoots at a cardboard target.

With my daughters, in dresses made out of window curtains because of wartime shortages, 1947

The villagers soon discovered that it was best to put at their disposal a certain amount of food and livestock: an expensive arrangement, but one that was safer in the end, even though it began the disruption of the economic system of a community which made it easier for the Party to "take over" later. The problem of the women was a more serious one, and there were terrible, unbelievable scenes of which I cannot write. Not even old women were spared. The terrifying part was the methodical brutality with which everything was done. The Russians did not seem to enjoy either their power or their sins. Slowly I began to see the horrible tragedy of these people, who had been robbed of their very souls, so that their reactions were not even animal but purely functional. I finally understood, also, what had at first seemed so surprising to me: that they robbed rich and poor alike. They had no standards by which to distinguish between one person and another. In Russia everything belongs to the state; the individual has no personal property apart from the minimum of bare necessities. To the Russians, even the poorest peasant had in his home possessions which seemed luxurious to them, and they took ruthlessly whatever they walked past.

It became dangerous to go even to Bran Poarta, and since of course I could not get to Brasov at all, it was fortunate that I could keep in contact with the hospital there by telephone. Their great trouble at first was that they had some German wounded who were prisoners, and that they also had as patients some of the *Tudor Vladimirescu.* This was an organization of Romanian prisoners who had been in slavery in Russia since the early days of the war, completely cut off from their homes and families and given entirely false information by their captors about what was happening in their country. Both pressure and eloquence were used upon them to induce them to become the leaders in a "new Romania"— which, Ana Pauker and other gifted Communists assured them, had the complete backing of both Great Britain and the United States. Eventually Lieutenant Colonel Nicolae Cambrea, who had always opposed the alliance with Nazi Germany and had himself been captured at Stalingrad, was persuaded to assume the leadership of a group to be called "Tudor Vladimirescu," a name in the heroic Romanian tradition which had the atmosphere for our people that a "Lincoln Division" or a "Nathan Hale Division" or a "Rodger Young Division" might have for you, and which certainly had no association with Communist aims. Since at this time Stalin had been successful in deceiving the representatives of both Great Britain and the United States as to his intentions, it does not seem remarkable that these hopelessly starved, exhausted, and oppressed soldiers could also be deceived. In fact, as I learned more about it, it was a source of pride to me that so many of the hundreds of thousands of mistreated, hopeless, homesick Romanian prisoner-slaves resisted both punishment and persuasion, and refused to make any sort of terms with their ancient enemy.

Understanding what had happened to them, however, made the Tudor Vladimirescu no less difficult to get along with, especially when they first returned with the Russians. It was some time before they fully realized how completely they had been deceived about conditions at home, and before they understood that they had been used simply as gullible tools of the Russians, thrown into the war against the Germans and killed in large numbers, so that at first only those who were wounded were allowed to be sent home. These men were arrogant and demanding to begin with, so that in the Red Cross hospital in Brasov, for example, they had "ordered" that all the German wounded must be thrown out of the place at once! They were made no less difficult to deal with by discovering that the Romanian wounded regarded them as traitors and fought to avoid even being in the same ward with them. The initials of their organization, "T.V.," were embroidered on their uniforms as part of their insignia, and the other Romanians promptly took the position that these initials stood for *T'ai vandut*—"You have sold yourself"—a taunt which of course infuriated the Tudor Vladimirescu.

Conditions became so difficult that I finally determined I must somehow get to Brasov, and I got help from the workmen at my hospital, where some last construction was still going on. A group of them going to town in a truck offered to take me with them. It was a most amusing drive, with the truck crowded with all sorts of people, all determined to seem cheerful and show the Russians that they were not going to get the better of us; we could still govern our lives to some extent, and get from Bran to Brasov when it was necessary! They found it great fun to have me with them, and when we had arrived safely in Brasov they deposited me at the hospital door, promising to stop for me again in the evening. It was a sweet illusion for both of us!

I was received with open arms and decided relief, and when I did the rounds we all behaved as if I had been away for ages, so much had happened since we last saw one another. It was sad for me to find among the new arrivals some of the boys whose feet I had washed on that day when they marched through Bran! My contact with the Tudor Vladimirescu was strange. I could see their old feelings fighting with the new, and leaving them uncertain how one should behave to a princess-nurse in the "new" Romania; therefore, I treated them just as I did the others—as wounded men who, because of their wounds, had a claim on my care and love. As time went on I found that this was the right way to handle them, and in fact as I heard their stories and realized how their pain and hunger and their despair of ever seeing their homes and families again had been played upon, and how they had been deceived as to the purpose of the Russians, I came not to blame them so much. At the same time, however, my admiration for the great majority of our officers and soldiers, who had resisted this pressure and who, therefore, had remained in slavery, became almost a reverence for their courage and endurance.

We finally installed our German prisoners in an attic on the top floor, where we made them as comfortable as possible and put them in charge of their own doctors. The entire hospital staff behaved wonderfully in this difficult situation and met it efficiently and calmly. Simone and Nadeje were excellent, as usual, and when the T.V.'s still showed signs of being difficult, Simone proposed that they and the German prisoners should exchange wards if they really thought the attic more pleasant—which settled matters for the time being.

It is a painful moment when one has to choose between two demands and two loyalties. I felt that I ought to stay at the Brasov hospital for a time, but I did not feel at this point that it was at all safe for me to leave my family. Therefore, when toward evening I received word that the Russians had taken the workmen's truck (so much for the Rights of the Workers!) and that I was stranded, I was anxious. Suddenly I thought of my friends, the firemen at the barracks, and they were quite happy to send me back on a fire engine, the one car the Russians never offered to take! Since most of us have felt the urge to ride on a fire engine, you can understand that it was an amusing occasion for me in spite of everything, even though the springs were not ideal and the road even less so.

The passing of Russian troops through Bran gradually decreased, and for a time dwindled almost entirely away. Most of the summer visitors managed to return to their homes in one way or another, which left me practically without nurses. Noelle had been obliged to move to other quarters for the winter, since the house of mine that she was using could not be heated. Although she remained in Bran she took up the work of buttermaking in order to earn a living for her family until her husband could find a position, and this meant that she could give little time to the hospital. The same situations began to occur in Brasov, so that the hospital there could let me have only one nurse, who did night duty for me. For the day there were the hospital cook's daughter and a girl who came from the village in the morning, besides me, but since only about ten of our cases were critical ones we were able to manage even though my two "assistants" were untrained and inexperienced. They were both willing and obedient, and then, too, soldiers are always good about making their own beds and helping one another when they are able to. We had a resident student-doctor who was very proficient, and one of the surgeons from Brasov visited us regularly.

It was this shorthanded condition of the hospital which started me on a phase of nursing which I had avoided up to this time. As the result of an accident, the toe of a workman from one of the nearby factories had to be amputated. The surgeon came, but the student-doctor happened to be ill, and there was no one else to assist. I offered my services, and since there was nothing else to be done the surgeon accepted them and instructed me briefly. We washed and put on sterile clothes and gloves, the man was brought in, a local anesthetic was given, and the operation started. I was more than nervous, and full of fear that I would not do the right thing, but all went well until I had to hold the flesh apart while he began hacking at the bone. I felt weak all over; perspiration ran down my back; a terrible nausea and faintness began to come over me.

"You *must* stand it now!" the surgeon said sternly, and by a great effort of will I did, but it was quite dreadful. From that day forward I decided there was to be an end of this weakness. I began to concentrate upon the operating theater. Slowly and painfully I overcame my sickness and abhorrence, until finally I could watch intelligently and understand what was being done. I read textbooks and made drawings, and at last I became a proficient assistant, able to do surgery myself in later emergencies—but this came about slowly and with the development of the hospital.

One morning I had another urgent call from Brasov. They were in great trouble, and I must come. I decided to "unbury" my car and risk the drive, since actually nothing was safe anyway, and I did get to Brasov without difficulty. What I found was appalling. The Russians were moving into the town in great numbers and with their wounded, and they had decided to take over the Red Cross hospital. We had to move out within three hours, and whatever was left behind at the end of that time would belong to the Russians. It was a stupefying situation. Even though the German prisoners had been moved a few days before to a prison camp, there were still more than three hundred fifty patients in the hospital, besides all our equipment.

My first instinct was one of revolt and refusal, but I was overruled. In fact, the moving was already under way, since a place had been found in a Hungarian Catholic convent. It was a horrid old, dark building, the inmates of which were anything but glad to see us. This was understandable from their point of view, but nevertheless infuriating from ours. Fortunately, the Saguna stood on a big square and public garden, and with the help of all the neighbors and any of the wounded able to walk, we carried out the seriously wounded in their beds to the garden, and heaped all our possessions next to them as quickly as possible. In this way the building was actually emptied of nearly everything in less than three hours, but it still left us with the problem of moving to our new headquarters. Since we had only one ramshackle ambulance and one truck, this was difficult, but we finally got help from the regiments near us and from one of the factories. We worked so far into the night that I spent the rest of it with friends and did not return to Bran until the next morning; something which made me anxious about my family because of this new approach of the Russians.

Simone and Nadeje were wonderful in setting up the hospital in the new location, but they now had to return to Bucarest to their own families. The Brasov chapter of the Red Cross had to take over the hospital, and I felt anxious because I did not feel that any of the women were really experienced enough to do this. So it proved, and eventually a fine woman was sent out from Bucarest; a nurse, who, having lost her only son in Russia, had no interest in life except to help the wounded. I myself was continually bound more and more to Bran, since the hospital there continued to grow and demanded my whole attention, and my visits to Brasov became rarer and even more irregular. Usually they were to smooth out difficulties arising in times of such stress, for to keep peace between the doctors, the nurses, the Red Cross workers, the nuns, and the wounded was not always easy. Everyone suffered from the cramped quarters, the enormous difficulties of getting provisions, the continual danger from the Russians, and the growing arrogance of the newly developing "Communist Party." Its membership was composed of various malcontents with their own axes to grind, few of whom had, a few months before, given so much as a thought to the Party.

More and more serious cases were in the meantime being sent to Bran, so that a resident doctor was necessary. At first we suffered from the impractical plan of a rotating system of different doctors. Hardly had we got used to one before he was changed for another, and while some were good, others were not. Since I felt that in the work of healing one should put forward one's best efforts, I had a few misunderstandings with one or two of our visiting staff who took their work a little casually, and I am quite sure there were those who disliked me intensely. It became more and more difficult to work this way, and finally—thanks to an inspection visit of the Commanding General, Vasiliu Rascanu—I obtained permission to have Dr. Dragomir, second surgeon from the Z.I. 161, the Brasov hospital, detached permanently and assigned to Bran.

He was a young but earnest surgeon, and we worked wonderfully well together. He entered wholeheartedly into my plans of coming to the assistance of the population around us in the mountains, even though this represented enormous work; for the hills were steep and the houses far apart. We spent nearly all our afternoons on these "rounds," for while we could take civilian men patients, we had no women's ward.

I well remember getting a telephone call one evening from a neighboring village where a woman was bleeding to death after a miscarriage. We rushed into the car and drove off into the night. It was dark and cold; a misty sleet was falling, warning us of the coming winter. After a little difficulty we found the house, far up in a narrow alley. We entered the badly lighted room where the woman lay on a bed which had been tilted up in the hope of stopping the flow of blood. Around her stood all the family and many of the neighbors; the noise was deafening, the air stale and bad smelling. The first thing to do was to clear the room of people, and then to get hot water and as much light as possible. Working chiefly with the help of my flashlight reflected from a mirror, and using the few instruments at our disposal, we gave her the necessary injections. While we worked, I made up my mind that we must plan to have emergency kits with the necessary instruments and dressings ready, and that somehow I must manage to have room for women in the hospital.

We managed to leave our patient fairly comfortable, and the next day we brought a specialist out for her. She was operated upon in my hospital, but had to be cared for in the civilian hospital in Bran, an inadequate building run by the village doctor, who had lorded it over everyone for years but had taken little trouble in practising his art. He had long since lost contact with modern methods, since he was much more interested in politics than in medicine, and I could not approve of most of the things he permitted in his hospital.

At another time we had a call about a woman far away up a distant valley to which we could get only on foot. We found her suffering from meningitis and beyond any help except what comfort good care could bring her. We rigged up a stretcher, as I had learned to do in my Girl Scout days, out of a rug and two stout poles, and in this way we got her as far as the car, and then to the civilian hospital. Once again I found much to be displeased with in the way she was cared for, but in her case it did not make any difference in the result, because death was inevitable.

The next woman patient I had was dying of a terrible tubercular abscess of the thigh, and since I could not bear the thought of sending her to the other hospital, I arranged a bed for her in the laundry at Spitalul Inima Reginei. When we saw her end was near we sent her home, since I knew how strongly the peasant wishes to die in his own home, among his own family. The doctor, the student, and I climbed the mountain every third day to change her dressings and to give her a few hours' rest with morphine. She died on Christmas Day, and our last visit to her was on Christmas Eve. I shall always remember that walk, which took us two hours because of the snow. It was a beautiful climb: the snow so sparkling, the sky so blue, the air so clean and clear! One felt that all should be well in a world so beautiful. Then in a moment there was the dark little house, with the poor girl on her bed of suffering. She knew that she was dying, and took a loving farewell of me, throwing herself into my arms and then blessing me—as is our habit—by making the sign of the cross on my forehead. Then I laid her down on the bed and blessed her in my turn, and no one's eyes were dry.

In November we had had to leave the castle and settle down for the winter in the house at the foot of the hill. This was quite a problem because it had not been intended to accommodate so many, and none of us had ever dreamed of spending the whole year in Bran. There were the six children, Anton and I, Frau Koller, Gretl, and Bittermann. In addition to these, I had with me Sandu, the blind officer I had first met in Austria, with his faithful batman, and the seeing-eye dog we had got him in Vienna. I had invited him to spend the summer with us, and now that he had no place to go he of course remained with us—we all liked having him, and the children enjoyed helping to care for him. The housing and feeding of all these people, however, was a problem, and there were also the doctor, the medical student, and two nurses who had to have living quarters provided for them. It was now two nurses instead of one because, by the greatest good fortune, a Red Cross nurse had almost literally turned up on my doorstep one day. She was strong, energetic, and capable, and the best night nurse I ever had. Her husband had disappeared, and she did not know whether he had been taken by the Russians or the Germans, so she begged me to take her in and let her help me and it proved a blessing to all of us. It was two years before she heard from her husband, who had managed to reach France, and later she was able to follow him there.

In spite of everything, our Christmas in 1944 was a blessed one, and included the visit to the mountain home I have mentioned. We had a tree in our small room, and even though not many people could get in at any one time, I kept to the tradition of having everyone invited. The village children sang carols under our windows, and we gave them cozonac, hot tea, and a few pennies. For the wounded I had a separate tree, which also was lovely; and of course there was a tree in Brasov at the Z.I. 161 as well as at the military hospital and at still another hospital which I visited whenever I could. At both these latter hospitals there were wounded German prisoners to whom I could speak in their own language—remembering how the year before I had visited the Romanian wounded in Austria— and I found among them the wounded Austrian from Bran.

I managed also to visit the prison hospital and to see there the son of one of our village priests, who was detained for political activity even though he was ill of tuberculosis of the bone. The Communists were beginning their drive against anyone suspected of being against them, and this boy at the age of eighteen had been given a sentence of twenty-six years in prison. I used every influence I could think of to get him out, but I did not succeed until much later—when it was too late for him, except that he could at least die in comfort in our hospital. However, thanks to my permission to see him, I was able to visit all the other sufferers, both the political ones and the ordinary delinquents, and to bring them a little Christmas cheer. This visit had no bad consequences for me, but I was never allowed to visit the prison again.

We had a heavy winter, with deep snow and tremendous drifts. The hospital proved easy to heat, and slowly it was getting more organized. We straightened out small difficulties, and we had regularly fifty or sixty patients—soldiers, factory workmen, and at one time three children who had been operated on for bone trouble in their feet. They were from a very poor quarter of Brasov, and the excellent bone specialist who operated on them asked us to take them because they needed special care. I had to put them with the soldiers, and while this worked out quite well, I realized that there must someday be a children's ward in our hospital.

One afternoon in January, feeling very tired and as if I were getting a chill, I had taken a bath and was getting ready for bed when one of my nurses, who was also a midwife, came to tell me there was a woman in the civilian hospital who was dying in childbirth. Nothing could be done for her in Bran; she must be taken to a specialist in Brasov as the only possible hope. I was appalled. For three days no car or cart had managed to break through the snowdrifts, and of course, since we had been "liberated" by the Russians, there were no such things as snowplows to clear the roads to unimportant villages like ours. Anton came in while we were discussing it.

"Why not try to get through?" he said. "Whether she dies here or on the way will not make much difference to her, and if you get through you may save her!"

With this encouragement I got up and dressed, although I fear not willingly because I felt so ill and the whole project seemed so hopeless. But Anton insisted that we try, and got the permission of the guard to come with us part of the way to help us through the worst of the snow. We went in two cars: I in one with the woman and her husband, the nurse, and Bittermann; and Anton and two gendarmes in the other. We crossed fields to dodge drifts; we got stuck and dug ourselves out again. The wind howled and cut through our wraps like a knife whenever we had to get out and dig in the snow, and it grew steadily darker. When at last we got to where a road was partly cleared, and Anton and his guards parted from us, the woman was moaning but at least still alive.

After what seemed another eternity we entered the darkened streets of Brasov, empty of course of all civilians, since no one dared go abroad after dark. The Russians robbed and murdered with absolute freedom whenever they felt inclined, and there was a death penalty for any man who defended himself from them. Only Russians were to be seen, and occasional shots were heard from all quarters of the compass. This last, by the way, is a specialty of Russian occupation; they seem always to be shooting, although the questions "At what?" and "Why?" remain gruesomely unanswered.

On this night no one stopped us, and we arrived at the hospital, where they had been warned by telephone to expect us. The woman was rushed to the operating room and put under anesthesia, while she hung on to my hand, crying my name, until she was mercifully asleep. This was the first confinement I had attended as a nurse, and it was such an unnatural one that it seemed to me miraculous that it could be accomplished. The child lived; the woman was saved; and I should have liked to kneel down there and give thanks.

After I had helped get the woman to bed I spent the rest of the night with a friend, and I found when I had time to think of it that I had entirely recovered from my own threatened illness! The next morning I went back to the hospital, after finding with difficulty some small presents to take to the new baby and to the other babies there, and I remained to stand as godmother at the christening. Later in the day we returned home safely, although not without getting stuck a few times. However, since we were not racing with death, none of us minded it as much as we had the night before.

The whole experience made me feel that, whatever happened, I *must* make a ward for women. The only space at the moment was a little cottage just across the road from the hospital, which my mother had built for summer guests. It was not equipped for winter use, so that I had to wait for warmer weather to open it officially, but I began collecting supplies at once. In the spring, I thought, Spitalul Inima Reginei would have a women's ward with five beds!

Ipeina
1951

TWENTY

O N DECEMBER 7, 1944, the second government under General Sanatescu had fallen, and had been replaced by one under General Nicolae Radescu, an old friend of mine who had once for seven years been aide-de-camp to my mother. Acting with a heroism which makes a flash of light in the dark story of Romanian oppression, he and King Michael battled against Russian domination. But the Yalta agreement was signed on February 11, 1945, leaving Romania helpless in the hands of her Russian captors. Finally, the end of February, Premier Radescu boldly addressed the Romanians directly in an open and violent attack on what the Communists Ana Pauker and Vasile Luca were doing, speaking of them as people "without God, without country, and without law." But in spite of this, and of the efforts of the American Political Mission in Bucarest—which Vishinsky, Stalin's emissary, completely and insultingly ignored—the King was forced to yield to Moscow's demands. General

Radescu's government was dismissed and the Premier himself was forced to take refuge in the British Military Mission headquarters to save his life. On March 6, 1945, Russia, with the tacit acquiescence of the other two Allies, imposed on Romania a Communist government, three of whose four heads were not even Romanian.

Political events had touched us but little in our valley, cut off from the outer world by the snow as we were during those winter months, until on January 5, 1945, we heard the horrifying news that all citizens of German origin were to be deported to Russia. All men between the ages of seventeen and forty-five and all women between eighteen and thirty, whether or not they had children, were to be taken at once. The protests of General Radescu's government against this decree, we heard, had been futile.

Terror struck at the hearts of all. The Russian troops came and surrounded village after village in turn, ruthlessly dragging men and women from their homes. Mothers were separated from their weeping children; husbands and sons from their wives and parents; young girls from their families. There were heartrending scenes, scenes that made one's blood boil. And one could do nothing—*nothing!* We all tried to help by hiding some man or woman, but the result was that then a mother or a wife would be carried off in place of the intended victim. Then at once the one in hiding came out of his own accord, for who can see a loved one taken in his stead?

Bran had many neighboring Saxon villages which had been in existence for eight hundred years; therefore, we witnessed our share of the mass kidnapings which in about three weeks sent 35,590 men and 32,748 women, crowded into unheated railway carriages in the middle of winter, to slavery in Russia. It was one of the most terrible things I have ever seen, and Mrs. Podgoreanu found these weeks more horrible than any of the other experiences she had had in the Brasov station. In one village near Bran, over eighty children were left parentless, and we were not permitted to help. They could only be collected and cared for by the old people left behind. Almost immediately it was also decreed that all Saxons were to be dispossessed of their property. Gypsies and ne'er-do-wells from the towns, who had no idea how to farm but who had eagerly embraced communism upon the assurance that it would pay them well, were put in possession of what had been the most productive farms in Romania. This, too, had disastrous later effects on the economy of the country.

In the general disturbance and fear that overshadowed the whole nation, the fact that during the fall Transylvania had been retaken from the Hungarians and declared once more a part of Romania did not bring much joy and elation to anyone. We were right to feel suspicious of the event, for the Hungarians in the province were quick to see their chance. They immediately joined the Communist Party in great numbers, and took the side of the Russians, so that they were allowed to remain in power and the Romanian people continued to be strangers in their own land. It was as if a blanket of sorrow had descended upon us all, and no matter how we tried to adapt ourselves to circumstances, the pressure was too great. Yet we struggled on, in literal truth "building up with worn-out tools," and often with no tools at all.

In February the hospital again had a visit of inspection by General Vasiliu Rascanu, who earlier had straightened out the matter of the hospital doctor for me. He was now, we heard, decidedly tinged with red and definitely working to gain favor with the Communist Party. In fact, because of his attack on General Radescu's government later that same month, he was to be rewarded with the position of minister of war in the Russian Communist-dominated government set up on March 6, to hold it until December, 1947, and to remain more or less in favor until the middle of 1948. After that, his usefulness evidently at an end, he was to be "purged" from the Party with other Romanians who had worked with the Russians for various reasons, and who were paid for it in typically Communist style.

In February of 1945, however, Radescu was simply commanding general of our region, and his announcement that he was arriving at the hospital for a visit of inspection with "an important gentleman" simply meant that another item had to be fitted into a busy day. The fact that he arrived late, which upset our schedule, did not add to our pleasure. Still, the inspection went well, and on the whole the General was quite pleased. The "important gentleman" did not seem particularly important. He was a civilian who looked middle-aged to me, although later I found that he was younger than I had thought. He had a strong, rugged face, intelligent but somehow ruthless. He wore his graying hair closely cropped and, although he was at first distant and reserved, his manners were pleasant. I soon found myself carried away with my hopes for the hospital, and I told him all my plans—for a women's ward, a children's ward, a chapel, a section for outpatients, and a building for contagious diseases; all things for which a great need was already evident.

"You must have vision," I told him, "and imagine all these things growing up around you!"

He was attentive and interested, and after the official inspection was over I offered them simple refreshments in my study, where Anton joined us. The conversation flowed easily; the "important gentleman" seemed less distant, and took a greater part in it. As the party was leaving he said to me quite seriously:

"I am——" and he pronounced a name which I did not hear distinctly— "Secretary of the Communist Party. I did not wish to come here at all; I only did so to please my friend, the General. Now I am glad I did come, for my opinion of you and of your work has changed. If—or rather when— we come to power, remember me. I will do all that I can to help you."

I murmured my thanks, and wondered who he really was. After the visitors had gone, we spelled out his name with some difficulty from his signature in the visitors' book: "Emil Bodnaras." I had no way of finding out more about him, since I had no one to ask.

I am now going to digress a little to tell of an adventure, or at least to tell the part I can relate without endangering others. I do not want to put it in chronological order in this story, for fear of involving some who helped me and who may be still alive to be punished. For the same reason I can tell only a small part of what occurred. It is a story which did not end for two years, and through all my other activities during that time it wove in and out of the days and nights, and thought had to be taken for it.

It began with the coming to me of two fugitives—whom I shall call by the nicknames we gave them, "Over" and "Under." They were different only in the length of their stay from many others who had to be hidden, for of course my underground activities began with the coming of the Russians and I was trusted by many people with their lives. These two came from opposite directions, but they arrived at about the same time, and in such circumstances that it was obvious we would not be able to send them on their way out of the country immediately. As a matter of fact, we kept Over for six months, and Under for two years before he was finally sent off with false papers.

The only safe place to hide them was in the castle itself. In winter no one went there, but this also presented complications. They had to be kept warm in some way, yet no smoke must be seen coming out of any of the chimneys. A room must be chosen which could be heated by electricity, yet it must be located where no one—the caretaker, for example—would be likely to go, and at the same time it must not be where its heat would melt snow on a roof above it. Anton and I studied the problem, and finally decided on a small, out-of-the-way room, inside which we built a sort of tent which could be kept warm without affecting the roof. The electricity was turned off during the winter, but Anton put in a secret wire which luckily the caretaker never noticed.

There remained the daily problem of food and water, and to get food for two men when food was scarce, as well as to carry it secretly to the castle, was no easy matter. Anton, Frau Koller, and I took it in turns to get the food to them, but it was my job to provide it. I did such things as inventing a poor, ill woman in the village to whom I wanted to send cooked food daily, and instructing the kitchen to provide it. Since everyone in my household knew everyone in the village, this did not work too well in my own kitchen, but it did succeed fairly well in the hospital, where the cook was a stranger to Bran. When there were heavy falls of snow it was also difficult, since not only was it heavy going to climb to the castle, but new footprints were hard to explain. The problems of "summer residence" were different but no less worrying, for there were many more people moving about the village and the castle.

All this provided us with plenty of excitement and thrills, especially since there were heavy penalties—usually death—for hiding any fugitives. I do not know to what extent the underground that had operated against the alliance with Nazi Germany carried over, but I do know that when I was first brought in touch with the underground against the Russians it was somewhat unorganized, and had not learned very well how to hide. At best, under Soviet law and police, it is a hard matter to set it up and keep it going. Over and Under provided us with examples of almost every possible difficulty in their long stay with us. There were plenty of incidents, both tragic and funny, but there was plenty of drudgery as well; something which seems rarely thought about in novels of adventure.

Perhaps one of the most dangerous periods of their stay was when Under developed a tumor on his breast which we thought might be cancerous. Its growth was rapid, and although we hoped it might be benign, an operation was the only way to make certain. I decided to entrust a certain doctor with the secret, and to ask for his help, and with real courage he consented to give it. Between us, we arranged that another operation requiring the services of a specialist should be scheduled at my hospital—something which happened often enough to make it entirely reasonable—and for this one we selected a specialist whom we knew could be trusted. When we confided in him, he also proved brave enough to risk his life. We smuggled out of the hospital the necessary sterile towels, dressings, and instruments, and Anton got them safely into the castle.

We had made an ostentatious preparation for asking the visiting surgeons to spend the night in Bran and "rest" before returning to their own homes. Separately, in the middle of a winter night, the two of them and Anton and I made our way into the castle, where Anton had chosen a room that could most safely be heated and prepared. There upon an improvised table the patient was placed, and Anton held him down while I gave the anesthetic, which was ether. (This proved a terrible bother to us later, by the way, for it is an odor which is almost impossible to get rid of for a long time.) While being put to sleep and while waking up, Under spouted endless reams of poetry to us, which gave a slightly hilarious touch to an otherwise mysterious and rather gruesome scene. The operation was successful, and it turned out that the tumor was benign—after a complicated and secret arrangement for sending the tissue for examination under the name of a legitimate patient in the hospital. In the meantime, however, I had great trouble in washing the soiled linen, for I had to get it all out of the way before morning, and bloodstains require soaking. It was also nerve racking to smuggle all the things back into the hospital, and when it was over I felt that I, for one, could be satisfied with a less exciting life if opportunity ever offered it.

Under had another adventure some time after Over had been sent on his way. This occurred during warm weather, when we were moving up to the castle for the summer. It was necessary for him to leave his indoor hiding place while the castle was being cleaned and made ready and until we were in residence and could hide him more safely. Anton and Stefan made him a "dugout" in the woods not far from the castle, but in a place where no one was ever known to go. They did this most expertly, and replaced turf and bushes so that nothing could be seen from the outside, although in his cave Under had plenty of room to lie down quite comfortably, and even to move about. He was enchanted with his new "palace," and we left him there fairly sure that all would be well, a conviction that was rudely shattered by—of all people—the village idiot.

This personage had gone for a stroll in the woods, his gaze lost among the upper branches of the trees, when suddenly the ground gave way beneath him and he found himself sitting in a hole staring at a man who was stretched out comfortably underground reading a book cozily enough by lamplight. As soon as he recovered his breath he uttered a yell of terror, climbed frantically out of the hole, and went tearing off downhill through the woods. Most fortunately for us all, the first person he met was Anton.

"Archduke! Archduke!" he wailed. "*Necuratul*—the unclean one; the devil—is in the forest! I fell in on him! He was under the ground reading a book!"

Realizing what must have happened, Anton assured him that he knew all about it and was taking care of it, and that if the idiot would go home and tell no one what he had seen, his soul would undoubtedly be safe. Happily he did *not* talk about it to anyone else, which showed how truly terrified he was; but actually his fear was nothing compared to that of poor Under! He simply disappeared, and it was some time before Anton found him and could devise another hiding place for him.

As I have indicated, the Communist Party early in 1945 began coming out into the open, agitating strikes and putting on "manifestations" which were protected and sustained by the Russian troops. This led to the speech by General Radescu which I have mentioned, and which made him a great hero to the nation. He had voiced what we all felt, and was therefore in great danger from the new masters of our country. During the time he was in the British Legation, and the months he was a "protected" prisoner, we all felt anxious about him, and when his escape was arranged over a year later we breathed more easily. We felt that with his safe arrival in Cyprus, and later in the United States, a spokesman for Romanian freedom was abroad to represent those of us behind an Iron Curtain. I was deeply proud of my old friend, whom I was able to visit secretly during his imprisonment. I had known him since I was a little girl, shortly after he had won Romania's highest award during World War I. With most people he was so silent and quiet as to have a reputation for being rather taciturn, but he had always been willing to talk to me. Now he had talked to the world, frankly attacking Ana Pauker and her colleagues, and it heartened us all. Even though it did not

Castle of Bran

change the plans of the Communists, it at least openly challenged them.

With the establishment of a Russian-dominated government on March 6, 1945, Petru Groza, an opportunist and a windbag for others to work behind, was declared premier.

"Did you see," Dr. Dragomir asked me when the announcement was made, "did you see that the 'important gentleman,' Mr. Bodnaras, has a position in the new government? He seems to be the 'Secretary General of the Presidency,' or at least I think it is he." Once more we consulted the guestbook and compared names. Yes, they were the same.

So he *has* come to power, I thought, but I did not give the fact much importance.

Now the persecutions began in real earnest, and in the open. The long arm of the Communist "law" reached out in every direction. Among the first to be arrested was our chief surgeon of the Z.I. 161. A petition was immediately set up to have him freed, and was signed by the entire hospital, including the Tudor Vladimirescu, but it had no effect. With what to my mind was an absurd, pathetic, and entirely misplaced confidence, I was appealed to. What could I do? My own husband was virtually a prisoner and my own freedom hung on a thin thread. But the doctor had been a good man and should be saved! Suddenly I remembered Bodnaras's promise. Well, let us see what he would do! I sat down and wrote to him.

It was like an episode in an adventure novel, for the orders to free the doctor came at the last possible moment. He was actually hauled off the train, which was to transport him who knows where, as it was leaving the Brasov station. And so that I would know who was responsible for this, I had a letter from Bodnaras telling me that he had done what I asked, and more than I had asked. He assured me that he had not forgotten my hospital, nor my vision, and that he had given the Ministry of Health orders to be of all possible assistance to me. So! I thought. Evidently he actually is a man of power, and he keeps his word.

In this way began my connection with the Ministry of Health, which was productive of so much good and which opened so many doors that I was able to help much farther afield than I had ever dreamed of doing. So also began with Bodnaras a queer—what shall I call it? Friendship? No, for it was not that. Emil Bodnaras and I were always openly on opposite sides. We were enemies to the very core of our thoughts and ideals. Yet a mutual respect for and trust in each other's honesty somehow bridged our detestation of each other's worlds, a detestation deeper than hatred, which separated us like a chasm. The survival of one of us would be the death of the other. Yet, strangely enough, he never, when he could help it, let an appeal of mine go unanswered, and I made many. Perhaps it was because my appeals were always impersonal so far as my own interest was concerned. Perhaps it was because he also had ideals, although these were false according to my way of thinking, and had suffered for them; therefore, he respected my willingness to suffer for mine—for he inevitably came to know that I dared much, and dared again whenever it was asked of me. He told me once that my time had not much further to run, but that as long as I was there he saw I had my job to do, and he would help me do it.

"Though it is vain, you understand. Just now you are still necessary, but soon you will go!"

"But why not you?" I asked. "That too might happen!"

"Might, but won't," he answered calmly. Well, he has won the first round, but so long as the world stands the whole story has not yet been told!

To me his first written offer of help from the Ministry of Health seemed a wonderful opportunity to go to Bucarest and try my luck for the hospital. The first question, of course, was where to stay; and here one of my mother's oldest friends stepped forward and offered me her home. She was a charming person who lived simply and quietly, and everything she had was put lovingly at my disposal. I shall never forget her welcome, nor the fact that I was able to go to her at any time without previous notice, something which was always a convenience, and often later was a serious necessity, for the telephone was a far from private instrument to use, and as time went on there were occasions when I needed to travel without announcing the fact.

I remember that one day I was so tired I allowed myself to become exasperated when I heard the little noise that meant my telephone conversation was being listened to and taken down. "Do you have your pencil and paper ready?" I inquired sarcastically. "Is it convenient for you that I begin speaking now? You must let me know if I go too fast!" There was a small, smothered gasp, and then only dignified silence!

In return for the kindness of my hostess, I could bring her delicacies from the country; especially meat, which in Bucarest was very difficult to get. I found great comfort in my flying visits to her, and we talked over many plans and hopes. It was while staying with her that I met the engineer Nicholas Malaxa, who was the proprietor of the factory which, under Colonel Serbu's direction, had built the hospital. He was a strange man, who liked to surround himself with a sort of somber mystery in his enormous house, but once one had got through all his noiseless, sliding doors, this great industrialist was most pleasant, and reminded me of his sister, who had been my mathematics teacher. I told him about the work going on in Bran, and of all I still hoped to be able to do. He listened attentively, and said he thought I was right in wanting to enlarge the hospital to include women and children, and that he would be happy to have the desired wing built for me! He would give the necessary orders, and when next I came to Bucarest we could go over the plans. In the meantime, he said, he would like to offer me a sum of money to get what I felt was most urgently needed for the hospital. For a minute I could hardly find words for my gratitude. My small staff and I had worked so hard to stretch our little resources over so many needs; there were such great anxieties and difficulties caused by the Russian occupation; we were constantly faced with so many situations our little hospital could not take care of adequately! To get such help seemed truly a miracle.

Emboldened by this unexpected answer to an unceasing prayer, I decided to go to the Ministry of Health and see what *they* were willing to do before spending any of this precious money. I found that, although the Minister thought himself a Communist, his organization had certainly not yet been affected; and since the Minister was a fine doctor himself, and one of our greatest brain surgeons, he did his best not to let politics hamper his work. Unfortunately, he himself was a very ill man, but after his death from cancer of the lungs—which he had himself diagnosed—his work was carried on by his wife, also an able doctor.

Once again I found that the years when I had been working and growing up with my country now made my opportunities for service greater and more far-reaching. Among the people I would have to work most closely with was a man whose wife had been a Girl Scout of mine; another Scout held an influential position in still a different department—and so it went on. At the head of one bureau, I found, was the aunt of one of the wounded Romanian officers I had known in Vienna. All this meant that I needed to waste no time convincing people of the seriousness of my purpose and of the fact that I had sufficient training and experience to carry it out. Even when later an old and convinced Communist was put in charge of the ministry, I found that he, too, was first of all a doctor, and one whose special interest was preventive medicine. Unfortunately, this was an aspect of the profession which had few followers in Romania, but I was one of them, and we thus met on the ground of a common purpose.

In spite of the good will I found at the Ministry of Health, many of the things I needed were missing from among their supplies. Because of the air raids, things had been dispersed all over the country, and wherever they had not been adequately hidden or guarded the invading Russians had helped themselves wantonly and stupidly. They had, for instance made saddles out of surgical gauze, drunk the alcohol, and found it amusing to pave the ground with tablets and capsules; yet at the same time their own patients were left without proper care so far as their dear "comrades" were concerned. One thing I could not get was abdominal surgical instruments, and I could also find nothing for electrotherapy. For these things I finally went to one of the biggest medical supply stores, which I found had been badly damaged by the bombardments. Hardly had I begun wandering around and observing the efforts being made to get things in order when I discovered that the proprietor was an old acquaintance. He had been the apothecary on one of the hospital trains that came to Vienna. He let me hunt out what I needed, and then told me that he would consider it an honor if I would allow him to contribute them to a hospital established in memory of the Queen, and that he would add to my selections some things he had stored away that were unobtainable on the open market; things made of rubber, for example.

Here was another miracle! I was getting almost all I needed, and the sum from Mr. Malaxa was still untouched! The heart of the Romanian is generous, and what made the gift still more precious to me was the fact that it was a tribute to my mother. Eventually I did find something on which to spend my money: thick materials to make gowns for the patients in cold weather. Also I got a quartz lamp and a short-wave diathermy set, as well as some rare surgical instruments for kidney operations. Not everywhere was I given wholesale presents, but I left no shop without their having volunteered a contribution of some kind. This would have been remarkable at any time, but now when these supplies were irreplaceable, and really beyond price, it was truly miraculous.

Can you understand why I so loved this hospital? It was because everything in it was a symbol of love. Behind each bit of it stood some act of kindness, some gesture of nobility, some memory dear to me; and woven through all were the hours of ordinary, essential hard work which made it truly a part of myself. (Once someone asked me how I had got "all that" done. "With my feet!" I replied. And this in many ways is true, for things do not drop into one's lap. One has to go and find them.)

This time my return to Bran from Bucharest was a triumphant one. I had gone there and back safely, and I had come home not only with my hands filled, but with many of my hopes for the future suddenly turned into immediate possibilities. I discovered that there was a second unused barracks at the Malaxa factory which could be used to make my maternity and children's ward, and I still had one of the old ones General Tataranu had given me. This, when moved and arranged somewhat differently inside, could be used as a storeroom.

Another wonderful thing was that there were things to be stored for the coming winter, in spite of the scarcities. I myself owned a little farm outside Brasov, and now I heard that two of my friends of the fire brigade were in great danger of losing their own farm. They were of German origin, and only the husband's position as an officer in the army had protected them up to this point. Therefore I bought the place from them, keeping them on as administrators on a percentage basis, and giving my share of their crops to the hospital. In this way a part of our food supply was independent and uncontrolled. This fact, and the fact that we had more than we could use for the hospital, meant that I could help provide food for those of the underground hidden in the mountains and for families of those designated by the Russians as "war criminals"; a term which, as I have already explained, could be applied to everyone in the country if our captors chose. Many of these families were dispossessed, and were forbidden to get work, so that those who did not starve must depend on the generosity—and ingenuity—of others.

Naturally these activities on the part of the hospital did not come about all at once, but developed one step at a time as conditions in Romania grew worse, a process which went steadily and inexorably on.

Ileana.
1951

TWENTY-ONE

THE QUESTION of "war criminals" now came up in a terrible way. There was a so-called "People's Tribunal" set up, which certainly had little to do with the Romanian people. It reminded one uncomfortably in its procedures of similar tribunals in the French Revolution. The difference was that this was an *imposed* way of doing things, regarded with disfavor and mistrust by the great majority of the people themselves, instead of being something which had sprung more or less spontaneously into being because of real public feeling. Like the other "demonstrations," which were reported as being the expression of the national feeling, it was artificially induced and supported, and the threat that gave it existence was the simple one of death to those who protested. Many did, and many therefore died; but there were of course always some who saved their skins by lending their names and presence to the Communist plans.

The first victims to come before the People's Tribunal were a number of generals who had fought in Bessarabia and in Russia, and who had been in punitive actions in the military campaigns there. It was interesting to note that even while the "trials" for such actions in time of war were taking place, Russians were doing much worse things in Romania in what was supposed to be a time of peace. The chief crime of the generals was actually that of their having executed orders, but it was those who had fought on "sacred" Russian soil who were singled out for punishment. Soon the horrible news arrived that they were condemned to death.

Now, the death penalty is against the Romanian Constitution, as well as against the religious principles of Romanians. It existed only on the front, in time of war, for spies and traitors. Since this sentence of the so-called People's Tribunal was therefore breaking one of the fundamental laws of the country, the point at issue immediately ceased to be whether or not the generals were guilty as charged. It became the question whether or not Romanian generals were to be condemned to a penalty contrary to the Constitution, in a court contrary to law (since officers can be judged only by a military tribunal), and by persons we did not count as Romanians. The indignation aroused everywhere was great, and all spoke openly about it but no one seemed really to be *doing* anything about it. Indignation was voiced, but no protest was really addressed to the authorities.

I was as indignant as everybody else. I stormed and raged and asked why no one protested. Then I thought to myself, After all, I am just as bad as everyone else. I am *doing* nothing at all. Why do I not go and protest? I thought it over from every angle, and decided that nothing could be gained without risking something: of the possible loss I refused to think. I would go and talk to Bodnaras.

This was not so easy to arrange, for I knew that this I could not write about, and that no one should know what I was planning to do. Finally, on the pretense that I had to go to Bucarest in the interests of the hospital, I arrived unannounced at the home of my friend, and was given the usual warm welcome. The next thing was to confide in someone who would be willing to cover my steps by accounting for my time. I could not use my hostess for this, since I did not want to have my actions compromise her if I failed, but I did confide in a friend not far away, who was both responsible enough and adventurous enough to be trusted with such information. Next I contacted a person who could carry to Bodnaras the message that I wished to talk with him. The answer came back that I could, but that it must be at night at his home and that no one must know where I was. Since it was at my request, I had to agree to the terms, and my adventurous friend agreed to say—if need arose—that I had been paying a visit there during the time I would be away from my hostess.

As I write this I have the same incredulous feeling I had at the time: a feeling of unbelief that a situation so like one of my father's and my favorite Bulldog Drummond stories should really exist in our Romania and that I should be playing a part in it. At the same time, I had now seen enough of what the Russians were like to have a most uncomfortable feeling of reality about the danger of the whole plan. I started out on my venture by going to say a prayer in a small, old church that stood quite near the house where I was staying, and I lit a candle for those whose battle I was going to fight.

The city was still under blackout regulations, so that it was in total darkness that I first stopped to inform my friend that I had begun my journey and then walked down the street to the agreed-upon corner, where a car was to meet me. It came; I recognized it by the number, and got in. There were two men, one driving and one sitting beside him, and although they proved to be quite harmless, they seemed most sinister to my imagination. Silently we drove through the darkened town, and soon we left the vicinity I knew. As I had no idea where I was going, my apprehension increased in spite of all I could do. I tried to keep count of the number of right and left turns, but in my excitement I was not able to remember them.

After what seemed to me a long time, during which I continued to think of various detective stories I had read, we drew up in front of a nice-looking villa with a garden. I was handed out politely, and there on the doorstep stood Bodnaras and his charming young wife. They led me into a pleasant room in which a fire was burning upon the open hearth; an anticlimax which of course made me feel that I had been a complete fool to be afraid. Later I grew to know that part of the city very well, since it was one of the most modern residential sections, built up shortly before the war while I was living in Austria, and therefore unfamiliar to me. Eventually it lost for me the terrifying aspect it had had on that first drive in the dark toward the unknown.

Mrs. Bodnaras served us some excellent coffee—a great treat for me, because it was a long time since I had had coffee—and after a pleasant conversation she left us. Now the great moment was upon me. *Help me, God, not to make a mistake now!* I prayed, and I plunged into the subject. At first Bodnaras looked both pained and horrified, and I had to sit quiet through a long tirade about all the crimes these generals had committed. I offered no protest, but my mind tried quickly to find a right approach. Finally I saw that the only hope was to point out what harm it would do the Communists if they began governing with such blood on their hands. "But crime must not go unpunished!" he responded. We argued for well over two hours, until at long last he said:

"Well, if the King decides not to sign the death warrant, I promise that we will uphold his point of view."

"You know quite well," I told him, "that the King will never of his free will sign such an unconstitutional document. If he does, it will be laid at your door, and before the whole nation your government will bear the blame. Surely you do not wish this additional handicap at this moment!"

He gave me no definite answer, but we parted amiably. What part my intervention played I do not, of course, have any idea, but the sentences were commuted to life imprisonment. If this was really better in the end or not, who can say? As long as there is life there is hope, one says, but that is a proverb which I am afraid does not hold true in the lands where

Soviet Russia rules. At the time, however, I felt that at least I had stood up for what I thought was right and that in so doing I was fighting the battle of my world—a world that was fast being destroyed. Perhaps somewhere where lost battles are recorded and counted, this one may stand to my credit.

I was taken back to the street corner in the same mysterious fashion, and although I was much less nervous this time, I was glad when I stood on the doorstep of my confidante and could report the result of my interview. After that I returned to my hostess, who kindly did not inquire too far into my long absence. Later, when I felt it was safe, I told her the truth about what I had been doing.

The following day I saw Mr. Malaxa and his architect, and they showed me the plans for the women's and children's wing, a grand structure indeed, with two stories. It seemed to me an expensive project, and one that would not at all harmonize with the rest of the hospital. Trying not to hurt anyone's feelings, I pointed out that the barracks they already had at the factory would do very well if we divided it more efficiently inside, and that it would cost less and look more appropriate. The architect was not especially pleased, but Mr. Malaxa laughed and said I was the first woman he had met who thought of spending less instead of more. Of course new plans would have to be made, but the time wasted that way would he made up by doing something simpler than the original design.

When I returned to Bran other changes were waiting for me. The Z.I. 161 in Brasov was being disbanded, but the Spitalul Inima Reginei was to pass over to the military hospital. This was a great advantage, as well as a compliment to the service my hospital was doing, since instead of being under the protection of a Red Cross hospital which was under the protection of the military hospital, we were now directly associated with the military one, and therefore sponsored by the Ministry of War. We could get supplies and doctors which, as a less carefully inspected private hospital, we could not have obtained at all in such difficult times. Less good news was the fact that Dr. Dragomir was being discharged from the army and wanted to return to the University of Jassy for further training. General Vasiliu Rascanu, who happened to be his uncle, was now minister of war and quite kindly disposed to his nephew, so Dragomir asked me whom I would like to have as a replacement for him. He felt that he could then ask the General to have that doctor detached and sent to me without my having officially asked for him myself. The appointment would be imposed upon me, so to speak, and I could then disclaim any part in it in case there was anything in his record which the Communists might later find they objected to, something always possible under the Russian regime. This, I felt, was most kind and thoughtful, for it avoided at least one possibility of future trouble for the hospital.

I inquired in various places and found that a good doctor would be Dr. Radu Puscariu, who was then still on the German front. His father, a native of Bran, was one of the greatest authorities on the Romanian language and a member of the Romanian Academy. The father was now living in Bran, but in ill-health because of a stroke he had had recently suffered, which had occurred shortly after the death of his wife. I knew it would be a great comfort to the family to have the doctor with them. The "family" consisted of the doctor's wife, their two delightful little daughters, and the doctor's sister, the wife of an engineer who had disappeared when the German troops retreated. She was a most charming friend, and had a daughter who was about the age of my Magi.

They were, all of them, most cultivated and intellectual people, although like so many of our Romanians they were only a generation removed from the peasant and had quite a number of "illiterate" relations. This is a situation which I find is often misunderstood by many Americans and Europeans, and I think it is because the history of Romania is not generally known. Our "peasants" are not the dregs of the population, who have gradually sunk down to the bottom of society because they had neither ability nor ambition to achieve an education. The Romanian peasant class does include such people, who exist in every country, but it also includes the most able, keen witted, and intelligent of people as well! At no time in her history has literacy been in Romania a test of brains, ability, or ambition. It is never unusual to find that a leading statesman, writer, military man, or artist has illiterate parents or is from a humble, peasant home to which he often returns for sympathy and encouragement.

One must always bear in mind that a comparatively few generations ago we were a Turkish colony; that since then the fight for freedom and for independence from other countries has been almost continuous, and not always successful. Under none of her foreign rulers was adequate education for Romanians provided in Romania, and there was a constant, though unavailing, attempt to stamp out the Romanian language, culture, and religion. Against this attempt Romanians still struggled to establish and maintain schools, but obviously the benefits of this kind of education under difficulties could not extend far. In Transylvania under the Hungarians, for example, there was almost no higher education for the Romanian unless he went to Budapest or Vienna, which few had the training or the money to do. The wonderful thing about this to me is that this contact with the Magyar and German worlds did not influence the national feelings of those few Romanians who achieved higher education, except to intensify their will for freedom. The only one I think of who did not remain a stanch patriot is Petru Groza, who lived to be a "front" for the Russian exploiters of his country.

Looking back upon our turbulent history, I feel that it was remarkable how much was done with education in a short time. I think few societies were more cultured, or had a more complete education and variety of interests, than the Romanian intellectual class, from whom teachers and professors were drawn to extend education to the remoter parts of the country. When Romania Mare began, in 1919, the serious work of extending education on an equal basis to eighteen million citizens, it was of course obvious that there would be a limit to the speed with which so many schools could be built and so many teachers provided. Yet in the short lapse of eighteen years, from 1919 to 1937, the rate of illiteracy became negligible in the generation then growing up. The number of students at the four Romanian universities averaged about 30,000 a year, with an average of 6,000 graduating every year. There were few countries in Europe where it was easier for the poorest student to get a university education, if he had sufficient ability, because tuition was entirely free and—by 1937—the government was paying all expenses of board and lodging for about 15,000 university students and nearly 30,000 high school students. It had never been a lack of ability or of ambition that kept the Romanian peasant from getting a formal education, as this one generation of opportunity vividly showed.

It was not at all easy to hold one's own in the Bucarest salons I knew during those same years. To speak French, English, and German as well as Romanian was considered quite natural; one was expected to be well versed in world history and literature and to be able to appreciate Romanian music as one phase of general musical development. Even in Bran and during the winter when we were cut off from the rest of the world, we had quite an active intellectual life, stimulated always at the holidays when the students were home from the universities for their vacations, for most families—as I have indicated—made the effort to send a son or daughter to one of the university towns.

At the hospital we instituted a series of lectures and discussions for doctors and nurses; there was a glee club, which I enjoyed even though my lack of musical talent prevented me from joining it, and which formed itself also into a church choir for special occasions. A literary club, which had functioned for many years in the village, owned and managed a lending library, which added much to our discussion groups. We had also a sports club, and although during the winter there was only the hospital team and the village team to play volley ball matches, in the summer we added the Y.W.C.A. and Telephone Company teams to our competitions. In the winter we also managed to arrange skiing contests with neighboring teams.

Besides all of these, there was that delightful habit of the peasants which extends far back into bygone centuries, the *sezatoare*. By this custom families met at this or that man's house to spin, or to take grain from the cob, or to do whatever work could be done collectively. The master of the house provided the food and entertainment, such as music for songs and dances. Young and old gathered to do the work and also to have a good time, and at these meetings the older men and women related the old tales and the legends that have for generations kept Romanian culture alive.

It was this which made the sezatoare more important than similar gatherings which exist for a time on the frontier of a new nation and die out when the need for them is past. In Romania it was not merely a matter of combining work which needed many hands with a social gathering for which there might not be any other time available. It was more than that. It was a means of preserving the individuality of a whole people. Thus through the centuries national history and literature and music have passed by word of mouth from generation to generation, and without books both language and faith have been kept alive. History has not come to the Romanian by way of study in the classroom, but at the fireside of his humble dwelling, as he listened in the evening by candle-light, in an atmosphere of good will and intimacy, to the respected voice of some loved one. History to him is not something he has studied but is part of his most intimate life, a conscious heritage. In the small, isolated dwellings in the remote mountains of my country, may this still be true! For the schools set up in the towns and villages in the days of Romania Mare have been made Judas weapons by the invaders, to betray our children and to destroy their heritage.

In the winter of 1944-45 the troubled outside world intensified our pleasure in this side of life in Bran, where we felt somewhat like an island, blessed and peaceful in a stormy sea. Each departure of one of our members and each arrival of a new one were of great importance to the rest of us. It was with real regret that we finally said good-bye to Dr. Dragomir, and our best wishes went with him. I was personally deeply grateful to him for all he had done for the hospital and the people of Bran, and for all he had taught me; for he had given me many hours of instruction in anatomy and other medical subjects, besides training me well as an assistant to the surgeon. I think that he, too, found it not easy to leave. Conditions in Jassy were hard and difficult after all the various occupations, both German and Russian, but for his career it was necessary that he take the further training. We shared many a memory and many a fight for the life of men, women, and children; and we had after hours of struggle many times looked into each other's eyes and found that response of joy and relief at winning a battle against death.

Some little time before Dr. Dragomir left, we had had a pleasant addition to our community: a young medical student who had reason to pass under an assumed name and to leave the field hospital where he had worked under one of our best surgeons, and where a friend of mine was head nurse. He came upon me one afternoon when I was alone and handed me a crumpled note, upon which in a few hurried lines my friend and the doctor had recommended the boy to me and had asked for my help. He was a nice-looking young man in a soldier's uniform, and he had a friendly, open expression, now showing considerable anxiety. It so happened that the student who had been with us had had to return to his studies, and therefore the doctor and I had been looking for an assistant.

"You are a godsend!" I told him. His anxious expression relaxed, and he took off his cap and threw it on the ground with delight. "That," I told him sternly, "was not a soldierly gesture!" —at which he laughed heartily and we became friends on the spot. For three years we worked side by side. He entered with passionate enthusiasm into all the hospital activities, and his energies never flagged. The children all came to he very fond of him, and finally Badillo—as we called him—fell in love with Gretl, the children's nurse. After we left Romania he married her, and he later got his doctor's degree in Austria, since he was among those I was able to take with me when I left.

The most important addition to our little community group, however, was Dr. Dragomir's successor, Dr. Puscariu, whom I have already mentioned. Since he had originally come from Bran, perhaps he felt it was we who were the additions, but he had been away so long that he was new to community life as it was then organized. He was a surgeon of wide experience from the University of Cluj, and because he had also studied in France, Germany, and Austria we gained greatly from his arrival, and the whole hospital was put on a higher level of techniques and efficiency. He was a real master of his art, so that as we collected the necessary instruments there was hardly any operation we were not able to perform. He brought forward a series of proposals for improvements, which I was delighted to carry through as far as it was possible for me to do. He was a musician, draftsman, and sculptor as well, and he had a delightful talent for telling stories, of which he seemed to possess an endless number. He was most pleasant to work with, and my only objection to him as a colleague was that he had no executive drive, and left all the unpleasant parts of the administration to me, even to keeping the ever-growing staff up to the mark. I have said so much because I feel it is fair to pay tribute to his real abilities, and because it was only gradually that a certain lack of personal integrity became evident. In the end, however, his behavior when the Communists took over the hospital was a surprise to everyone, and I can only feel in his defense that because he had been a victim of shell shock, it may be that he was not entirely himself.

The staff was growing considerably, too. I had to have an administrator, or business manager, because we had various sums from different sources to deal with, supplies to account for, and similar bookkeeping to do. For example, we had military rations for the soldiers; Dr. Puscariu, one student, and three nurses were paid by the army; the social insurance paid a small and insufficient quota for the workmen (and I was forever in the middle of arguments and discussions with them); the Ministry of Health later subsidized two doctors and three more nurses. The rest of the money came from other patients, from donations, and from my own pocket.

This financial support of the hospital was an eternal worry, from which I was never relieved. I got many donations in the way of medical supplies and even of food, but to be sure that I had the actual cash for salaries and running expenses remained a continual nightmare, especially now that my own personal resources were so much reduced and so undependable. Our reputation reached ever farther, and patients came from regions far beyond our own thirteen villages, so that there always seemed a little more demanded than we could quite give.

In the end I had Dr. Puscariu and two students; Dr. Lazarescu, intern, and his wife, who assisted him in running the laboratory; Dr. Herman, apothecary; and seven nurses besides the head nurse. This last appointment was finally necessary, because as time went on I had so much to do with general administration, getting provisions, and carrying on other activities that there had to be someone to whom the responsibility for nursing could be delegated while I was away. Besides this medical and nursing staff, there was the administrator and his assistant, a head for the linen room and laundry, two orderlies, four servant girls, and one gardener. These made up the hospital staff at the time we had reached the size of one hundred twenty beds.

It was for this that my small dispensary in Sonnberg and my first work with the wounded in Austria had begun to prepare me. Perhaps it was as well that I had not been able to look so far ahead, and to puzzle over how I could ever cope with such an organization—especially in a country first at war, and then under the rule of a foreign tyrant.

TWENTY-TWO

IN THE summer of 1945 the building for women and children was started at the hospital, but because Colonel Serbu was not there to see things through the whole thing went much more slowly and less pleasantly. It was not ready for use until the spring of 1946, but because it was roofed over by October 29, my mother's birthday, I used this occasion to have it blessed. The day also served as a reason for entertaining our benefactors and the authorities who were over us and gave us a chance to thank them and to show them what we had accomplished in a year and what the plans for the future were. It was a most successful day, which made those who had aided us feel that it had been worth while and that the hospital was a successful project they could be proud of having helped. It also inspired others who had held back a little, until they saw how it all came out, to come forward and offer their services! As it should be unnecessary to say to anyone who has put through a project of any size, there had been many difficulties in getting people to work together, but this display of our actual accomplishment did a great deal to end this. I was especially glad of it because there had been some difficulty with the Red Cross, a thing I regretted deeply. From now on there was no more of this, and we worked together and fought all major battles side by side. It was not long before the Communists attacked the Red Cross in a dastardly manner—but of that I shall speak later. Besides restoring and cementing friendly relations, the celebration inspired the army administration to pass on to me a mechanical laundry, which was surplus and would soon be taken by the Russians if it was not installed somewhere. It was arranged that it should be put into the old barracks-storeroom that General Tataranu had originally given me, but that project, too, was not finished until spring.

With the three years' drought that began in 1945 there came a terrible epidemic of typhoid, closely followed by typhus, diphtheria, and other scourges. Bran was not immune, but we did our best to combat the infections, and we were so successful that the ministry decided to put the local civilian hospital also under my administration, to be used as a contagious disease hospital subsidized by them. This was renovated and ready for use by the fall of 1946. You can see by these few items, out of what is in itself a long and varied story, that the hospital grew from sheer necessity, and from the growing trust of the people and the authorities in the seriousness and honesty of our work.

Soon the American Red Cross also became interested in us, and were most generous. Colonel Sigerist paid us a visit, with happy results for us, and through my much loved and admired cousin, the late Count Bernadotte, the head of the Swedish Red Cross, that organization also sent us considerable help. The Swiss Red Cross sent condensed milk, and the American Catholic War Relief also was most generous. As I have said, a part of all that I had available I used to help those to whom no official relief could be given. That, too, is a story in itself, and only small items of it can yet be told because I must protect others still at the mercy of the

Russians. I can give one example here of those other activities of mine which extended beyond the work of the hospital. I had been helping the Y.W.C.A. with their camp in Bran, but I also helped with a parallel camp run by former Y.W.C.A. secretaries and housed in the village school and neighboring homes that were available. This second camp was for Bessarabian girls who were refugees, high school and university students. It soon needed a great deal of both financial and moral support, for I have seldom seen such poverty and distress. These girls were nearly all orphans who knew their parents had been killed—many times they had been eyewitnesses—or who had seen their parents deported during the annexation of Bessarabia in 1941. They had originally been under the protection of the Romanian Ministries of Education and Labor, and were studying on scholarships, but now they were in continual danger of being claimed by the Russians as Soviet citizens, and "repatriated"—to labor camps or worse. The best we could hope for them was that they might be forgotten as far as possible by the authorities, and so we never dared insist too much on official help for them but must take care of them as privately and quietly as we could.

When we had them settled in camp we found that hardly any of them had a change of underwear and some had none at all. As many as ten would share one comb among them. In this country where personal toilet necessities are so freely advertised, perhaps I may mention frankly that it is difficult for those who have never suffered as refugees and fugitives, or who have never worked to help them, to imagine the physical discomforts these girls endured. One comb for ten girls; toothbrushes, towels and washcloths luxuries long since forgotten; and for their monthly periods only discarded newspapers to use as sanitary napkins. These are some of the small items that add to the miseries of existence for those whose home is the concentration camp, the labor camp, and the refugee camp. The girls lacked shoes and stockings; many of them lacked sufficient clothing to cover them from the weather; most of all they lacked the love and comfort of feeling that someone cared about them.

The leader at the head of the camp was one of the most loving and understanding, yet energetic, efficient, and self-forgetful women I know. She was an old friend; I had served my apprenticeship under her as quite a young girl when I was a Girl Reserve. I did all in my power for them, by getting provisions, clothes, and medical assistance from the hospital, by giving what I could from my own supplies, and by helping to beg and importune others to do the same. We did our best, also, to provide them with intellectual and spiritual food by organizing lectures and discussion groups, and by bringing in good speakers, both secular and religious. We met in my garden twice a day for these occasions when the weather made it possible, and often some stray holiday visitor would come in and add interest to the group. Yet always, whatever we did, there was the hopeless realization that for these girls who had lost parents and home, country and future, we were doing only small things even when we did all we could.

I was not always present at their meetings because I did have my program at the hospital, which grew always more exacting as I advanced in my knowledge and understanding of medical science. Besides, I often had to rush off to Bucarest in answer to some call for help, for there were many demands of all sorts finding their way to me as people heard that I was able to get a hearing from those in the government. Perhaps the thing that was hardest to bear was the criticism of those who blamed me bitterly for this contact and said—more often to others than to me, of course—that it, would have been far more "suitable" had I sat aloof in proud dignity and ignored the Communist interlopers! To this I could only reply that I would give more weight to this criticism if those who made it were not always so quick to run to me at their first difficulty, and to ask my help to get news of their dear ones or to try to get some member of their family out of jail or prison camp. On the day that no one asks my help, I once said bitterly, I will have time to be aloof and proud—but that day never came.

They were most unexpected and curious requests. The most usual, of course, were to find out where someone was imprisoned, or how to get food and medicine delivered to someone in camp or prison, or to get someone out of trouble with the ever-vigilant police, but there were many others. To stop the destruction of acres of rice fields, the water for which had been shut off to spite the proprietor because he had been a general; to get someone into a hospital; to spirit away some Bessarabian or Bucovinian who was on the verge of being repatriated; to save some deposit of food or clothing belonging to an institution from being confiscated for the use of the Party; to arrange for the transportation of provisions—and so on and on, endlessly.

Perhaps I should here give you an example of an incident of this kind which happened the following summer, when I was still more accustomed to a variety of appeals and had learned even more ways of "getting around" a situation. It was, you can understand, quite contrary to the Russian policies to have relief or help sent into Romania. Not only did such action draw the attention of outsiders to the miserable condition of the country, but it made the Romanians feel that they had friends "outside" interested in helping them, and this would never do! A constantly increasing succession of difficulties was put in the way of the foreign organizations trying to help Romanian organizations, and individual efforts to help individuals were, by 1946, pretty well taken care of by putting a large and prohibitive duty on packages of food or clothing, including CARE parcels, sent from abroad to Romania. Since no one could afford to pay the duty, no one benefited by this attempted help; and eventually the CARE organization simply closed its depots in Romania.

One day I was appealed to by the Romanian Seventh-Day Adventists. Members of their church in the United States had collected and shipped seven railway cars full of used clothing, and these cars had now arrived in the freightyard at Bucarest. However, the duty put on them was not only more than the clothing was worth but far more than the church could afford to pay. Could I not try to have the duty waived, since none of the clothing was new and it was all for charitable uses? I realized that this was a hopeless idea, for the Communists knew all this. An idea struck me, however. I told the church group that they must make me, personally, a present of the seven carloads of clothing! Since members of the royal family were still privileged to receive gifts duty free, I thought that if we moved fast the scheme might work.

Everyone did certainly move fast. The church members made the necessary arrangements to "present" me with the clothes; I got permission from the Queen to have the freight cars moved to the private station within the palace walls; and in less than a week, working with every imaginable kind of transportation and a great deal of manpower, church members had unloaded the cars into the palace, and then quietly and efficiently taken the clothing away and distributed it. To show their gratitude they gave me some of the clothing to distribute from my hospital, for which I was deeply grateful. And to do the Communists at least this much credit, I never suffered for this particular evasion on my part. In fact, the Minister of Health was quite good humored about it when next he saw me, and said only:

"Well! You certainly fooled us that time!"

However, there was little humor in most of the requests for help, and there was always a certain amount of danger in putting myself forward in these matters, as I was always being warned even by the Communists themselves. To be criticized for doing this, then, was hard; but at least it saved me from any possibility of feeling proud or self-satisfied! Instead, I was constantly forced to re-examine my motives and to redecide whether or not I was acting according to my highest intelligence—a mental state which made the whole thing harder.

When we had left Romania in 1948, and I was beginning to feel at the very end of my endurance, I remember being challenged a little patronizingly by a person who had herself begged and insisted that I use my connections in an important matter. What had I really got out of it in the end? she wanted to know now. Was I not in the same position as all the others; an exile, condemned as an "enemy of the state" to the loss of my citizenship and my property? I could only remind her of a discussion we had had while still at home, when she had once somewhat more kindly drawn my attention to the risk I was running.

"You will remember what I said then," I told her. "I would say the same thing if it were all to do over again: 'There is little hope for us, and the end is coming whatever I can do. My activity makes no difference to *that* end result. Yet in the small daily accounts it *does* make a difference, for everyday that I can keep someone out of jail, or keep strength in those who are in jail, is a day gained in the ultimate appraisal. It is a blow struck for our side, which may encourage someone else to strike another blow; and such an endless chain of small efforts may eventually affect the larger issues. Therefore, if I am going to lose my head, at least as long as it is still on my shoulders I am going to use it to the best of my lights!'"

Well, miraculously my head is still on my shoulders, and I am still using it as well as I can to serve the same cause, and to fight for the same liberty.

Do I need to tell you how tired I often was? How sick of heart and weary and discouraged? Often I got to the point of not being able to sleep at all—a condition which became quite serious for a time after I was finally forced to leave Romania. I seemed eternally to see before me all the suffering, both physical and mental, that I had witnessed during the day. Even worse than this was the heartache for those I had been unable to help; whose misery I had not been able to alleviate that day. Before me was the thought of the tortures many of my people, many personally known to me, were enduring in the camps; their punishments, their hunger, thirst, cold, or heat. The continual pressure being brought to bear in this way on families and friends to make them come to heel—all this oppressed me endlessly, even though eventually I realized that this was something which could break down my resistance as well.

There are so many cases I can never forget, cases which are perhaps only stories to you but to me are living memories of crucified flesh and blood, minds and hearts. I cannot, of course, tell you of many of my successful efforts, for to do so would endanger many people still in Romania. It is safer to tell you of my failures! There was, for example, the charming young girl studying medicine who one day was stricken with polio of the lungs. Her adoring mother and father and her friends kept her alive for thirty-five days by giving her artificial respiration, not stopping for a single moment, until an iron lung was flown to her by the American Mission. A present from the Red Cross, sent all the way across the ocean! When this precious instrument arrived all hopes grew bright, and she began to show marked signs of improvement.

Just at this moment the Communists found that her father had been a technical adviser in the Antonescu government for three months, and was therefore a criminal. He was arrested under the very eyes of his suffering daughter and taken to jail, to be condemned to hard labor. The family's house could now be confiscated at any moment; their modest income was in jeopardy. An aunt came all the way to Bran to appeal to me for help, and as soon as I could I went to visit the poor girl and her mother. It was my first sight of an iron lung, which is sad enough without such further tragedy and loss as that which was hanging over the family. I said all the encouraging and hopeful things I could think of, while I turned over in my mind what I could do.

I invited Mr. and Mrs. Bodnaras to dinner—they could now come openly to see me at times, since apparently Ana Pauker had given permission. I had a photograph of the girl laid casually on a table, and eventually Bodnaras' eye fell upon it. I told him the sad story of her disease without saying who she was, or what had happened to her father, and his sympathy was immediately aroused.

"But a monument should be erected to such a mother!" he said.

"The best tribute to her would be to let her husband share in the care of their child," I answered.

"What do you mean?" he asked quickly.

When I told him, he looked upset and worried. "That is not at all easy," he objected, but I insisted that he try. Yet after weeks of effort, and even after I had taken Mrs. Bodnaras, under an assumed name, to see the girl for herself, I could obtain nothing except the assurance that the family would be allowed to keep their house and money. In the end the girl got influenza, and it was clear that she could not live. Everyone—the King, the head of the American Mission, General Schuyler, who had arranged for the iron lung in the first place—everyone used pressure to get permission for the unfortunate father to come and see his daughter before the end, but it was useless. The child died, calling in vain for her father. This man's worst crime was that of serving his country in a minor capacity when called upon by the heads of his state. The only concession made was to allow him to come to the funeral under a heavy guard, and to grasp briefly the hand of his wife, without speaking to her.

I did not go to that tragic funeral nor did I ever visit that home again. I had failed, and I could not bear facing the bereaved mother. Now I often reproach myself for my lack of courage.

There was another instance when I had not the courage to give bad news. A famous professional man came to ask me to find his son, who had been an officer and attached to a foreign mission because he had studied abroad in that country. One day this young man disappeared without a trace. I used all the channels I knew of, and found there was no doubt that he had been taken to Russia. For this I knew nothing could be done, and I thought, *Perhaps it is better for them to go on hoping, and to think that I have not really tried to find out or that I was not able to learn anything, rather than to know the horrible truth.* But was I right?

It was cases such as these; it was the information—"accidentally" allowed to leak out—that this night a person was being tortured to make him confess; it was such things that drove away sleep. It is, of course, part of the system of terror to allow such news to leak out, and later to allow people to verify the fact that such apparent "slips" are often accurate. Then every rumor adds to the despair and distress of those who are for the moment left in physical freedom. The victim himself, if he returns alive, will never speak of his treatment. It is only his body—seen in secret;

seen in a hospital—or his deadened expression that testifies to the truth. In this way fear spreads, while its cause is "officially" denied by authorities and victims alike.

IPeana

TWENTY-THREE

T HE SUMMER of 1945 brought the political situation in Romania to another climax, which for a time made us hopeful that help might be given us by the other two Allies. Great Britain and the United States had refused to recognize the Communist-imposed Groza government, which had been put into office on March 6. The Potsdam Conference during the last of July and the first of August called, among other things, for having a "recognized democratic government" in Romania, and shortly afterwards President Truman, speaking over the Voice of America, reaffirmed this, and added that "Romania, Bulgaria, and Hungary . . . are not to be the spheres of influence of any one power." The next day the British Foreign Minister, Mr. Bevin, followed this up by stating that he did not believe the Romanian government represented a majority in the country; that he believed "one kind of totalitarianism was being replaced by another."

After these public recognitions and condemnations of the kind of government that had been imposed on the Romanians, the representatives of the United States and Great Britain serving on the Allied Control Commission in Bucarest said in a note to King Michael that their governments refused to recognize the Groza government; that they could neither re-establish diplomatic relations with it nor invite it to the peace conference in Paris. King Michael, therefore, felt that he would have the support of those nations in establishing a more representative government in Romania, and he requested Premier Groza to resign. Groza, after an appeal to Russia and a promise of her support, refused to do this. There followed a difficult period during which King Michael declined to see any representatives of the government he had asked to resign, and during which this same government, aided by Russian force, continued to carry on the business of the country. Papers without the King's signature were legally invalid, but it was soon evident that anyone who refused to accept government decrees and documents simply because they were legally invalid got into serious trouble.

It was a time of a most difficult impasse, which Russia used for her own advantage. In return for Stalin's support of the Communist government under Groza, many additional concessions were made to Russia by this government, and Romania's future was loaded with still more chains of hopeless slavery. It is no doubt too early to know exactly the motives from which the Allies acted. Perhaps they felt that Russia would back down before sheer force of words, for certainly no one in either England or America felt enthusiastic about actually going to war with Russia over what she was doing in Europe. Too little was known by the general public in both countries about the real purposes of Russia, and the futility of "appeasement" policies.

August, September, and October passed. The Romanian people waited, enthusiastically loyal to their king but with no way to take over authority. The Romanian army also waited, loyal to their royal head but helpless in the face of the well-armed and ruthlessly poised Russian forces occupying their country.

On November 8 came the name day of King Michael, on which his birthday also was celebrated. Usually there were no great festivities for this occasion, but people went to sign their names in the visitors' register at the palace, and a *Te Deum* was sung at the *Patriarhie*—the church where the Patriarch, who is the head of the Romanian Orthodox Church, resides and carries on the church government. This year any observance of the day was discouraged by the government, but the opportunity for a public demonstration of loyalty was not surrendered by the people. Although the King was in Sinaia, they went in throngs to the palace in Bucarest, carrying flags and singing the National Anthem; men and women, old people and children crowding the square. Russian trucks full of armed soldiers drove up to disperse the crowd. The people, in the face of the bullets, by simple force of numbers overturned the trucks and set fire to them. Larger forces had to be brought in, and literally hundreds of the people were beaten savagely and dragged off to arrest before the crowd could be broken up. Perhaps there are few peoples who have allowed themselves to be shot in order to wish their king a happy birthday!

It was a moving demonstration, but it had the powerlessness of a man attacking a machine gun with only his fists to help him. The Communists tried to minimize it by hastily announcing that "Fascists and capitalists" had shot and killed the "poor, unarmed workmen." They quickly collected as many of the bodies of the dead as possible, taking them away from their protesting and unwilling families, and put on a tremendous funeral procession for these "victims" of the "Fascists"; a procession which deceived no one except those outside the country who read and believed the news dispatches. A special mass grave was dug in one of the big public parks which has in itself been made to follow the Party line. It was originally Parcul Jianu, named for a Romanian hero, but under the Communist government it was rechristened "Tito Park." Since Tito's fall from grace, I hear that it has again been renamed. Now it is "Stalin Park."

Following this demonstration of loyalty to the King, increasing pressure was put on Romania by Russia and her imposed Communist government.

Finally, at the Allied Conference in Moscow in December, the King was advised to accept a "compromise," which was largely a matter of adding one minister without portfolio from each of the other two political parties to the Groza government. Since these two parties actually represented the vast majority of the Romanian people, and since the position of the two ministers was obviously a "figurehead" one, this amounted to forcing the King to accept a situation he had previously been encouraged to repudiate. If it had not been for the great love and respect felt by the people for their king, his prestige would have suffered seriously. As it was, the action served to discredit the other two Allies in Romanian opinion, for it had been made clear that they would not seriously oppose Russian actions.

The entire lack of power of these two added ministers was brought to my attention later, when I was appealed to for help needed by the National Peasant Party—one of those thus "represented." To my great joy I was able to aid one of Mr. Maniu's favorite nephews, by working through an acquaintance I must not now identify but who used my name and went directly to the Russians. It is the only time I agreed to this being done, but the circumstances were special ones, and I am glad that it was a successful effort.

During that same fall of 1945 my own difficulties again became great with the recurring problem of the children's schools. The three eldest all needed work more advanced than they could get in the village school. The Catholic Sisters of St. Mary in Bucarest offered to take Minola and Alexandra. They had for many years conducted one of the best high schools for girls in the country, and my family had a close connection with them because my great-uncle, King Carol I, had helped them start their community. I was deeply touched by their offer, and I accepted it without asking anyone else about it. No trouble for any of us was caused by this.

The problem was not so easily solved for Stefan. He had passed his examinations successfully for the previous year, but there was no doubt that he was getting insufficient instruction because of the informal and irregular teaching that had been the best thing we could manage the year before. In Predeal, in the mountains above us, there was a famous military school which gave by far the best and most democratic education in the country, and which had been founded by Nicolae Filipescu when he was minister of war under my great-uncle. The fundamental purpose of the school was to train peasant boys of outstanding ability for officership, but there were a small number of places open for boys of other classes as well. I asked a former aide-de-camp, who was on the Board of Trustees, if there was any possibility of getting Stefan into the school, and he promised to see what could be done.

My joy was great when he told me that everything had been arranged, and that if Stefan could pass the examination there was no reason why he should not be enrolled. I realized that the whole matter was very delicate, for I was still not supposed to communicate with or to see the King. I felt it was best to have no direct contact myself with the Ministry of War, on which the school depended, because of the equivocal political situation that had existed ever since March 6, when a Communist government had been imposed upon us. This time was, of course, at the very beginning of the months when the King ignored the government and the government, supported by Russia, ignored the King; but I was not at all aware of what the situation really was. Having discovered that asking too many questions usually resulted in everyone's saying "No" because he was afraid to assume any responsibility, I decided to ask no questions at all, but to accept the trustee's statement at its face value. Stefan left for Predeal, accompanied by Bittermann because I was at the time ill in bed—something which proved to be very lucky for me.

Stefan was received in person by Vasiliu Rascanu, now minister of war, and a great fuss was made over him; something which we did not want, naturally, and which put me in the false position of being friendly with a government discredited by Michael, who was not only my nephew but also my king. I still did not understand what had been done to me, even when I heard of the public reception, When I heard Rascanu had announced that the King had given his consent to Stefan's enrolling in the school, I was delighted and immediately wrote to thank Michael. It then developed that Michael had known nothing about it at all, and he was very angry at the way the situation had been used as a political weapon. I was ordered to remove my son from the school.

This, I felt, was both unfair and unwise. I had acted in an orderly way, and it was neither my fault nor Stefan's that others had used a harmless request as a political football. It seemed to me, as it had from the beginning, a dreadful thing that the grandson of King Ferdinand and Queen Marie should be refused an education in their country, and I even felt that my own work for Romania deserved the favor of permitting my children to attend school. I went to Bucarest to try to see the King, but I was told that it was not possible for me to be received. My friend of the year before, General Aldea, who still had access to the King, pleaded my cause; but—politics being what they are—he was told that I had put myself hopelessly in the wrong, and whether it was through ignorance or not made no difference. Stefan would have to leave the school in which he had immediately felt happy and at home. I was informed that on the following weekend I must take him away.

I hoped and prayed that something might intervene, but the week passed uneventfully. On Friday night I made one more desperate prayer, and then went to bed, but not to sleep. Finally I said, "Thy Will be done. If it is right for Stefan to remain, then he will remain. If not, he will have to go." Suddenly I felt at peace, and I slept. On Saturday morning I awoke to a tremendous fall of snow, unexpectedly early in the season. The drifts were waist deep; not even a sledge could be moved. For me the answer was clear. Stefan could not come home, and I felt that I had been granted a miracle.

I used the respite given me by the snow to insist with fresh courage and more strongly that the King receive me. He finally agreed to do this, but I was not able to see him until shortly before Christmas because the roads remained impassable. Even by that time I had quite a struggle to get to Bucarest, and Stefan had to come home from school on skis for the holidays. It was a joy to see Sitta and Michael again and to feel once more the warm comfort of one another's company. We talked everything out, and I could then understand how terrible their position had been. They, too, then realized that, cut off from every contact with them as I had been, I had had little idea of the intrigues that had been going on, or of how I was being misrepresented to them. It was not the first action of mine that had been used in this way, but at last those who wished to separate us for their own purposes had gone too far. They had defeated their own end by making me feel sufficiently desperate to insist upon seeing Michael, and we were together again in fact, as we had always been in mind and affection. We were now able to see one another almost normally, which was a great comfort to me; and I was able with time to be of service to them, to my great joy.

The winter of 1945-46 also presented new problems at the hospital. The epidemic of typhus which I have mentioned hit the hospital hard, and I found myself with nearly all the staff down with it, including Dr. Puscariu and Badillo. The worst difficulty was to get someone to nurse them, because there were on duty only two nurses besides me, and I was recovering from a slight operation, as well as having to cope with the difficulties in regard to Stefan's school. Happily Frau Koller and Gretl could step in to help, and since all the nurses were not equally ill, and were not stricken at the same time, they could also help one another. The military hospital sent me a doctor, who was pleasant even though he had not had much experience, and we also refused to take any new patients for the time being, so that we could get a chance to locate the cause of the epidemic and to disinfect everything.

In spite of all this, we kept the Christmas festivities as well as we could for our own family and our patients. I even went so far as to put on all my finery, which seemed to please everyone very much indeed. In fact, Badillo, who was the most seriously ill of all, told me later that it was the one clear and happy picture he had of those difficult days. Dr. Puscariu had been taken to a hospital in Brasov, for he developed phlebitis in the

leg. I had to make the journey to Bucarest to get him the necessary medicine, and it was a terrible one because of the snow, but I did get back
with the medicine in time. One of the nurses in Bran—not to be outdone
by the doctor, we told her!—then developed phlebitis in her arm; a rare
occurrence which gave us much worry for a few days, and which she got
over by a miracle, we felt.

When at last everyone crawled back to health and we could again
begin normal work, I was more than thankful. The last to return was
Dr. Puscariu, although at least we were able to bring him back to his own
home for his convalescence. The military doctor had returned to Brasov,
so that Badillo and I ran the hospital as best we could between us, visiting our chief daily to tell him all that went on and to ask for his instructions. I remember those visits with especial pleasure. We really got to
know him, and we were enchanted with his wit and intelligence. Badillo,
being young, developed a fine case of hero worship, and later when he
discovered his idol had feet of clay, as so often happens, his grief was
great. I had fewer illusions about people, but I still enjoyed this intelligent
man greatly and learned much from him.

It was during the time Dr. Puscariu was convalescing that a woman in
labor came to us. The midwife had found that it would be quite impossible for her to give birth naturally, as she was very narrow and not at
all young, and this was her first child. She must have a Caesarean. I had
assisted at a Caesarean but Badillo had only watched one. Did we dare
do it? Then I remembered there was a woman gynecologist spending her
vacation in a valley village not too far off. We were much relieved. We
could get her and she could operate.

She was delighted to come, and gave us good advice all the way from
her house to the hospital. In fact, by the time we got there she had reor-
ganized the whole place, moved into it, and turned it into a first-class
maternity hospital with herself at the head. When I mentioned that the
hospital really was already organized and had a head, she waved this
aside as quite unimportant and assured me smugly that *she* stood well

with the regime in Bucharest! Badillo and I looked at each other, divided between indignation and amusement. Once in the hospital, our doctor looked the woman over and after many important-seeming and time-consuming examinations announced that a Caesarean would be necessary. Then she told us calmly that she had never operated; Badillo would have to do it, she would assist, and I could attend to the instruments. Again Badillo and I looked at each other grimly and settled the question between us. She could give her name as operating, but we would do the actual work.

To save her face she agreed, but she carried on the ruse by washing up and pretending to assist. She finally got into our way so much by ordering me about, telling me how to set up the instrument table, and in general making a nuisance of herself that I did what I rarely allowed myself to do. I got on my royal high horse, as it were: firmly put her in her place; shoved her gently but decisively aside, and set to work. It was comforting and flattering that the patient's confidence was entirely in me, and she took the anesthetic calmly. Badillo and I managed well between us, the child was safely delivered, and all was well with the mother. Need I tell you that we were relieved and glad, and also not a little proud?

The lady doctor departed less pleased, and never ceased trying to get a footing in the hospital by using her influence in Bucharest, but happily she did not succeed. What made it difficult for me was that she was the wife of a man who had been kind to us, and we did not like to hurt his feelings. It was with some trepidation that we made our daily visit to Puscariu and told him what we had done. He did not scold at all, but instead commended our courage and initiative and said that having a registered doctor present saved us before the law. The experience gave Badillo and me more confidence in ourselves, and Puscariu seemed pleased that he had found two good pupils. He proposed that later in the year we might try to arrange a visit to the University of Cluj to visit the clinics there. Of course, we looked forward to this, and it was a most interesting experience, but it is one of those things which belong in another story.

As soon as the weather permitted, the new wing was energetically started again. It was not too easy. Mr. Malaxa had left the country for the United States, the factory was constantly changing directors, and the engineers were more interested in their own profits than in the hospital. This class of people were affected to a greater extent by the Communist regime than the workmen themselves, who seemed to remain much more conscientious and willing. On one occasion only did I have any difficulty with a workman, and he was a patient who I am sure had been "worked up" to find fault with the hospital in order to make an opening for those who would have liked to take it over "so that it might serve the interests of the people"! In fairness I must say that those who wished to do this, and those who were affected by Party propaganda, were the discontented and incompetent "small fry," who had been passed over in their own professions because they were mediocre and were now looking for opportunities to show their devotion to the regime so that they could profit by it. They seemed to feel also that in this way they might "get even" with a world which had not rewarded their lack of ability. The higher authorities never listened to them, so far as the hospital was concerned, and did not uphold their efforts to harm the work I was doing, but it was not always easy to find time to deal with the difficulties they sometimes introduced into our daily program.

One instance like this occurred when the construction was at last finished and only the painting remained to be done. The engineer in charge of the work announced triumphantly that there was no sum allowed for the cleaning that would have to be done before the painting and that we would have to take care of that somehow ourselves before he could do any more. Naturally we had no money to spend on hiring extra hands, so I made an appeal to my staff that they should help clean the building in their free time. Everyone volunteered, from the doctors down, and we had great fun washing the walls and scrubbing the floors. We sang and laughed and worked away gaily, and in the middle of it who should appear but our engineer, coming in, I suppose, to observe our disappointment and frustration. He was apparently surprised to hear the cheerful songs, and he asked rather pointedly where *I* was.

"There she is!" said someone, pointing down the passage to where, with an old dress tucked up around my waist and a red kerchief tied on my head, I was hard at work on my hands and knees, scrubbing the floor.

"Why," he said mockingly, "I was under the illusion that you were *directing* this hospital, not scrubbing the floors!"

"Indeed?" I replied. "Well, I do whatever is necessary: scrub floors, operate, or interview you in my office, where I now invite you to come!"

I let down my skirt, took off the kerchief, and preceded him to the office. He followed silently and we transacted our business with as few words as possible. At the end of the interview he excused himself a little lamely.

"Yes," I told him, "you made a mistake there. Work should never be laughed at, and today it is also extremely imprudent to do so."

On another day we had a visit from the new head of the social insurance. He was an ordinary workman, a Communist, but I do believe an honest soul who thought he could do something for his fellow workmen. He arrived decidedly the worse for a few glasses of wine, and full also of the jargon of the Party. He greeted me offhandedly, reeled a little unsteadily ahead of me into my office, and sat down at my desk to interview me. Inwardly amused, and remembering Shaw's "Apple Cart," I asked him if I, too, could sit down. To my great delight he immediately answered, just as does the man in the play:

"Oh, don't stand on ceremony with *me!*"

An inspection of the hospital followed, during which one could see him visibly rearranging his conception of how the "bloodsucking royalty" lived. In the end, he took hold of the collar of my uniform and, giving me a vigorous and affectionate shake back and forth, assured me that in spite of my being a princess I was quite a decent person, and my work deserved support! Actually the man was really full of good intentions, and when sober he had plenty of good common sense. He repeated his visit several times, and we became good friends. He felt that I was interested in seeing that the workmen got back in benefits more of the money they had paid in for years in compulsory insurance, as of course I was. They had never really got back a fair amount. What was paid me for their care actually covered only the food, leaving nothing for medical supplies, nursing, or operations, as the records plainly showed, and many hospitals were not able or did not wish to make this up from other funds, as I did. The "graft" in the compulsory system of social insurance was one of the things that even the strongest anti-Communist believed would be corrected by this party with its avowed purpose to help the worker. Of course, nothing of the sort was done, and abuses were simply increased by the party for its own benefit. This was discouraging to everyone, but it was terribly disillusioning to those who had honestly believed that communism had any good intentions whatever.

My poor inspector became more and more saddened by the way things were going and confided many of the details to me. He told me how the administration of the insurance, instead of being simplified so that the money really would go for the care of the patients, was constantly being made more involved. More and more "spongers" were being put in all the time.

"It is not being run to the advantage of the poor or the workmen at all," he said sadly. "I cannot understand it; I really cannot! And I have *lived* for this day!"

I felt sorry for him, but he was only one of a number of people—several of them highly placed—who had been deceived in the purposes of the Communist Party. I know of many whose hearts were almost literally broken by their disillusionment as time went on, and whose deaths were due to nothing else than their realization that they had been deceived into betraying their country. As for our inspector, since he was a simple man and did not understand the intricacies of administration, he was eventually removed on the plea of his incompetence and a less honest and more pliable person was put in his place. This new man was a good bookkeeper, and since he had been installed ostensibly as the "people's" representative, they could not protest against his dishonesty without being told:

"But you put him in yourselves! He is your representative!"

This is one of the Communist methods of getting things into their power. An institution is put into the hands of the "people" themselves. Then, as events prove they naturally cannot manage a complicated post for which they have not been trained, a *real* Party member, dishonest and ruthless, is put in. Any protest is sabotage against the state, which is presented as being something which expresses the will of the "people" themselves. Eventually, to their entire bewilderment, the workers find they have become enslaved to something which they are told is their own will and they do not know how to disentangle themselves. When you discuss this with a Party member who is "high up" in communism, he tells you glibly that "the individual must be sacrificed to the interests of society." What I wanted to know, and never succeeded in finding out, was: *When* does the individual become a part of that society which profits by all this sacrifice? For if there were some definite period of probation, or apprenticeship, after which one could be sure of being admitted into the inner circle and getting some of the mythical benefits this sacrifice produces, I am sure everyone would be more spontaneously willing to leave his home at a moment's notice with what he can carry in his hand, or to crowd strangers into it and sacrifice his privacy—to mention only a few items which the individual contributes to "society." However, there never seems any answer to my question, as I have said.

Instead, "privacy" is labeled as one of those perverted "bourgeois" notions fostered by "Fascists." In Romania about this time the word "Fascist" began to be bandied about in the most incongruous way to denote anything not Communist. I once read in the same article references to "Anglo-Hitlerists" and "Monarcho-Fascists," among other strange creatures, all mentioned in the *Scanteia*, a leading Communist paper. Phrases like this were supposed to be swallowed whole by the faithful, but the desired result was not always attained because Romanians tend to be mercilessly critical and mocking toward anything that is not intellectually irrefutable. In the past we used to consider this "taking to pieces" of everything a destructive element in the Romanian mentality. Someone once said, "Romania is the only country where success has no success!" But at this moment such a critical attitude stood us in good stead, for the wholesale propaganda did not go down as quickly as the Russians evidently expected. People were not impressed inwardly, even when they had to conform outwardly.

I remember the time the hospital was visited by *Apararea Patriotica*—the Patriotic Defense—which was one of the leading Communist associations. I found them in the wards distributing small gifts, and since I was busy and did not pay much attention to their remarks, I made the amusing mistake of thinking they had said they were from the *Civil Defense*. It was only at the end that I grasped who they were, when they said they would like to come again with a play and songs which would enlighten my poor patients with the *truth*. I thanked them politely, but showed them that we really had no space for a stage or such things, and said vaguely that perhaps later on something could be arranged.

A few days afterwards when I came into the wards in the morning I was not greeted by the usual "*Satraiti, domnitza!*" Instead, everyone who could walk about was doing so in a vague and groping manner, as if he were in a fog; and the bed patients were rubbing their eyes and shading them with their hands while they peered at me as if they had suddenly lost their eyesight. I realized a joke was intended, but I could not understand what it was, so after I had laughed as I was supposed to do, I asked what they were about.

"What?" they said in mock surprise. "Do you not know that this is a house full of darkness, and that you are preventing any light from reaching us?" I still did not understand. "Aha!" they said. "That comes of not reading the papers!" And they showed me an article in the *Scanteia*, telling of the visit with which we had been honored, and ending with the accusation that I had refused to let my poor, downtrodden, unhappy patients be told of all the lovely things in store for them in the brave new world.

"Or is this great lady"—the article ended—"afraid that light might penetrate into this house of darkness and show her up?"

The bombastic words had tickled the sense of humor of my "poor, downtrodden, unhappy patients," and the joke was good for quite a while. They knew it was not true, and they laughed. I laughed too, but today I think it less funny. Today I know that this is the only kind of literature one is permitted to read, and that the young people who have nothing with which to compare it will not only be deceived by the content of such articles but will not know how poorly written they are by purely literary standards. The whole level of culture and education is being lowered, in addition to the corruption of ideas that is going on, and one wonders how long there will be any people left who know this, and who dare to show it.

In Brasov when posters everywhere urged that people "buy and spread abroad" the *Scanteia*, the public quite spontaneously reacted by buying it in quantities and "spreading it abroad" by tearing it up in small pieces and throwing it all over the place. Even in Bucarest, with the machine guns of the Russians uncomfortably in evidence, the compelled and policed "spontaneous" parades and demonstrations of the workmen were always getting into difficulties. The tired, irritated workers, anxious to get home to supper, shouted witty and unrefined remarks about the Party members whose portraits they were carrying as posters, or used these banners for quite rude and disrespectful purposes. More than once I was recognized by some of the annoyed marchers, who stopped the procession to inquire cheerfully how my children were getting along, or to ask me the names of the Russian Communist "heroes" whose pictures they were carrying, and to comment in a free and uncomplimentary fashion on the appearance and probable ancestry of the gentlemen in question! I always got away as quickly as possible, for fear of getting them into trouble with the Russians, and as I left I would be divided between pleasure at finding that they were not really deceived by our captors and anxiety for the economic condition of the country—for of course all these parades and demonstrations are during working hours, and are paid for by the employer; something which tends to disrupt production.

The "less than one thousand" membership in the Communist Party when a Communist government was imposed on Romania was a true reflection of the Romanian attitude toward communism, and I am not speaking of the upper classes alone, but of the back bone of the country: the peasant and the middle class.

TWENTY-FOUR

A T ABOUT this time Bodnaras said he thought I should make the acquaintance of the rest of the government, and would I accept an invitation to a dinner party at his house? I thought it over and saw that it had its advantages. Since the King had accepted the compromise urged upon him at the Moscow Conference and there was now a political relationship between him and the government, there was no real reason to say no. I accepted the invitation, and when I arrived at the house, there they all were! It was the first time I had met Groza, who had a cheerful manner and certainly knew how to get a party going, with his loud laugh and his far from conventionally refined jokes. Sitta once told me that of course one could always be grateful at these gatherings for his complete insensibility to atmosphere which allowed him to fill all gaps in the conversation noisily and with entire self-satisfaction. There was Ghiorghiu Dej, the former railway mechanic, big, burly, and not unpleasant looking;

Maurer, whose appearance was perhaps more well bred than that of anyone else in the group; Lucretiu Patrascanu, the Minister of Justice, with
his beautiful, talented wife—the only smartly dressed woman present; and
there was the small, unpleasant Theohari Gheorghescu, Minister of the
Interior, who did not even pretend to be amiable.

Last, but most certainly not least, there was Ana Pauker. A big, stout
woman, with short, untidy gray hair, fierce blue eyes under lowering eye-
brows, and a fascinating smile which was not spoiled by the fact that her
upper lip hung over her lower one, she made one know that here was
a real personality. I have always felt when I was with her that she was
like a boa constrictor which has just been fed, and therefore is not going
to eat you—at the moment! Heavy and sluggish as she seemed, she had
all that is repellent and yet horridly fascinating in a snake. I could well
imagine, simply from watching her, that she had denounced her own husband, who in consequence was shot; and my further acquaintance with
her showed me the cold and dehumanized brilliance by which she had
reached the powerful position she occupied.

On that first evening we talked but little. It was at a later time, when I
was trying to ease in some way the terrible treatment of those in prison,
that I conceived the plan of inviting her to dine with me and the children
in Bucarest. Somewhat to my astonishment, she accepted. All the children
were present, and as usual before sitting down to our food the youngest
one said grace—and there was our atheist standing up respectfully with the
rest of us. She was quite charming in her manner of speaking with the
children about their studies and schools, and after they had gone to bed
we sat down to a most interesting talk which lasted almost three hours. At
the end I was surprised and a little amused to have her say: "Now should
you dismiss me, or should I leave? I have enjoyed this charming conversation so much that I have forgotten just what the protocol is!"

It was not a conversation in which I distinguished myself, for I was
no match for her brilliant array of half-truths and slightly distorted
facts, which she used dexterously in meeting arguments. Sometimes she

answered questions frankly, with such an open lack of all we mean by the term "humanity" that she reminded me of those first Russian soldiers I had seen in Bran.

I remember asking her to explain some of the Communist principles and methods; why, for example, they used so much violence, when violence never convinced anyone.

"It is not intended to convince," she replied calmly, "but to frighten. When one replants, one first destroys everything that grows, root and branch. Then one levels the earth. It is only afterwards that one can plant successfully."

She was quite frank about the reason for their treatment of the people. She said that it was not possible, unfortunately, to destroy a whole generation and have only the young left to train. A certain amount of physical work had to be done—road work, agricultural work, industrial work—to support the children in their youth. It was for this that the older generation had to be left alive, but they must be too frightened to dare to interfere with the Communist training of the children. Moral and physical threats of every possible variety were used to produce this condition, and in doing so it was not necessary to have any regard for human life. There would be enough of the "expendable" generation, too old to train, for purposes of labor, no matter how prodigally they were used and destroyed.

Finally we got around to the subject of prisons, and she told me of her own imprisonments, amounting to nine years in all. "And did you change?" I asked her.

"No," she said, "but I have already told you that we are not seeking to change people in prison. They are too old to be convinced; their habits are too strong. We are only getting evil out of the way when we jail them."

"But why not kill outright those whom you intend to punish most severely?" I asked her.

Again there was the feeling of utter, ruthless, impersonal inhumanity. "Simple death would be too good and too easy," she said. "And it would not frighten the others sufficiently."

Once for a moment I did manage to put her in a corner, but it was only for a moment. We were still talking of conditions in the prisons, and she assured me good-humoredly that many things were exaggerated; that actually they were not so bad as I thought. I said that I wished I could believe her.

"Why," she said, "you could see for yourself, if you just went through one or two jails, that really it is not so bad!"

I took her up promptly. "Then let us go now, at once!" I said. "I will be glad to have you show me that I am mistaken!"

She hesitated for a moment, obviously taken aback, but recovered quickly. "Oh, but, my dear," she said smilingly, "what would people say— your people and my people—if they should see us going through the prisons together!"

Perhaps I do not need to add that my pleas for the relief of the dreadful suffering and torture were useless.

We talked also of America. As I was to notice many times, the hatred of the Communists for the United States was of a deadly bitterness which exceeded their hatred for anything else. Ana Pauker, like other Communists with whom I talked, was specific about their plans in regard to this country. Actually I was not so much impressed at the time as I have been since I came to the United States, for my own knowledge of conditions here was relatively slight. It is only now that I begin to appreciate the careful and detailed information and appraisals with which the Communists were so familiar. Since at the time Romanians still thought of this country as a powerful rescuer who might at any time end the Russian occupation if it wished to, I was shocked by Ana Pauker's calm disregard of this as a possibility.

Many years later, in 1954, Ileana appeared before the Communist Committee for Aggression in the USA.

She explained to me quite brilliantly and—so far as I have been able to determine from newspapers and magazines I have now read here—quite correctly, the industrial setup of the United States, and I remember that she stressed particularly its dependence on electric power. She had figures and statistics to prove that if electric power were destroyed, the entire country would be so completely disorganized that it could not possibly recover before the government was taken over by those prepared to do so. Another easy method of attack, she explained, was offered by the kind of water system on which a high percentage of the population depended, and which could be destroyed or polluted simply and easily. She explained that these and other similar possibilities existed not only because an urban population had forgotten the basic fundamentals of food raising and food preparation and conservation, but it was also because the system of food distribution itself was such that it could be seriously disarranged by only a slight effort, and completely destroyed by a little more. Experiments along this line had already been carried out on a small scale in the United States, she assured me, so that information on overall methods had been checked and made extremely accurate. Small and strategic strikes, she thought, might make atomic bombs unnecessary; but only a few properly placed bombs would do the work if that seemed a better method. For good measure she explained casually just why this was impossible in Russia, where an entirely different organization was in operation.

Was she correct? How can anyone tell that now? As I have said, she was a brilliant talker, utterly and unhumanly a weapon of a force which is the very essence of evil. The venom of communism is as impersonally malignant as that of a striking snake. Certainly the facts she presented seemed correct, and the conclusions she drew seemed at least one of the possibilities of the situation. She had, of course, left God completely out of the picture, and I cannot do that because I have seen His power. Yet I do not think it is in accordance with His will or His plan that we trust in our own ignorance to protect us. I believe that it is His will that we trust in a Love and Wisdom which today do not seem manifested often enough in the lives of men. I have, after all, seen Nazism take over one country, and communism another. One country is not yet wholly free, the other is still in total slavery. This perhaps makes me more conscious of possibilities, and of the need of intelligent recognition of them and defense against them, than I might otherwise be. But this is forgetting my story!

In the summer of 1946 I at last got a holiday, for I seemed completely exhausted and it was felt that I badly needed a change. I had tried to arrange my days so that I could spend a regular time with the children and Anton, for it was sometimes hard for them to remember that the work I was doing was not only for others but for them as well. My activities protected them. Our whole life, even to the seventy acres of farmland I owned, would have been under much severer control if the hospital, serving a demonstrable use to the country, had not been a part of that life. From small privileges up to the greater one of the children's education, I was allowed certain freedoms because even the Communists recognized that my life was indisputably a hard-working one.

In general I tried to stick to a daily pattern which began at 6:30. I was in the hospital at 7:00, home for breakfast at 8:00, and walked with the little ones to their school, which stood directly across from the hospital, at 8:30. Dr. Puscariu came at 8:45, and we made the rounds; then we had outpatients and operations until about 1:00, when I went home for lunch. I tried then to take a half hour's rest, and to spend the afternoon with my family, but it was often necessary to combine this with some of my work. Sometimes, for example, I took the children for a walk so that I could visit some patient, and I tried to interest them in my activities. I would delegate errands to them or ask them to follow up the progress of some child dismissed from the hospital, and one summer my two older daughters, under the supervision of Gretl, ran the children's ward while the nurse was on her vacation. At 4:30 we had our tea, usually in the garden in the summertime, and from 5:00 until 7:00 I was back at the hospital. At 7:30 we had dinner, after which there were games with the family. Monopoly was the favorite, but sometimes I would read aloud to the younger children while Anton played bridge with Frau Koller, Gretl, and one of the older girls if they were at home from school. I tried to be in bed by 9:00, and on days that had been very strenuous I had supper in bed.

This program was often varied, sometimes by an afternoon picnic or a swim in our pool, which the hospital staff were always invited to use. At other times it was varied by the fact that I had to spend all day and a good part of the night at the hospital during some emergency. Also, I occasionally departed from the usual program so that I arrived at unexpected hours for inspection, to see that everyone was at his or her post during the slack hours of the afternoon and night.

Now it seemed that I must get away for a few days, for my visits to Bucarest were anything but relaxing even though they provided a change from the hospital routine. I accepted an invitation from a friend and took the three older children with me. I had not at first wanted to go because of the fact that Anton was still not allowed to leave Bran, but he insisted that I needed the rest and must take this opportunity. Cella, who had also been a friend of my mother, had a country place in Oltania, a beautiful part of Romania which is enclosed between the Carpathians, the Danube, and the Olt. The Olt is a large river which winds through Transylvania to join the Danube, and which is supposed to have carried the tears of the Romanians enslaved there to their brothers south of the mountains, who were more free.

Unfortunately, the drought that had begun the year before still continued, and it was a sad sight to see the parched land and meager fields. Conditions were bad in Oltania, and I could hardly believe it when I saw that the great Olt had become almost a puny stream. Normally it is one of our largest and swiftest rivers, winding its way through magnificent gorges and entrancing meadows, and sweeping past the feet of lovely old monasteries. Yet in spite of the drought I was delighted to find myself in this part of the country, which historically is the cradle of Romania.

It was up the Olt that the Romans had come to attack Sarmisegetuza, the stronghold of the Dacians. It was here also that the first Romanian *voevod*, or prince, lifted his standard in the thirteenth century. The city of Curtea de Arges, not far away, was Wallachia's first capital, and it is there, where her first rulers were buried, that my parents also were laid to rest. It is an extraordinarily beautiful part of the country, which seems to present a picture wherever you look. The peasant costumes here are the most lovely and varied of all those Romania offers: every valley seems to have one of its own. Although I have never lived there, something about Oltania pulls quite specially at my heartstrings. When I think of the Romanian soil, it is there I feel my roots go deepest.

My mother also loved this part of the country. She had a special tenderness for these villages; for the simple, frugal people so proud of their past; for the convents and monasteries always built on the most lovely mountain slopes, with the white walls of the fortified buildings standing foursquare against the green forest, and guarding in their centers the exquisitely painted churches. The beauty, dignity, and peace of these places—monuments which have withstood the vicissitudes of countless wars and occupations—had always enchanted both of us.

It was in one of these convents, that of Hurezu, that I trained and started my first company of Girl Scouts. I remember the last day of our camp, and how my mother came to take our pledges. I still see the square formed by the blue-uniformed girls in the white-walled courtyard with the lovely old church behind them, their outstretched arms and clear young voices carried on the clean mountain air while they made their pledge to their queen, as she stood on the old, carved stone gallery above. That evening we had a campfire around which we all sat, with my mother in the lovely dress of the region telling us stories of her girlhood. The night descended and gathered beneath the forest trees, and slowly closed around our circle about the fire. The flame died down and we became silent. We needed no more tales, we were living such a lovely one ourselves. It was out of deeply grateful and happy hearts that we sang the evening prayer of thanksgiving, and as we wound our way back through the trees to our dwelling, each carried something precious, something I think we all carry to this day in a world which has destroyed so much of what we lived for. Of the thirty-two of us there that night, I alone have escaped to freedom. You cannot know what it is to endure such a thought!

I was happy to be able to show my children all these places I had loved so dearly when I was young. Cella's house was not beautiful, but it had large, cool, whitewashed walls and a view that was deeply satisfying. There was an untidy garden, full of flowers in spite of the drought, and corn- and wheatfields running down to a road bordered by large old willows. In the evening I loved to walk down this straight and dusty road under the trees, and to see the carts drawn by the big, patient gray oxen slowly creak their way back from work in the fields. Then we would leave the road to walk through a cornfield and come out upon the banks of the Olt, which was here less broad and turbulent, though still swift. Cella and I would sit under a tree and let the children go swimming—something which would have been dangerous in normal times because of the current. Even now they were often swiftly carried away on the brown waters, but there were plenty of sand banks to stop their passage.

As we sat there, a peasant or a passing gypsy would come and talk with us, and I found it moving that so many remembered my mother's visits. We would speak together of those happy days in the past, when we were allowed to do as we wished with our "poverty." Once the family of Cella's husband had been owners of almost the whole region. Now they had hardly anything left, and that little was being reduced still more by the new agrarian reform; yet in many ways things had not changed. The peasants still came to the boyar—the lord of the manor— with their troubles and needs;

Romanian peasant house

with their misunderstandings to be settled and their ills to be cured.

We would return through the gathering dark to a country meal of chickens cooked on a spit out in the courtyard, served with vegetables and fresh cheese made of sheep's milk. We ate by the light of oil lamps, and afterwards Cella would play a Chopin prelude or a nocturne. Then we would retire, each to his room, with our candles, and find at our bed-sides a jug of iced water and a spoon of *dulceatza*—the thick Romanian jam that is served on all occasions with a glass of water. I loved to blow out my candle and look at the moon-silvered world of fields and trees and little white peasant cottages gleaming white among the shrubs. There was a haze of smoke from the cooking fires still floating over the whole in the quiet air, and giving it a dreamlike look. I would climb between the cool sheets and fall peacefully and restfully to sleep, listening to the distant barking of dogs and to the song of the nightingale, both part of the Romanian night. Forgive me if I have taken too long to describe what is so dear to me, but the thought of it rests me even now in this strange, new life I am beginning.

After those too few and short days I felt greatly rested, and on our way back to Bran we stopped at Curtea de Arges to visit the graves of my parents, which my children had never seen. The drive there through the hills was beautiful, even though the drought had done great harm here too, and not only were the roads bad but we had to make quite a detour to keep out of the way of the Russians. Curtea de Arges lies in the south-ern hills of the Carpathians, in the valley of the Arges, which is another one of our largest rivers. As I have told you, it was once the capital, and it still shows the ruins and foundations of the old palace of the voevods, or princes. The old church still stands, and careful restorations and exca-vations have brought to light the beautiful old frescoes, and the grave of Neagoe Bassarab, a prince of the sixteenth century.

It is not within the old church that my great-uncle and aunt and my parents are buried, but in another church which my uncle had restored according to the fashion of his time, when they literally rebuilt the entire church, although following in every thing the old plans and painting. This stood in a great park, with a big brick palace in the background. Half of this building was used by the resident bishop, and half was reserved for the royal family, and it was comfortable even though it is to be regretted that it did not at all harmonize with the jewel of a church, all white and blue and gold. With beating heart I drove the car to the church and walked up the steps—to find the door locked. A monk soon appeared and opened it for us. His eyes filled with tears when he saw me.

"We are not permitted to keep it open. Too many people come . . ."

We stepped within the cool interior, with its frescoes and dim light. To the right as one enters are the graves of King Carol I and Queen Elisabeth (Carmen Sylva) and of their four-year-old daughter and only child, Maria. Beautifully carved and slightly raised marble slabs cover them; and to the left, under a window behind arching columns, other similar stones cover the graves of my father and mother. Here I knelt first in silent prayer, thanking God that they were at rest and could no more be hurt by all the sorrow that had befallen their land and their children. I could weep for ourselves, but not for them. Then I knelt by the other three graves, and after going up to the altar to pray there too, and reverently kiss the icon on the right, as is our custom, I turned sadly and wordlessly away. I felt like a ghost from the past visiting the past. Had I known that it was for the last time I came there, how could I have borne it? God is merciful in that we do not know what awaits us.

I have heard that these graves are among those destroyed by the Communists; the bodies dug up and burned; their ashes scattered. Not so easily can a spirit be destroyed!

The royal church at Curtea de Arges

TWENTY-FIVE

AFTER MY five days in Oltania, I came back to the work at the hospital with renewed vigor. It was about this time that I bought a small but pleasant house in Bucarest, for it became necessary not only for me to have a house of my own to go to but also to have a place for Minola and Alexandra to come on their free afternoons and weekends. It was not only complicated to get them to Bran for short periods—a distance of about a hundred eighty miles through the mountains—but it was also not a little dangerous. I had had several unpleasant experiences myself, one of which occurred when I was driving to Bucarest with Noelle and her husband in the car.

When the Russians "thumb a ride" they do not do it as it is done in this country. They stand in the middle of the road with a machine gun pointed at you, so that of course you stop. Then, if you are lucky, the charming cavalier sits beside you and with grunts indicates the way he expects you to take. If you are not so lucky, he kicks you out—if no more—and takes the car himself. In this case I was lucky. My unwelcome companion got in beside me, after waving Noelle and her husband to the back seat. To leave no doubt as to his intentions if I disobeyed orders, he jammed the muzzle of a gun into my ribs and indicated that I was to drive on. I did. After about twenty miles he grunted and indicated that I should stop. I did that also, wondering what next. To my great relief he grinned at me, expressed some sort of thanks for the ride, and waved us on; but this kind of experience was always a harrowing one.

On another evening we were coming home from Bucarest—Bittermann driving and the car full of people, as always, for transportation was so difficult that always someone wanted a ride—when on one of the numerous curves in the Timis valley we passed part of a Russian column. They chose to take offense at this, and shouted and sent a few bullets after us. We rushed down the hill, afraid to stop within range. At the bottom there was a control barrier for both Russians and Romanians. Would they let us through quickly enough? One more curve and there was the barrier—shut! But as we desperately approached, it lifted. The guard had formerly been one of our guard in Bran, and since he recognized the car he let us through, and shut the gate behind us. We did not pause to look back, and when Bittermann asked me laughingly if I had felt cold about the back of my neck, I quite unashamedly admitted I had.

Such experiences made me increasingly uneasy about having the children on the road, and what happened to Stefan and Niki, when they went one day to Brasov in the car with the caretaker of the castle, did not encourage me. The man left the two boys in the car, and a group of Russians approached to take it. Whether they recognized my children or not I do not know, but the market women did! With angry cries they collected a crowd, and brought pails of hot water to fight off the Russians. There was a great row, with the police being called by the Russians, but unexpectedly (at least to the Russians) taking the side of the children! In the end, the boys were forced to take eight of the Russians into the car and deliver them somewhere, but it was agreed by the Russians that they would not harm the children or take the car.

All this made me feel that it would be better if the older girls stayed in Bucarest during the school year, except for the long vacations. Arranging the new little house was great fun, and I felt that it would be an advantage to be able to meet both foes and friends freely, without compromising any of the friends. It also gave me another place to deposit things, for I was being helped more and more generously, as I shall explain later, with supplies which I could pass on unofficially or to the underground, and it was best not to have everything in one place.

During one of my discussions with Bodnaras, when I was trying to get permission for political prisoners to receive parcels from their families regularly, he asked me if I did not find Anton's prolonged "arrest" in Bran hard. I said that it was indeed not easy, especially because Anton himself was worried about conditions in Austria and longed to get back to see for himself what had happened.

"You have never asked anything for yourself," Bodnaras reminded me. "I think it is time you did. Better still, I will ask it for you. Your husband must be set free."

In spite of his good will on this subject, it took a long time before the order was put through. The King also was kind about the matter, and spoke of it repeatedly to Tatarescu, Minister of Foreign Affairs. This man had played a doubtful part in Romanian politics, and I never felt in any of my contacts with him that he was running a straight course for anyone. Although with me he was full of words and promises, nothing happened. However, once I had been encouraged to ask for Anton's freedom, I fought for it with all my might, and at last the longed-for release came, near the end of 1946, with a Romanian passport so that he could go abroad. He left for Switzerland, and remained there until the spring, trying in vain for permission to enter Austria. All he could do was to have long talks at the barrier with Colonel Zwilling, the administrator of my estate in Austria. Colonel Zwilling had only unhappy news to tell of the wanton destruction at Sonnberg by the Russians and the damage done to the property of other friends and members of Anton's family under the continuing Russian occupation; but it was a relief for both of them to be in touch with each other.

Except for the fact that Anton could not be with us, the Christmas of 1946 was a happy one. When I say "happy" I mean it in the modified sense we were becoming accustomed to. We had no critical cases at the hospital at the time, no major disaster overtook us, and the winter was not so severe as the one we had had the year before. The Turku Canal, which supplied our electric current, lacked water, so that we were often reduced to oil lamps. I rather liked this at home, but it was a serious problem in the hospital.

Far more serious than the problem of light, however, was the specter of hunger looming large everywhere, about which I shall have more to say in another chapter. Even in the preceding year children had been taken from their starving families in Moldavia and sent to regions where there was more food. This was badly organized, however, and I shudder to think of what many of those children suffered and how few of them ever found their way home; especially those who were taken out of the country and given over to the care of Big Brother Russia. Some of the children, of course, were more fortunate and found good and loving homes.

Eventually I had taken two of them, although at first I had felt unable to do this because I was already responsible for a number of stray children who had in some way or another been left to the hospital. The first one, a tiny baby whose mother had died of hemorrhage after being brought to the hospital when she was already beyond hope, I had taken into my own nursery, and the children and Gretl tried hard to save our poor little Ilie. He had not been strong enough to survive the hard winter, however, and he died. Later we had Suzi, whose suddenly widowed father brought her to us one day; then a woman came with her starving son, Gheorghitza; then a grandmother brought a deformed granddaughter—and always the parents or those responsible seemed to disappear, and the child remained with me. There were also the women who could not find work because they had young children, and to help them I finally found myself with quite a collection of half-orphans to care for, so that a nursery was started.

When this was done, I added to these so-called "resident children" the healthy children under three of mothers who needed hospital treatment. I had found that many women would not, and in fact *could* not, come to the hospital because they had no one with whom to leave their small children. Now we took them into our nursery free of charge while their mothers were being treated, and I found this one of the most useful things I ever instituted. More women came to us in time, and could be saved before their ailments became too serious. The peasant conviction that a hospital was a place where one came to die was gradually altered as they saw that one could be cured there. As one patient recommended the hospital to another, confidence in us grew, and our death rate became very low.

We had one most happy event in our immediate circle. Our dear blind officer, Sandu, while studying in Vienna, had fallen in love with a Romanian girl studying medicine there. She was lovely to look at, and—more important still—she had an utterly lovable nature. The war had trapped her in Austria, and we had had absolutely no news of what had happened to her; a circumstance which would have been dreadful for any young man in love, but which seemed even sadder because of Sandu's blindness. We all tried to keep him from being depressed. He was studying for his Ph.D. in philosophy, and I had organized several willing friends to help him with his reading.

It happened that he was in Bucarest when I received a telegram from his fiancée, whose name was also Ileana, that she had arrived at the frontier and was on her way to Bran. She knew that I would know where Sandu was, and was coming straight to me! It was perhaps one of the most happy telephone messages I was ever able to give, and at this time of suffering and despair, when everyone braced himself to expect that any news would be bad, it brought me inexpressible joy to be able to transmit good news.

They planned to be married at once, for they felt their one long and anxious parting had been enough, and as soon as she had gone to Constantza to see her parents, the wedding was arranged to take place at Bran. We had only Ileana's parents and Sandu's father and sister to stay with us, for the other guests—his brother officers and a few close friends—came only for the day. To save the expense of a wedding dress, Ileana wore one of my most beautiful national costumes, and she looked truly lovely. I wished more than ever that Sandu could see her. When I brought his bride to him, I tried to explain what she looked like. He went up to her and gently passed his hands over her, finally kneeling so that he could better picture her skirt and shoes. Never will I forget that scene: his kneeling there in front of her, "seeing" with his hands, and she with a happy smile looking down on him. I turned away and tears smarted in my eyes. I felt that I had intruded on something that was not for me to see.

A year later a son was born to them in my hospital, and became my godson. They made their home not far away with Sandu's father, who came to live with them. They ran a small farm as well as a tobacco shop in Brasov, which made it possible for me to visit them often and see how they were getting along. Ileana was so beautiful that I had sometimes feared for Sandu, but I was wrong. A more happy and harmonious couple could hardly be imagined, but the fight for mere existence was a terribly hard one. Sandu had won the highest war medal, which gave him certain awards, but he had won the medal and lost his sight outside of Odessa, on "sacred" Russian soil, so that it was nearly impossible to get any of his "rights and privileges" from the Communist government. My heart contracts painfully when I think of them today. I heard once through a third person that they had had a little girl and had lost their farm, but even that news is now old.

One of my best friends during this time was General Aldea, who in the first days of the armistice had been so good to me. After he fell from power he did not cease to be active for his country, and soon he was the head of one part of the increasingly widespread underground movements. For a relatively long time he was suspected but not caught, and was fairly free in his movements. I saw him often, although Bodnaras warned me against him and drew my attention to the fact that in his circles my association with Aldea was looked upon with disfavor. I replied that I had never let others choose my friends for me. If I had, I reminded him, I would certainly not have him for one of them! He laughed at this, but continued to disapprove. For my part, I saw to it that I never inquired too deeply into all General Aldea did, but helped where I could, asked for help when it was needed for someone, or passed messages along. I felt that the less I knew the better, since what I did not know I could not repeat—willingly or unwillingly.

One evening I had met the General at the house of a third person in Bucarest, and an amusing evening I remember it to have been. There were some exceptionally clever people there, and the conversation was full of sparkle. As we were about to break up, one of the party came back to report that there was a high-powered car waiting just behind the General's car, and evidently on the watch for him. Aldea confessed that he had been followed for some days by Ana Pauker's men, but that he thought he had given them the slip. This, I am afraid, was his great fault: he was brave, daring, and determined, but he was not wary enough, and so he was finally caught and dragged many down with him.

On that evening, however, we devised a method to get him out. I was to drive off as usual and go around the block; he would be on the watch, and on my return I would slow up, he would make a dash for my car, and we would try to run for it. Our little strategy worked well, and we got a fairly good start on the other car. I shall never forget that mad ride; up streets and down, through traffic lights, around corners on two wheels! It had all the thrills of living in an adventure movie, I assure you. When we felt we had pretty certainly lost our pursuers, I left the General at a corner not too far from his secret dwelling. It was amusing a little later to find the heavy car once more hot on my trail, and to lead my pursuers for another mad chase up streets and around corners before slowing down and driving sedately up to my own door! I am afraid I found that great fun.

Finally General Aldea was caught red-handed, and imprisoned. With him went the lady in whose house we had met, and another friend. For these two women I was able to be of real help, and to have them released, but for the General there was nothing I could do, although I tried in every way I knew. His organization was too widespread and effective for the Communists to let him go. All I could do now was to send his wife vitamins and some drugs which he was badly in need of, and here my original plea for parcels to the condemned now served my friend. With him to the prison went others I had been fond of, or had known when I was young, and the discovery of his activities brought me into serious danger as well.

One evening Mr. and Mrs. Bodnaras had dinner with me, and as we sat out on the terrace of my house after the meal, Bodnaras asked to have a few words with me alone.

"I have always warned you against your friendship with Aldea," he said, "and see now what he has told of your share in his underground work!" Taking a paper out of his pocket, he leaned forward to catch a ray of light coming from the house, and read me a part of Aldea's "confession." Every word was true! It was a stunning surprise.

I thanked God for the semi-obscurity, and kept my face in the shadow. I was also grateful for the long royal training that taught us to keep our feelings to ourselves. Even for the Gestapo and their "housesearchings" in Sonnberg I spared a grateful thought, as I quietly and firmly denied everything. I hated myself for finding prudence the better part of valor, and for dissociating myself from my friend. I would have preferred to stand up beside him, but this would have been of no use to him and would have betrayed others who were concerned as well, and who had a right to my protection. I lied smoothly and logically, and so far as I know I was never found out, nor were two other people closely concerned in his activities.

But the imprisonment of Aldea was a great sorrow to me. I was genuinely fond of the man Mr. Markham called "the distinguished and fiery General Aurel Aldea." His counsel had always been good, and his courage and valor an inspiration. What could they have done to him to make him talk? I wondered. In those days the methods of Communists for extracting "confessions" were not so generally known as they are now. It was the only lapse I ever heard of; everything else was to his credit and showed not only his own personal bravery but his ability to keep courage alive in others. I was in Argentina when I heard from someone that Mrs. Aldea had been to Aiud, the big state prison of horrible repute, to get her husband's body. God rest his soul—"in a place of light; in a place of greenness; in a place of rest."

Another great sadness awaited us in the spring of 1946. Prince Stirbey's health had been failing for some time. His wife had been for many years almost completely an invalid, and he had cared for her with touching love and devotion. Only duty ever took him from her side, and now it seemed incredible to see him ill and unable to answer her calls. I can see them in my memory now, both of them in the Princess's delightful green boudoir in Buftea, the lovely spacious home in the English-looking park; the one place that had remained completely unchanged since my childhood. It was not far from Bucarest, and I loved going to visit them whenever I could.

Although Prince Stirbey had completely retired from active political life after the unhappy armistice and "peace," he was deeply concerned over events and followed them with the burning interest of a great patriot. I had always connected him with all that was stately and fine; he preserved his dignity in the most difficult situations. Always near my parents, as their chief friend and adviser he had helped them through all the years of their successful life. As I visited him at Buftea I felt I was watching the end of the last life that bound me to the past I had loved so dearly. His advice was always something to lean upon, and his reproaches so logical and kindly that one could not be hurt by them—at least I never was. I treasure among my dearest memories those last visits I had with "Good Man," as I had named him in my childhood. His death was a shock because no one had expected it quite so soon—yet how much better it is for those who have gone. "Wherefore I praised the dead which are already dead more than the living which are yet alive" (Ecclesiastes 4:2).

His funeral was turned into a national expression of mourning even though this was frowned upon by the government. "Father" Stalin had chosen a few days earlier in a public address to insult the Prince. Nevertheless, high and low filled the church in Bucarest where the memorial service was held, but what touched me most was the ceremony in Buftea, where the peasants and the workmen from the factories on his estates followed the coffin to the family crypt. I was also deeply impressed by the dignified sorrow of the widowed Princess.

"I have been so blessed for over fifty years," she told me, "that it is now my turn to suffer." And she who spoke of her blessedness had not walked for twenty years. Three months later her youngest daughter died in Switzerland. Today, driven out of her home, Princess Stirbey is still alive but so poor that she cannot afford stamps to write to her daughter in America, the daughter who is unable to free her mother. Yet Nadeje Stirbey is one of those who never had anything but kindness for all in her heart.

One by one the representatives of the life we had known were passing away. Death and prison claimed them, and with each one died a little of our hope. We struggled valiantly against the depression and sadness, against increasing despair. We would not give in! A miracle would happen! Our friends from the West would come and help us! Surely they must by this time realize that the tide sweeping over us would not stop at the Romanian border!

Then came the news that Antonescu was again in Romania. "They" had brought him to Bucarest. No one had really known what became of him except that shortly after his arrest on the night of August 23, 1944, he had disappeared into Russia. Now he was back, to be judged by the mockery of the so-called "People's Tribunal." He was tried and condemned, not because of any mistakes he had made in governing his own country (for such mistakes could only have been judged by his own countrymen), but because he had expressed by fighting against Russia his undying conviction that Russia was Romania's enemy. It was not the voice of any "people" that spoke through that travesty of justice, but the voice of the Soviet; harsh and metallic as the mechanically magnified sound of the loudspeakers that picked up the artificial "demands" for Antonescu's death from Communist sympathizers—as I myself witnessed—and broadcast them. It was strange that I should happen to drive through University Square that day and so be able to see how this "demonstration" of the "popular will" was staged.

The square had for me many associations with the past. Every year, as far back as I could remember, I had seen the parade pass through here on our National Day, the Tenth of May. Here my father had reviewed the troops, my mother riding past him in her uniform of honorary colonel of the 4th Rosiori Regiment. Now, on this summer day so many years later, a small, uneasy crowd had assembled, and I stopped to see what they were doing. Trucks, with armed Russian soldiers on each one, were bringing loads of working men and women from nearby factories, putting them out in the square, and then returning empty for more loads of the "people." Still more armed Russian soldiers presided over this "enthusiastic" assemblage, but in spite of their presence men and women were constantly slipping off down side streets and alleys, and between the houses. For this reason the "crowd" never increased, even though the trucks continued to bring their unhappy loads to the square. Through the crowd went Party members, trying to incite and stir up cries of "Death to Antonescu! Death!" They had small success, but the voices of these artificial leaders were picked up by microphone and rebroadcast out over the square, as they were broadcast to the world, and to the courtroom where Antonescu was—no, not on trial for his life, but merely waiting the sentence of the Russians. The harsh, unnatural, inhuman sound of the amplifiers "Death! Death!" rang in my ears for a long time afterwards.

Another coincidence which I did not know about until later was that on the day Antonescu's death warrant was brought to the King, who was forced to sign it, a great feeling of inquietude was in my heart. I was still in Bucarest, and I suddenly felt that I should try to see Antonescu's old mother. I did so, leaving my car on a side street and starting off on foot from a friend's house. The elder Madame Antonescu was nearly blind, but extraordinarily active and alert. Her composure and her pride in her son were inspiring to witness. We talked long of many things, and she showed me the food parcels she had prepared to take to him that very afternoon. "For," she said joyfully, "they are at last letting me see him!"

She was allowed to see him, and he did not tell her that he would not need her loving offering, since he had only a few more hours to live. He played his part in their conversation as if there still was hope, and his mother belongs with the great mothers of tradition. When given the news she took it with calm pride and dignity. The last glimpse I had of her was some days after her son's death. She was sitting on the balcony of her house, dressed in black, the tears running slowly from her sightless eyes. I saw her from the street, but I felt there are sorrows one may not intrude upon, so I bowed my head and went on. When later someone criticized the King to her, because he had signed the death warrant, she spoke quickly and decisively.

"He had to do so, to save the country from something worse," she said. "Do you not know that if my son had had to choose between me and his country, he would not have hesitated to have had me shot?"

In her there is a picture of a Romanian mother long ago, whose words have become a part of our national heritage of pride. When her son, Stefan Cel Mare—Stephan the Great—returned, wounded and at night, from a battle in which his armies had been defeated, she spoke to him from a window of her locked and barred castle, and her words sent him back to victory.

"No son of mine would be returning alive unless he was victorious!" she told him. "Go back! You have a right to make Moldavia a nation of graves, but you have no right to leave it a nation of slaves!"

The news that Antonescu's death warrant had been signed came to me while I was walking up from the hospital to the castle. "Our death warrant has been signed, too," I said. Even now not enough facts have been told to enable history to make a judgment of Antonescu as a statesman and soldier, and I have attempted no such judgment—then or now. In my heart I have wept for the Antonescu who was my friend.

It would not be safe to tell you now how I was able to see Marshal Antonescu's widow, who had also been imprisoned in Russia, for it was a difficult arrangement involving several other people, and it was a dangerous thing for all of us. I found a sad, white-haired woman with a face almost as white as her hair, dressed in a simple, neat, black dress which was darned at the elbows and at other spots where it had evidently become threadbare. It was almost unbearable to see how she had changed. I took her in my arms and she sobbed with the dreadful hopelessness of a child in utter despair.

It was some time before she could find words to tell me about herself. Finally in a monotonous voice she began telling me of how she had been taken to Russia; of how she was changed eleven times from one prison to another, but always at night, so that she had never known where she was; of some of the tortures she had undergone; of how for a year she was kept in utter silence, and never heard the sound of a human voice; how the guards made only signals to her, and whistled when it was necessary to communicate with one another where she could hear them, so that when she was spoken to after that year she could hardly bear the pain of the unaccustomed sound. She told me how in desperation she had tried unsuccessfully to cut her veins; of how she was forced to lie with her arms outside the blanket, and that if she fell asleep and drew her arms under the folds because of the cold, she would be rudely awakened. She had had pneumonia and typhoid, and yet she did not die.

"Why?" she kept asking me desperately, tonelessly. "Why had I to live?" What impressed me most dreadfully of all at this meeting was the moment when one of those who had made my visit possible came to warn her that she must go. Terror, stark and inhuman, leaped into her eyes. Wordlessly, wringing the hands clasped in front of her, she turned to scurry away like a beaten dog. I jumped up and once more embraced her, but I felt that she was out of reach of any human sympathy.

She had been separated from her husband on August 23, 1944. She was permitted to see him once before he was killed. The Russians thought of an additional refinement of cruelty: Marshal Antonescu was made to tell her that he had been condemned to death but was not allowed to tell her the day and hour, so that for many, many days she was kept in suspense, wondering if he had yet been shot. It was a long time before she heard the story of that death; of his final courageous statement; of how the men ordered to shoot her husband missed their mark again and again; of how an officer finally finished off the wounded man with his revolver.

Later Madame Antonescu was allowed out of prison so that she could live with her ailing mother, but they were given no ration cards and so were forced to live on the bounty of others. They were guarded constantly. Madame was permitted one hour's walk every week, still under guard. One could visit them—not, of course, without risk, since a list of their visitors was sent to the government. I am glad to say that there were many who were glad to take this risk, and that even some who were more fearful at least sent supplies by the hands of the braver ones. She was one of the last people I saw before I left Bucarest for the last time. She was also one of the people who had begged that I would get through the hospital a poison she could take to avoid another imprisonment in Russia. How is it possible for you who live safely to understand a life so twisted that the kindest gift one can give a friend is a deadly poison?

Mr. Iuliu Maniu, the great leader of the National Peasant Party, was the next focus for the destroying forces of communism. His was a fine, upstanding character. Cold and reserved, he did not attract the affection of others, but all respected his integrity, whether or not they agreed with his politics. I had known him since the first days of Transylvania's union with the Greater Romania, and I grew to know him better during the government in the time of the Regency, from 1927 to 1930, when the baby Michael was king because of his father's renouncement of the throne.

Mr. Maniu had behaved with great nobility throughout the German ascendancy and the Russian occupation. As I have said in an earlier chapter, he worked constantly for an accord between Romania and the Allies, even when Romania was forced to fight on the side of Germany. During the Antonescu trial he was called to give evidence, and when he left the stand he stopped to shake hands with the already condemned man. This, Maniu told a friend later, he felt was simply the act of a man and a Christian, which he would have been a coward not to do; but it added to the Russians' hatred of him. Posters of his "crime" in shaking hands with a "criminal" were immediately pasted up everywhere by the Communists, but they only added to Maniu's already enormous popularity and to the conviction that Antonescu had been unjustly tried and condemned. Next to the King, Maniu was undoubtedly the most popular man in the country. He and his party came to stand for everything that was lost: freedom, equality, democracy, justice.

The elections of 1946, which followed the "compromise" of the Moscow Conference, when King Michael had been forced to accept a discredited government supported only by Russia, were supposed to be "free." They were instead carefully organized by the Communists to be anything *except* free, after a systematic reign of terror at gatherings throughout the country, designed to show Romanians that it was not safe to oppose the Communist government. To make sure that the Communist Party received a convincing majority, a large number of the electorate were deprived of their votes: for example, all known non-Communists, all men who had fought on Russian soil (and their families), and all those who had held any office between 1940 and 1945. To make up for this, all foreigners who had entered the country within the past three months (especially Russians) were given a vote, and those felt to be "dependable" were given five to seven votes.

Nevertheless even these precautions did no good. One of the "dependable" women said laughingly to me, "I'll vote one for them, because I have to or I would be caught, but six of my votes go to Maniu!" To the surprise and fury of the Russians, the vote went eighty per cent against the Communists, and nothing was left for them to do but to suppress all *facts* about the election, and simply announce the lie that the Communist Party had received over eighty per cent of the votes cast! The fraud was so flagrant that official notes protesting the election were sent by Great Britain and the United States. No attention was paid to these notes by the Soviet government.

The fact that the people almost to a man had voted for Maniu added heavily to the counts against him, but he was permitted to live out of prison until the summer of 1947. Then Romania was invited to join the Marshall plan, and the Groza government, under pressure from Russia, refused. Maniu's paper, *Dreptatea (Justice)*, wished to publish this fact, but it was of course a piece of news immediately censored. *Dreptatea* then went to press with the resulting empty spaces filled by quotations from the American Declaration of Independence. A few days later Maniu and his chief follower, Mihalache, were arrested, and the paper forbidden to be published. The National Peasant Party was liquidated and outlawed in July, 1947, and Maniu was condemned to life imprisonment on November 11, 1947, after another travesty of a trial.

In Romania it was as if one stood on an island of sand, the sides of which were constantly falling in great chunks into the sea, leaving the space on which one was standing ever smaller.

Communist rally in Bucharest

Ileana
1951

TWENTY-SIX

IT WAS not possible for me to think only of the difficulties I knew in Bucarest, for there were also worries at home. A new epidemic of typhoid broke out in the summer of 1946, and we settled down to an attempt to cope with it on a larger and more systematic scale then we had used before. The investigations we made, and our struggles with everything from superstition and inertia to red tape, would make too long a story to tell here, but I must mention that the hospital staff and I made regular personal contributions, as well as official ones, to this concentrated effort. We worked to educate the people in the most hygienic methods of defense; in the free use of DDT and of inoculation. Every Sunday all of the doctors and nurses would scatter up the various valleys to the churches, where we could be reasonably sure of finding the villagers all together, and would try with the help of the priest to convince the people that they should be inoculated. Since the injections bring a painful reaction, it was not an easy matter to get them to come a second and third time, and the keeping of records was far from simple. Because the houses were widely spread over hills and dales, many miles of real mountain climbing had to be done before the job in any one area could be considered at all complete.

It seemed to me an irony of fate that my son Dominic should at this time come down with typhoid, and I found myself terrified at once. My youngest brother Mircea, whom I had adored, had died of this dread disease during World War I. Long after he was no longer conscious of anything, his baby voice called my name, hour after hour, and it was something I had never forgotten. Always the work with children was hardest for me, in all my hospital experience, for the cries of a child in pain or delirium brought back those anguished days of my own childhood when I had lost my baby brother. To my deep joy, Niki's case proved to be a light one, and I was able to nurse him at home because my invaluable Frau Koller volunteered once more to be isolated with the patient, as she had done when Minola had scarlet fever. I found also that Niki's illness had a good effect on the peasants in our countryside. They seemed to feel that if my son could get typhoid no one was safe; and they came in greater numbers to let themselves be inoculated.

During the fall I found that my back was giving me increasing trouble. I had always suffered to some extent from arthritis, but now I developed a severe and hampering pain. In addition to my regular work, there had been too many occasions when I must lift and carry heavy bodies, or strain to push cars, or shovel snow when we were forced to travel in bad weather. I was advised to have X-ray treatment, which had to be done at Brasov at a very early hour, and which complicated my daily schedule no little. This was the beginning of the crippling condition that is still under treatment, although I was able to keep fairly active until after we had reached South America.

I have spoken of the Christmas of 1946, when Anton was in Switzerland trying vainly to get permission to go to Austria, and I mentioned that it was a quietly happy one, with no major difficulties, and with the typhoid epidemic at last definitely seeming to be ending. What I did not mention was the fact that to our parcels in 1946 were added some from our very special American friends, and I would like to speak of them now. Many people came to look at Bran, for it was a unique and lovely castle, but few really stayed and took an interest in the inhabitants of our little village. Some did not wish to and some were not able to; but there were some who did, and who have remained staunch friends ever since—not only to me and my family, but to many of my countrymen and to Romania in general.

The first I would like to mention is Bishop O'Hara (now Archbishop) of the Roman Catholic Church, who was appointed regent of the Apostolic Nunciature in Bucarest in May, 1946, but because of delays in obtaining a visa did not arrive in Bucarest until January, 1947. He was the first American to be appointed to our country in this capacity. The former appointees had kept within the strict official confines of their duties, but Archbishop O'Hara had a different view of what his work should be. He decided to know this country he was accredited to, and he toured it from one end to the other, visiting not only his own churches but going to other places where he had heard there was distress. I can say with envy that he has explored parts of Romania where even I have never been! He not only visited but he seemed to love and understand the country and the people. A great quantity of food and medicine had earlier been sent by Pope Pius XII to Romania and distributed by the Romanian Red Cross, but in March, 1947, the Catholic War Relief was organized on extensive lines. This was an untold blessing that reached far out to many an abandoned village, where food, medicine, and clothing were distributed without regard to religion or nationality. Archbishop O'Hara did not confine his own personal efforts to those of his own church, and I have never known him deaf to any appeal of mine. It was in great part due to him that we were able to run the camp for refugee girls that I have already mentioned.

In one instance he was, to be sure, indirectly responsible for getting an innocent man into trouble, but no one could have foreseen this would happen! Archbishop O'Hara had sent extra food to the school that Stefan attended, but the directions on the boxes were printed in English. The Commandant bought an English dictionary in order to translate them, and the poor man was instantly pounced upon as a "capitalist sympathizer," and nearly lost his position. Because of this and other similar incidents, so typical of the Russian Communists, the labels were later printed in Romanian, which made things much easier. The Archbishop remained at his post, working under difficulties which one day may be more widely known, until he was forcibly obliged to leave the country in 1950. He is a great Christian and a great American, and the Romanian people will long be grateful to him.

Another American friend was Sergeant Wilmer Park, who with his friend Mr. Albanasi came once to visit someone staying with us, and then came often after that to visit us. It was through these men that I got the first messages over to friends in the United States, and it was they who got for me the badly needed American textbooks of nursing that became wells of knowledge and help to me. In gratitude I feel I must list them here. They were for me the substitute for the medical schools and libraries so easily accessible to you in this country, but which I did not have: *The Principles and Practice of Nursing*, by Harmer and Henderson; *Nursing: an Art and a Science*, by Tracy; *The Textbook of Anatomy and Physiology*, by Kimber, Gray, and Stackpole. I have those very volumes now on the bookshelves of my home in Newton. The Communists, you see, allowed me to bring those books with me, since they were texts which would enable me to earn a living as a "worker," instead of remaining a "parasite" upon society. All other books which had not already been destroyed by the Russians in Sonnberg were retained as the property of the state, including those irreplaceable ones autographed and given me by my mother.

These American textbooks were a priceless gift to the work of the hospital. I began translating chapters to read to my nurses. I adapted certain charts and diagrams, and I was inspired by others in the texts to create original ones for our use. I dreamed of one day getting permission from the authors to translate and adapt the books for Romania. Perhaps, I thought sometimes with a determined cheerfulness, they might be our first texts in the School for Nurses that I hoped to establish.

Among our new friends was also Lieutenant Colonel Krichbaum, M.D., who was medical attendant to the American Mission. He, too, traveled the country far and wide. He grew to know and love it, and to understand the spirit of the people and the depth and strength of their resistance to the Russian oppression. Colonel Fred G. Sigerist, the head of the American Red Cross, also was unfailing in his efforts to help, and we have him to thank for the generous gift from the President of the United States, in March, 1947, of a shipload of rations for the starving population of Moldavia.

The kindness of these men, so different from one another and yet so alike in spirit, was my first experience of the generosity of the Americans, of their lack of resentments and of their desire to help the neighbor. Their gifts under our Christmas tree reminded me of the night so many years before, when Father Christmas had come to a little Romanian girl in Jassy. There were so many small kindnesses done, which I cannot mention here for lack of time and space. I shall never cease to be grateful, for example, to those who gave me the Armed Services Editions of American books, which did so much to help me escape for a little while in my mind to a different world.

In February of 1947 we received the wonderful and heartening news of the shipload of food from President Truman, which was to be distributed by the Red Cross to the distressed regions of Moldavia. What seemed most extraordinary to me was that the Communist government had accepted this, under certain restrictions, and had given the necessary authority to the railroads for transporting the supplies. It was, of course, a tremendous undertaking to distribute the food, and it needed a great deal of technical knowledge to plan it so that nothing could go wrong. The problem was solved in an interesting way. The Red Cross appealed for volunteers, and nearly the whole of the General Staff of our army, besides many other officers—all of whom had been forced to resign in 1945—offered their services to this project. Mr. Costinescu, President of the Romanian Red Cross, gave full powers to General Mardari, a most capable general and a former royal aide-de-camp—and one of those victims later deported to Russia by the Communists.

The whole plan was set up like a veritable military campaign, under the supervision of the Red Cross and representatives from the American Military Mission under Brigadier General Schuyler. Experienced civilians and former Red Cross workers filled up the ranks. Since at this time the hospital was running quite smoothly, I volunteered my services, and asked my dear friend Mrs. Podgoreanu to go too. She agreed to come with me, and certainly she is to be thanked for the good results we obtained, and for the orderliness and thoroughness with which our branch of the expedition worked. I only smilingly carried out and passed along the orders she had thought out, with perhaps a little more tact added than she would have used.

I had asked that if it were possible I might be permitted to go to the region of Piatra Neamtz, in the northern part of Moldavia and in the valley of the Bistritza. During World War I, I had spent a happy summer there, away from the horrors of Jassy and the war, and it was there I had first learned to love and respect the Romanian peasant. There, too, I had obtained the foundation for my really quite thorough knowledge of the Romanian language, for it is the peasants who are its real guardians. It is a truly beautiful archaic language, and my mastery of it is one of the things I do pride myself on.

The Red Cross agreed to my request, and so did the King and the government. I then asked if it would be possible for me to be housed in a railway carriage, so that I could avoid the necessity of accepting anyone's hospitality, for I realized that anyone who entertained me might endanger himself. I half hoped that I could have my old carriage, in which I had traveled so widely all over the country in the days before I was married. It had been decorated according to my own taste, and because I was so passionately fond of the sea I had had it made to resemble a ship. However, it existed no more, for it had been destroyed in one of the bombardments, and therefore a ministerial one was found for me. It was fairly comfortable, and it not only could be heated independently, but it had a sort of kitchenette in it, which added to its usefulness. I must say that I felt a certain thrill of pleasure when everyone assembled and we left from the central station of Bucarest. My party included Mrs. Podgoreanu and two of my nurses, with three other girls from Bran, and seven people chosen by headquarters, making a "team" of fourteen. We traveled all night, so that we would reach Piatra, the capital of the region, well ahead of the first trainload of provisions.

It was a raw and cold March morning when we arrived, but the sun was shining. Although I had been warned that this was a "Red" town, I was given a fairly large reception and invited to have breakfast in a private home, where I began finding out exactly what the situation was in the city. To my delight I met there my father's old librarian and trusted friend, who was a great help to me. I learned that the most difficult person to deal with would be the Prefect, the administrative head of the region, who was a strong member of the Communist Party. He was described to me as a capable administrator, however, and by no means a bad man, but as one who was not at all friendly with the Red Cross, and was aggressively on the alert for anti-Communist sentiment and activities.

Immediately after breakfast I called the local authorities together for a meeting with the Red Cross executives, Mrs. Podgoreanu and myself. I explained that I was only a woman, with little knowledge of how to direct activities and with absolutely no information as to the town's resources, the state of the roads, or how many supplies would have to be transported. However, I said, I knew that they would be able to take care of the situation, since Mr. Prefect was known even in Bucarest for his splendid talents in organization, and I was leaving it all to him. He and the men of the Red Cross could work it out, I was sure, and I would follow the lines they laid down for me. The supply train was due that evening, and would they please come to my carriage at five o'clock so that we could decide on any final minor details? At six in the station waiting room, I suggested, we could meet with our different teams, including the local organization, and Mr. Prefect would lay the plans before them and give them their instructions.

I could see that I had won the first round, so I bowed politely and left the meeting. I spent the intervening time seeing some old friends, for it was deeply moving to me to return to this little mountain town, so proud of its past, which I had visited often as a child when we spent that war-time summer in Bicaz. When the group met again I found the arrangements could not possibly be improved upon, and the meeting in the station went off equally well. Later I was told that in the last three years no one had dared mention publicly the King, the Americans, or God: I had mentioned all of them in my speech, and neither had the heavens fallen nor had Mr. Prefect walked out on the meeting!

Our work began the next morning at six o'clock. Mr. Prefect was there promptly, keeping a wary eye on me, but this did not at all disturb me. In fact, I was delighted to have him with me, because in that way I also knew more or less what he was up to. I had no intention of allowing the American Relief to be made into a Party weapon. We watched each other carefully: we were inseparable companions for at least fourteen hours of every one of the next sixteen days. Neither of us could have done much harm in the remaining ten hours, for we were much too tired. I once said to him, "What will you do when I have gone?" and he replied grimly, "Sleep and eat!"

That first morning we had to take over the control of the goods shipped in, and have those for the Bistritza valley carried into a narrow-gauge train and into trucks. This was done by soldiers and workmen, and we had to watch carefully because they, too, were very hungry, and to see such quantities of food was a great temptation to them. It was a cold and thankless job to check the transportation of these supplies, and it was exhausting both physically and emotionally. The American observer for our section, a nice officer whose name and rank I am sorry to have forgotten, appeared in the course of the morning and advised me to take a rest. He offered to share his breakfast ration with me, so I invited him to my carriage—which he found, I think, much less grand than he had expected. In fact, I could find but one plate for the lot of us.

"But," I said, "notice that it has a gold rim, and don't say I did not treat you royally!"

This broke the ice, and we all laughed together. I returned to my post warmed and strengthened, and soon everything was loaded and we were able to start off on the day's round. A gentleman had kindly put himself and his car at our disposal, and although the car was both antediluvian and temperamental it plowed surprisingly well through mountains of snow and rivers of mud. It was really extraordinary how well it did get us to most places, although I could not help teasing the driver once by telling him that I had pushed his car more miles than I had sat in it. Mr. Prefect had been forced to push, too. He had at first been a little surprised that I evidently expected him to help, but he soon joined me quite cheerfully. This really assisted us in becoming friends of a sort, for two people cannot remain stiff and hostile after they have many times been pushing together at the rear of a car that suddenly bounces forward and leaves them to fall face foremost into the same snowdrift. Sharing a military ration and breaking an apple in half and in half again to make it go around also are things which make for a certain creation of mutual sympathy.

Mrs. Podgoreanu went in another car so that we could cover greater distances and at the same time "follow up" on the distribution, for our routes were arranged to cross each other. In this way we visited thirty-eight villages in sixteen days, which was quite an accomplishment when one considers the condition of the roads and the terrible, changeable weather, which shifted from snow storms to sudden thaws and back again. A team was sent to each village, and they were responsible for the fair distribution of the provisions and for controlling the lists. Mrs. Podgoreanu's car and ours then drove from one village to another to see how things went, to settle difficulties and misunderstandings, and to explain things; tasks which were far from easy.

The misery we saw was appalling. The first thing that struck me was the extraordinary emptiness of the villages. Normally they would have been overflowing with people, children, and all kinds of sheep, dogs, geese, and hens, but now there were no animals at all. Anyone who had a cow was fabulously wealthy, he who had a few hens was rich, and the man who had flour or corn in his house was considered amazingly blessed with earthly goods. To choose which families were poorest was not simple where all were hungry, and yet there was not enough to give each family something. Lists of those who were to be helped had been made up in advance, and each list was read out to the assembled villagers for their agreement to it. Rarely did they suggest that someone's name be taken from the list, but always they named those left out who were still more unfortunate than the ones selected. Very well, the team would say, then who shall be taken off the list in their place? But they were all so poor! How could anyone decide?

I cannot make clear to you who have not seen it the heartbreak of such a situation nor do I wish to burden you with pictures of distress. Yet it is people in such conditions as these about whom I have heard Americans say, "But why do they not revolt against the Communists?" One does not always remember that not only is a certain physical strength required to *revolt* but also that prolonged misery produces in the end a dazed and stunned spiritual and moral state which leaves the individual partially paralyzed. Perhaps one illustration is enough to show how things were, and I choose one more pleasant than many I saw. One afternoon when I had gone hack to my carriage in the railway station I was eating an apple, and I threw the core outside. It fell into a dirty puddle of black, slimy water, but a child standing near threw himself ravenously upon it and gobbled it up. At first I stared, horrified, and then I rushed in to get him the rest of my ration for that day, but I could do that very seldom. Mrs. Podgoreanu, Bittermann, and, I were allowed American five-day rations, which made up the bulk of the provisions sent from the United States, for our own use, but we had to be extremely economical with them. We had to share ours with the two soldiers sent to guard me, whom the authorities found it unnecessary to feed, and with the railway attendant. Fortunately, the rest of our team of fourteen had been lodged in the town and received rations there.

When we arrived at Bicaz, where I had spent the summer of 1918, I felt a tremendous emotion. Every corner spoke to me of my father and mother, of my sisters, and of our loved Canadian friend, Colonel Boyle, whom I called "Uncle Joe." I looked into the dear white house on the very edge of the rapid Bistritza, where I had spent so many hours as a little girl watching the swiftly passing rafts, but I found it ravaged by the invaders. My mother's room, kept always as she had left it, was now empty and its windows were broken. I wanted to share my memories with someone, but of those who had come with me there was no one who had been there before. I left the house and returned to the waiting peasants, and from the crowd stepped a woman.

"*Domnitza, nu'tzi amintesti*–Domnitza, do you not remember?"

What sweeter words could I have heard? Of course she remembered, and so did many of the others. There was hardly a village, a monastery, or a convent which I visited where I was not greeted by these words. There were women I had played with when they, too, were children, and older people who remembered many of the details of events I had almost forgotten. It was always hard to leave them; there was so much we could have talked about. But I had work to do, and I could spend little time in talking of things past, no matter how much it might have warmed my heart. Often, too, I found not only the past of my childhood, but also a bridge between those days and the present. Once at a small station there were police holding the crowd back, and suddenly a disturbance began far at the rear. A hand appeared, waving a paper, and a man's voice cried:

"But I must see the Domnitza! She is, I tell you, my friend! See, here is a card she wrote me!"

When I insisted that he be allowed to come to the car I found that he was one of my Romanian wounded, a soldier who had lost his arm and had been in a hospital in Leipzig. To those men so far away that I could not visit them as regularly as I did the ones in Vienna I tried to send postcards at frequent intervals, and this soldier had kept a picture of Sonnberg through all these years. With him, too, there were many things to speak of and remember, but only a little time before the train had to go on.

On the whole, the help sent to Moldavia was greater from a moral standpoint than from a physical one. The five-day rations we distributed as evenly as possible did not add a great deal to the total food of any one village, and they were completely foreign to the peasant. He naturally could not read the English directions, which in each village we had to explain, while we also supplied a mimeographed translation for later reference. A piece of coconut chocolate meant little to a peasant child who had never tasted coconut or chocolate. It was difficult to make his parents understand that a little pouch of powder could produce a satisfying and nourishing soup for the family. The excellent crackers did not make up to them for bread or *mamaliga*—the thick corn porridge that is the basis of their diet.

Yet morally the effect of this distribution was much greater than one might realize. The people felt that indeed they were not forgotten; that the friends in America whom they had never wanted to fight had understood, and had sent them help. I witnessed many touching scenes, when in spontaneous speeches, under the disapproving scowls of the ever-present Communists, I was delegated by the people to thank the Americans for what they had done. I shall be happy if in some measure, through the medium of this book, I am able at last to transmit to my American readers the truly warm and unfeigned thanks of my people who have remained behind the Iron Curtain, and, as a nation caged and enslaved, cannot voice their thanks for themselves. For my own part, I am deeply grateful also for the opportunity those days gave me to revisit another part of my distressed country before I was compelled to leave it forever.

There was another thing about this distribution of the American Relief supplies which I believe would have touched you. It was the almost reverent appreciation of the peasants for the sacks of peas that came with the rations. In every village, before any were eaten, people waited to see whether or not the peas would grow if they were planted, and when they found the seed would sprout they set it aside to plant. You must remember that these people had no seed for the coming year and no tools with which to work the ground. Everything had been carried away, even to the hoes and spades and rakes, so that they would literally have to use their hands to plant and cultivate the soil. Hungry as they were, they still set aside something which could be multiplied for the coming year, even though it meant that more of them would die in the meantime. It was the supposedly Communist ideal, which the Communists actually do not practice, here carried out by the free will of the people. Because they themselves were honest they could in truth sacrifice themselves as individuals to the good of "society," even though they would not have described their action in such terms. But no such plan can be *imposed* on any group, for this imposition not only fails to determine whether there exists the necessary integrity but destroys such integrity if it does exist.

Ileana 1951

TWENTY-SEVEN

THE WHOLE project of the American food ship was an immense success, and it did more to restore a faith in the friendship of the American people than anything else could have done—except, of course, an implemented effort to assist the Romanians in regaining their freedom. However, even the good impression made by this gift of food could not but annoy the Communists, and they turned almost at once to increasingly open disapproval of the outside relief agencies in Romania. The Romanian Red Cross itself was one of the first to suffer, both the organization and its individual officers and members being attacked. The government first arrested the General Secretary for dishonesty, a charge which they were never able to prove, and which was particularly cruel because he was very ill at the time. I visited him regularly, and realized how seriously such an undeserved accusation had affected him, both mentally and physically. Somewhat later the government arrested the Honorary President, Mrs. Irina Sturdza, a woman of such integrity of character that the injustice of the act was apparent to everyone. With her to prison went her husband, her two sons, and a daughter-in-law. Since the Honorary President in the Romanian Red Cross had an important role in the organization, this arrest struck deep, The Queen was in Sinaia at the time, and sent hurriedly for me to go to Bucarest and do what I could to liberate Mrs. Sturdza and her family.

I was more than happy to do so, not only for the Red Cross but also for Sitta, and I did not encounter too much opposition in my efforts. Almost at once I was able to have Mrs. Sturdza, one son, and the daughter-in-law released, and later her husband was freed, but it was six months before the other son was out of prison—partly because I had great difficulty in finding where he had been taken. It is a feature of the Communist system to make those arrested simply disappear, so that one not only knows nothing of the charges but has no idea whether the victim has been killed, sent to Russia, or is around the next corner being secretly tortured.

In making inquiries about the Sturdzas I discovered that the general feeling was an unquiet one and that radical changes in the entire Red Cross were being demanded by the government. I suddenly found myself in the position of mediator in the matter, a position which absorbed a great part of my time and energy. I had endless discussions with Bodnaras, the Ministry of Health, and Ana Pauker. I arranged interviews between these government officials and the leading Red Cross representatives, taking care not to be present myself at any of the meetings in order to remain as impersonal a go-between as possible. Colonel Sigerist, who had been in Geneva for a time, now returned in the interests of the deposits left by the American Red Cross, since these were in danger of being sent to help the Communist Marko in Greece. To my surprise I found myself also mediating in the American interests, which showed once more how little the Communists cared what Americans said or did. The hatred and disdain that the Communists nourish for all things connected with the United States, and that amount to an obsession, were once more clearly in evidence, but I was happy to be able to bring about a successful interview between Colonel Sigerist and Bodnaras. It was now the summer of 1947, and I had hoped to go to the sea for two weeks with my family. Everything had been arranged: a friend had lent us a house on an isolated beach south of Constantza, with the delightful name of Man-japunar, and we were all looking forward to the expedition. However, the fight for the survival of the Romanian Red Cross in a form acceptable to the international organization dragged on and on, so that finally I decided to send Anton and the children on ahead. I saw them off, wondering if I would really ever manage to get there. It was hot and dry in Bucharest, my back troubled me increasingly, and the discussions continued endlessly. At long last things seemed to be settled in a possible fashion, and I also could leave—but my rest was short-lived.

Only a few mornings later I came downstairs to find a messenger from Bucharest literally sitting on the doorstep. He brought word of a new law being passed which would arbitrarily change and thus destroy the entire Red Cross, but it had not yet been signed. Could I not return to Bucharest and try once more? A ten hours' drive over impossible dusty roads by day, or a night on a train with no sleeping accommodations! I felt an overwhelming exhaustion at the thought of facing either possibility. Then a brilliant idea came to me. Ghiorghiu Dej, Minister of Communications and one of the supreme heads of the Party, was taking a vacation in a smart residence nearby, at what had formerly been a fashionable summer resort. I walked to the next village, which had a telephone, and to the enormous astonishment of the operator I asked for Comrade Minister Dej. And who dared such a thing? Domnitza Ileana? Not possible! But at last I did get put through to this great "representative of the people," and he graciously agreed to sacrifice one or two of his remaining hours of rest to see me, for he was about to leave for Bucharest.

Up I drove in my car to a grand and extremely well-guarded residence. Certainly these days, I thought, the "representatives of the people" leave nothing to chance nor to the "love" of the people they are supposed to represent! Dej himself I had always found quite a nice man. He was simple and childlike in his enjoyment of the situation which had made a workman "top dog," and he could not help boasting about it every second minute—a bit of human behavior which made him somehow pathetic, until one reflected on the ruin that had been brought on the country by using such well-meaning but stupid people as the tools of intelligently evil forces. I once more pleaded the cause of the Red Cross, and he promised that he would not sign the decree: a promise he kept, although eventually it had no restraining influence on the course of events.

I may as well finish the story now by telling you that eventually a general assembly was forced upon the Red Cross, in an attempt to make the desired changes appear to be brought about legally. When this move was blocked, the meeting was stormed by ruffians and a real fight took place in which several women were severely injured, among them two nurses who had served at the front. The disturbance was promptly blamed on the Red Cross by the government, and a new executive committee was named, a so-called provisional one. Some of the former workers were kept on, but there was a divergence of opinion as to whether one should try to work with the new organization or express disapproval of it by withdrawing. I personally felt that as long as no Red Cross law of procedure was broken and the members made no political moves, they should try to remain long enough to save for Romania whatever materials they could by large and rapid distribution, for once more there loomed up the danger of everything being sent to Marko's forces in Greece.

Eventually this policy was adopted, but too late to save much. I remember that when the Communist guard came to supervise my leaving Bran I still had a whole roomful of former Red Cross supplies which had been desperately distributed at the last minute but which I had not had time to send along to the underground. The guards were Communists, but they were also Romanians and knew the suffering of their own people. Rather than confiscate the packages for foreign Party members, they allowed them to be sent over to my hospital, where they could continue to serve Romanians. But this is getting ahead of my story. The fight to keep the Red Cross of Romania a part of the International Red Cross was finally lost. Other organizations, including that of CARE, likewise went down to defeat. Swedish Relief, including a special "Save the Children" fund, which had fed 60,000 children daily for six months, was forced to withdraw in 1948. Monsignor John C. Kirk, Secretary of the Nunciature, had been in full charge of the Catholic War Relief services in Romania since the spring of 1947, when the government had refused permission for the return of Mr. Thomas Fox, who had opened the service a few weeks before. I have already spoken of the vast area these services had covered, but the difficulties of operating them increased constantly until in the fall of 1948 Monsignor Kirk was finally forced by the government to terminate this Relief.

My own vacation at Constantza had been cut short, as I have explained, but even the time I spent there was complicated by a number of difficulties which ranged from the serious to the somewhat amusing. By this time the entire country was in a state of nerves, and people hardly dared trust anyone. The most absurd stories were avidly picked up and circulated, and all sorts of improbable rumors were seized upon by the secret police in an effort to prove to the Party headquarters how alert and active their representatives were. An unfortunate family out on a rubber raft one afternoon had incautiously waved gaily to friends on shore and called "Good-bye! We're going to America!" They had promptly been arrested, and the raft impounded by the police. Anton, not knowing any of this background, tried to arrange to borrow the "detained" raft, and at once the rumor spread that we also were going to escape to America in that inadequate and unlucky craft. When I came down from Bucarest and the Red Cross meetings there, Bodnaras had told me that if it was necessary for me to get back quickly he would send his plane for me, and I mentioned to someone the fact that I might be leaving by air. My remark was at once added to the "escape" story, and later Bodnaras showed me with considerable amusement the detailed report of all this, made to him by the local Communist police. He found it extremely funny that it was *his* plane for which the vigilant guards watched, in order to prevent my leaving for America in it.

But none of this seemed really humorous to me, for it spoke sadly of the wreckage of what had been a happy, growing country. All about me were other examples of this destruction. I love the sea, and Constantza had been the dream place of my childhood holidays. The Romanian navy was small but good, and because our mother had been the daughter of a sailor—her father had been commander first of the British Mediterranean Fleet and then of the Home Fleet—we children were brought up to know and love all that had to do with the sea and ships. From childhood I had known all our ships, both those of the Royal Navy and the commercial vessels. Later, as a young girl, my love for the sea and sailing led me to take up the study of navigation. Then, because I found that no one thought I was serious or knew what I was talking about, I took my Master's examination at the Royal School for Navigation in Constantza, and passed with quite a good average for a girl, especially one who had had to do her studying at odd times. Later my son Stefan, filling out an application blank for his admission to the Massachusetts Institute of Technology, was to be quite cheered when he remembered this, since it enabled him to fill in the blank for schools from which his mother had graduated!

Constantza meant much to me, and I wanted to show it properly to the children, and to arrange a sail for them. I was therefore bitterly disappointed not only to find the town terribly damaged by the war, but to be forbidden by a Russian guard to enter the port. Finally the Romanian Admiral turned up and intervened. He had when young once been out sailing with me and five others on a memorable occasion when we were caught in a storm, and driven before the wind for a good part of the night. How long ago that seemed! And now we met again, arguing with our Russian oppressors. I told him that I had wanted to see our ships, or at least those the Russians had deigned to return to us—for in 1944 they had quite unjustly seized our shipping. His eyes filled with tears.

"They are in a terrible condition," he told me. "And no one can go on board without permission from Bucarest."

I turned away, heartsick for both him and myself but feeling still more bitterly sorry for our country. It was finally arranged that the family could all visit the big sailing training ship, *Mircea*, and have a sail on one of its boats, but it was not like the old days. We were received on board with royal honors, for the officers and men had insisted on this, once our visit was known to be permitted. The children were pleased and amused to find themselves "piped over the side" by the bosun as they came on board, and to learn that this was a relic of the old days, when honored visitors were hauled on board in a basket, and the bosun's whistle was the signal to pull it up. The sailors formed ranks, the officers formally presented themselves, and a guard of honor stood at attention, but the spirit was dead even though we tried to pretend that it was a happy reunion and that we did not feel the presence of spies and traitors among us. For on the *Mircea* there was one who had returned with the Tudor Vladimirescu, and who wore the hated sign on his arm. This boy had belonged to an aristocratic family with a proud tradition of service to their country, and he was the only son. When he returned he went at once to his home, but his father looked at him without recognition.

"But do you not know me, Father?" the young man asked. "I am your son!"

"No, I do not know you," the old gentleman had answered. "I once had a son, but he died in Russia!"

Knowing the story, I looked at him as he stood this day in the group with the rest of us, and I felt sorry for him, for though he was not openly excluded from the others, there was a wall between him and them which he could not pass.

I made one more attempt to bring back the past for my children. We paid a visit to the magnificent beach of Mamaia, upon which my parents had built a lovely Italian villa. There as a young girl I had occasionally given dances on August 15, our Navy Day. At first I could not find the spot, so many houses had grown up around it. They were all ruined now, and as we walked about among them I suddenly recognized the villa by its shape. It, too, was a ruin. Wiring and piping had been wrenched out of the walls, the fireplaces were broken to bits, and out of the floors over which our dancing feet once trod so lightly weeds were growing. Why had I tried to go back? I thought. What sad pictures the children would carry of these places, once green and gracious. My vision of what had been was not strong enough to be transmitted to them. One should never try to revisit the past.

But I must not be ungrateful. Manjapunar held for me no memories, and there the sea and the sand and the open spaces brought their healing and gave me strength to return to what lay ahead. I thought much, however, during those days by the sea, of my children and of their lives. In a way my attempt and my failure to re-create for them my own small part of the past in Constantza was a picture of the inevitable failure I felt I was facing in trying to re-create for them the past of my country: a past which had held freedom and a brotherhood of striving for the common goal of our Romania Mare.

An intellectual plague was slowly creeping over us, which was far more serious and fatal than the epidemic of typhoid had been. Slowly but surely Communist doctrines were being instilled into all the schools. History was being changed to suit the Party line. In one of the schools attended by my older daughters this was done quite simply and openly. The teachers collected the history textbooks and carried them to the courtyard, where they put them ceremonially on a fire around which the entire school stood in a circle. In this way the girls could clearly appreciate the lesson that the past and everything taught about it had been wrong and false, and must be destroyed. In other schools the old textbooks were confiscated and others were substituted. It was forbidden to mention any historical event not listed in the text, or to supplement the Communist account and interpretation of these events. I had been shocked to discover that in these new histories the reign of King Carol I was mentioned only in connection with the revolt of the peasants in 1907. Nothing else in his reign of thirty-three years was referred to, although he had freed Romania from the Turks and made it an independent country. The reign of my father—thirteen years in which Romania Mare had been established and had prospered in its development—was referred to once only, where it was said that "the uprising of 1919" took place under his rule.

Needless to say, the truth of the "uprising" was not told, and because I remembered it well the implications of this new history text seemed unbelievably flagrant in their lies. In Bucarest in 1919 there had been indeed a small riot, lasting less than a day, which had been fostered by the Communists but which had died down at once. I remembered how, when my father heard of it, he and the very popular Prime Minister, Marshal Avarescu, had got into the car—after a small altercation as to which one should drive, won by my father—and had gone to the square with no thought of guards or weapons to protect them. There they found a mild fight being carried on between the only troops then in town and the workmen who had been stirred up. It ended almost at once in colossal cheers for the King, who then made arrangements to adjust whatever grievance of the postwar conditions it was that had been used to get up a crowd.

In the same arbitrary way in which history was rewritten, many poets and writers were "purged" from our literature. They no longer existed: they had never been. Pictures of Romanian kings and queens, of heroes and statesmen, were taken out of the schoolbooks and those of Stalin and Groza were substituted. In Stefan's school the infiltration was more subtle and gradual. Textbooks were abandoned rather than solemnly burned, but the students and teachers were not allowed to have them in their possession. "Lectures" were substituted for texts in all classes except mathematics, where it was permitted to use printed problems. The indoctrination in Communist theory was introduced as a course in "general education," said to "supplement and round out" the formal courses. Like the camel in the tent of the Arab, this course gradually absorbed more and more of the students' time and became more and more specifically directed. The method of instruction used deserves more time than I can give it here, but in general it cleverly directed the students so that they believed they were drawing their own "impartial" conclusions, when actually they were being driven blindly along in the desired direction. It is a method characteristic of the Communists, and it has been used on a smaller scale by individual instructors who are Party members and hold positions in schools and colleges in many countries.

Eventually this course in "general education" not only used time and energy, but the grade in it counted fifty per cent of the total grade for the year. All other courses of study, all grades in military drill and in conduct, were averaged together, but counted only fifty per cent of the mark. This put the Party representative in the school in absolute control of the student body, since failure in the "education" course meant failure for the school year, and there was no possibility of re-examination or of appeal. Besides the disruptive effect of this policy on the other studies, the morale of the school was destroyed by the gradual setting up of a spy system, so that each boy knew he was being spied upon by some of his fellow students. Rarely did he know who was doing it, of course, although Stefan was warned by one of his "watchers" because of the real and deep friendship they had always had. A pressure system was used to enforce this spy system, which in a few rare cases attempted to work by rewards, but which because of the high moral caliber of the boys finally depended on blackmail and threats involving the safety of some member of the boys' families.

In the village school still attended by my younger children there had originally been a less noticeable effect because of the age of the group and because the teachers were at first left in comparative freedom. After all, it took a little time for the Party to "get around" to everyone! The children were forced to attend Soviet propaganda films and to learn songs and recite pledges of love and loyalty to the Communist government, but even in the primary schools there was resistance to the process. When the pictures of the King were taken down from the walls and those of Stalin and Groza substituted, all the children wore little "buttonhole" badges made out of stamps that bore the King's head on them. Soon all badges were forbidden, to stop this, and then the children wore them under their lapels. For a time the teachers were able secretly to teach some of the truths that had been eliminated from texts and courses of study, but as the spy system was built up these teachers were found out and removed. Once more the truth could be taught only at home, as in the very old days, around the family fireside at night—and then only until the children's minds should be so warped that they would spy on and betray their own parents.

In the little village school at Bran we, too, were forced to "celebrate" all the holidays commemorating our unity, political and "cultural," with our dear big brother Russia. There we all stood respectfully for the Russian Anthem and for the Internationale, which my children sang lustily and uncomprehendingly with the rest while I squirmed! Not too much, of course, was ever understood by these younger children. I remember one incident which is amusing enough now, but which at the time made my heart stop beating for a second. It was on the occasion of one of these Russian celebrations, when many songs and much oratory about the grand and glorious union of Romania and Russia had been produced. (The oratory was prepared by the Party, and handed to the luckless "speaker of the evening" just before he took his place on the platform; a fact which everyone soon learned, and which kept us from blaming any of the orators for the sentiments expressed.) An artificial atmosphere of cheers and smiles was kept alive under the watchful eyes of the local Communists, so that to a casual glance the event would have seemed a most joyful one. But at the end my small Magi said to me, in a too audible whisper:

"Mamma! I don't quite understand! Are we all rejoicing because the Russians are leaving at last?"

Reported in the right place, her remark could have sent all of her family to labor camps in Russia, and I admit that I was terrified. When nothing happened, I realized that those who had overheard her felt that she spoke for them too, but it was not a pleasant situation. It was encouraging to know that the teachers were not being very active and thorough in their Communist "instruction" to the children, but I could see that things were becoming steadily more dangerous. How does a mother warn a seven-year-old daughter so that she will not innocently condemn her family to death or slavery? How can she happily choose for a fourteen-year-old son between the truth that may cost him his life and the lie that may destroy more than his body?

All these things I thought of there on the beach at Manjapunar, while the children played in the sun, and I looked at the horizon wistfully. Perhaps it would be better to embark in the rubber raft, after all! But to try to escape with my own family from the oppression to which my people were condemned could never be the right solution of the problem for me. It was my duty to stay with the country that had given me life and held my heart, and not to desert it in a time of stress. I was not simply an individual, a mother who had only her own children to think of. I was also a symbol, a member of a royal family which had stood for service to its people. For that very reason I and my family could perhaps do more than other families to help strengthen and keep alive a small secret flame of hope for a Romania Mare of the future. I resolved to try harder and more courageously. I returned with the family to Bran, carrying this resolution in my heart and not knowing that soon all decision would be taken out of my hands.

When we arrived at the castle we found that Anton's long-awaited permission to enter Austria had come. He was eager to get off in order to have plenty of time to go and come back before Christmas, and Frau Koller was to go with him. She had been a dear and faithful companion to me for more than eight years; she had lived through many difficult times with us, and I had often found solace in the presence and friendship of this older woman who had helped us through hard and rough moments. She had been good and kind to the children and had patiently borne a country life which could not have been easy for one brought up in Vienna. I could not believe that now we were really parting, and I was saddened also by the reason for her leaving. Her daughter, an actress in Dresden, had escaped the Russian occupation unharmed but had died a year later in tragic circumstances, leaving a young son. Frau Koller was now going to him, after endless difficulties in getting her papers.

It was hard to see her leave, and I knew that Gretl also must soon return home because her mother was ill. I wondered what I would do then, but this problem also solved itself. Gretl left Romania when we did, and on our way to Switzerland she remained in Vienna. Then, although I was ill, I was free of other duties and could care for my own children without help.

But I did not foresee this in the fall of 1947. I was astonishingly free of any premonition of the end of my life in Romania. I went on planning for the future. Thanks to the generosity of a rich industrialist, I began building a small chapel, exactly resembling that built by my mother in Balcic, which should stand in the center of the hospital courtyard. There I planned to place my mother's heart, so that it should remain always in Spitalul Inima Reginei, which had been dedicated to her memory. I found a talented painter to design the frescoes for the walls. I even began to build in the garden a log house for winter use, which would substitute for the house in the village, and would give my big family each a room of his own. Our winter home I planned to transform into a dormitory for the School of Nursing I wished to found.

My arrangements for paying for these things had been given a terrible blow because of a financial move by the Communist government in August, 1947. Everyone in the country, excepting the top Party members and the Communist propaganda institutions, who were naturally exempt, was compelled to take part in an operation which, our leaders assured us, would stop the serious inflation in the country and restore normal conditions. It was simple. Everyone had to surrender all sums of money he owned, including his savings, and in return everyone received 125 lei, or about three dollars and a half in United States money. Whoever had actual gold or other valuables could deposit these at the national bank and get the new kind of paper currency, but those who did not have their money in such a form could start a new life with three dollars and a half. This move hit the peasants hardest of all, which was a planned step in the economic enslavement of the country, but it was something that might have seemed a little surprising to anyone who took the Communists' word that theirs was the people's party. I myself was left with my farms and my woodlands, which although greatly destroyed and restricted could still, with careful management, bring in a little income; so I had gone on planning and working.

At this time I was also busily engaged with a new project for coming to the aid of the intellectuals, the families of political prisoners, and other people whom one could not help openly. I had found that quite a number of people at that time were still left in possession of their houses.

This number has since greatly decreased. One room is sufficient for a family. And if, in the bedroom where a man and his wife and a few children and an old mother must all sleep, there should be hung a curtain to give some semblance of privacy, that room has been divided into two rooms by the curtain, and another family is put into one of the "rooms." It is things like this that make me understand the anguish in a letter recently smuggled out of Romania to me—a letter in which a friend writes: "We no longer ask for freedom. We ask only for the decencies of existence."

In 1947, as I have said, I found that many of these families still left in their homes were willing and anxious to help those less fortunate, but food was so scarce that this was increasingly difficult for them to do. I thought of setting up a plan to help people to help others by giving them the necessary provisions to do so. Each of these homes, therefore, became a supply depot, to which, apparently quite casually but actually according to a carefully planned schedule, "friends" were invited in for a meal—at regular intervals.

In this activity Archbishop O'Hara co-operated, and he became one of my regular sources of provisions, which of course had all to be delivered as secretly as possible. The Seventh-Day Adventists, who had once, you may remember, "presented" me with seven carloads of used clothing, also helped in this, as well as the Missions from the Norwegian and the Danish Red Cross. The Queen, too, became enthusiastic about the plan, and shared her extra provisions and donations with me to use in this way. In spite of the informality of the arrangements, and the necessity of keeping it entirely secret and undercover, the number of families and students we were able to help ran up into the hundreds, and the plan was only well started when I left.

By numerous and devious means, which I cannot describe now because too many others were involved, we prepared and distributed parcels of food and clothes to families of political prisoners and others who must be helped secretly. I had a wonderful band of co-workers who labored long hours by day and by night. Why the activity in the basement of my Bucarest house did not attract unfavorable attention I have no idea, except that perhaps the policeman at my door felt that he had better let well enough alone. After all, I had always received a great many people, and did not the ministers of the government and other highly important Communists come in and out? I confess that it gave me an exquisite joy to entertain these people while my friends worked down below! Once I even blandly showed the workroom to a group of highly placed officials, and explained that here we were making parcels for the village children of Bran. I am afraid I am still not ashamed of that lie, which I hoped would protect our work from investigation if any rumor of the activity got out. And of course, truthfully, the village children of Bran were not forgotten, for thanks to the Red Cross of Switzerland I had set up a milk canteen to run all through the winter.

Have I succeeded in making you realize how many of my activities were in their beginnings, as well as how many were being carried on intensively? Then perhaps you can understand the shock of an end to all these things coming, not naturally, but as if a knife had rudely cut through a whole life in a moment. It condemned me, not to death, but to a living death.

It was the end of 1947. A strange, bitter winter had begun. We had thunderstorms when lightning mingled with the snow, and there were icy winds of such force that I have seen great snowballs, as large as cartwheels, driven along the plains at a furious rate. Nature itself seemed to be in revolt.

Ileana 1956

TWENTY-EIGHT

KING MICHAEL and his mother, Queen Helen, had gone to the wedding of Princess Elizabeth of England. Everyone was delighted at this—even the government, who of course hoped the King would not have the courage to return. His family and his people hoped that he would find a bride, and soon whispers began creeping back that he had done so. Everyone was happy for him, and eagerly waited for the public announcement. It was rumored that the government was considering the matter, and it was taken for granted that everything was awaiting the King's return, which had been set for December 20, 1947.

I was in Bucarest that day with Stefan, and we had been asked to go to hear a new Christmas Oratorio to be given that morning by the Opera Choir and the Philharmonic Orchestra. I did not say that I could come until the last moment, in order to avoid any kind of demonstration, but we did as usual sit in the royal box, I in my Red Cross uniform and

Stefan in the military uniform of his school. It was a beautiful concert, deeply moving and inspiring, but I felt that I must leave during the second intermission in order to be on time to receive Michael. Therefore, at the end of the last chorus in that part, I rose from my seat, and, as the custom was, bowed to the performers to indicate my thanks and appreciation. They rose as one man, and the entire hall rose with them, and there I received the greatest ovation of my life. It is true that whenever I had gone to a public hall, however informally, I had always received a cheer—especially during the last two years. But this was something quite different. There was an agony in it. It was the expressed emotion of a people in distress calling to one of their royal house to understand. I stood at that moment not for myself as an individual, but for the institution of which I was a part. Their shouts and cheers were an expression of almost anguished love for all that was being destroyed, of bruised and dying hope for the salvation of a country. I felt this to the very marrow of my bones. I tried to leave, but again and again I was forced to return, the cries mounting ever more strongly and engulfing me in a volume of almost unbearable sound and echoes.

At last I was able to tear myself away, deeply shaken. Stefan and I drove along the empty streets, guarded so that no one could approach the station where the King was to arrive. There I found the representatives of the government looking glum and silent. Only Groza, Bodnaras, and Ana Pauker came to talk with me, Ana commenting affably on how Stefan had grown. After the hall I had just left, coming into this gathering was like falling into ice water, in which I must smilingly go on swimming.

The train drew in, and there stood Michael in uniform, tall, good-looking, and with a smile of inner content which even the frigid, formal reception did not succeed in wholly destroying. Sitta, too, looked decidedly better for the change, and it did my heart good to see them. As I drove with them to the palace I tried to convey to them something of the real love and fidelity of the people, who were unable to reach them to express it. For not only were all the streets that gave access to the station closed and guarded, giving a strange and unnatural air of desertion as we drove along, but the exact time of the King's arrival had been kept secret.

They on their part had more pleasant things to talk about. In the first place, there was Anne. Her photographs were taken out, and Michael's beaming face showed his happiness. He and Sitta were full of plans about how things would be arranged; about how they would transform the Foisor—Michael's residence at Sinaia. Then there was all the news of our English cousins and the other relatives and friends, and it was wonderful to listen to it. It was like a breath of air from another climate. I returned to my own house much happier, although the two contrasting events of the day had worried me. What would the outcome be? I knew in my heart what was inevitable, but I refused to accept it.

Christmas at Bran was a pleasant one for the children. Anton arrived just in time with surprises and gifts bought in Switzerland, and also with unobtainable necessities for the hospital which he had been able to find for me. There were the usual celebrations, and for the very last time I wore my beautiful sapphire and diamond diadem. Perhaps because it was the last Christmas in Romania, that day stands out clearly to me, not for any special event, but because every minute since then has made it dearer to me. The snow was deep and crunched underfoot; the sky was full of stars; the songs of the children were clear and joyful; all faces seemed to smile and love one another; the gifts had been made with care and forethought. It was one of those times which warm the heart and make it content.

The next days also were peaceful and uneventful. We drove over to Sinaia to see Michael and his mother, and found them well and full of their plans. When I was alone with Sitta, however, she confessed to a deep uneasiness. The government had not yet given its formal consent to Michael's engagement. Why were they holding off? But still we tried to cheer each other into believing that soon the thing would be settled. My family and I drove back to Bran, with no feeling that it was their last visit to Sinaia.

On the evening of December 30 I went over to Noelle's house for a cup of tea. Another friend was there, and we sat around the fire in the lovely living room of the house Noelle and her husband had built with such effort, and where they were so happily and courageously carrying on their new life. Outside there was a blizzard, and I felt I must not stay too long or the roads would become impassable even for my "jeep." As I drove into our courtyard, the headlights of my car fell on the white and terrified face of the caretaker.

"Domnitza!" he cried to me in anguish, "Domnitza! We have no more king! We are lost!" I can still see him clenching and unclenching his hands. "We are lost! It is the end! No king!" he repeated.

I ran indoors, and found all the family sitting around the radio in the children's room. There was the message. The king, seeing he could now no longer serve his people but was only an impediment to their advance, had freely abdicated and wished his people well. Slowly the room filled with the doctors, the nurses, and other friends who had heard the news. No one of us spoke for a long time. The end had come.

Later that night my administrator from Bucarest called to say that Groza wished to speak to me: would I come in to town at once? The King, he told me, was in Bucarest but was returning to Sinaia. Naturally I could ask no further questions over the telephone.

Early the next morning I drove off with Stefan, Bittermann, and Badillo. It was snowing slowly and relentlessly. The world was still. I parted from Anton and the younger children with a great fear in my heart, but still I felt that I had to go, for the safety of all of us. Besides, I must find Sitta and Michael and speak with them. We met little traffic on the way, and those who recognized us only bowed sadly and silently. At Sinaia I decided to take the risk of delaying the journey a little, and to drive up to the Foisor. When I came to the gate I found the two guards standing there, but as I looked more closely I saw that they were unarmed. I stopped and talked to an officer standing near, and with a voice choked and hoarse with emotion he explained.

"They disarmed us by force last night. The Tudor Vladimirescu have taken over. We obtained permission to stand this one last guard, to welcome his Majesty for the last time. He is still in town—pray God they will not harm him. We mean to greet him this time with '*Sa ne revenutzi, Majestate!*' ['May you return to us, your Majesty!'] and then they can shoot us!"

I drove on up the hill, past the dignified castle of the Peles, past the beloved old Pelisor, happy home of my childhood, to the Foisor to wait for Sitta and Michael. The servants were sad and anxious. None of us talked much—what had one to say? After two hours I decided to risk a telephone call to Bucarest, and surprisingly enough, I was permitted to speak to the Queen. They had been delayed, but were on the point of leaving. It would be best if I, too, would leave and take the road for Bucarest, so that we could meet on the way.

The snow continued to fall. Sinaia was wrapped in whiteness. There was something not quite real about it all; the whole drive was a long drawn-out nightmare of white confusion. In Campina we met the royal party, and we stopped so that I could get into Michael's car and drive out of town, where we could more easily talk. He and Sitta told me how they had been called to Bucarest, and had gone, thinking it was about the question of Michael's engagement. Immediately upon their entering the palace they had been separated from their suites. There were strange guards at the doors. Then Groza and Ghiorghiu Dej had laid the abdication before Michael, informing him that guns were trained on the city and that they would fire on the people if he refused to sign. It was as if a revolver had been held to his head: there was nothing for him to do but sign.

Now they were returning to Sinaia to pack, and were being sent to Switzerland as soon as possible. Michael had asked about his two aunts, my sister Elisabeta and myself, and had been told that we could remain, if we wished, as private individuals. What, I asked him, did he wish me to do? He said that he thought I should try to stay, but that he could express no outright opinion because he did not want to ask me to risk my life and the lives of the children further. I should see and judge for myself.

This conversation went on in low, controlled voices, with no show of emotion on the part of any of us. None of us could have borne the expression of emotion then! So we parted there on the roadside, not knowing what would come next, or when we should meet again, or how. When we did meet it was at Lausanne in Switzerland. We were all alive and well, but we had lost too much for it to be an occasion of rejoicing. We felt nothing more than a bare gratitude for life.

The moment I entered Bucarest I knew I could not endure to remain under such a regime. There were the red flags, the posters with insults to my family, and—which seemed worst of all—the guards standing sloppily in their places, leaning carelessly against the palace walls smoking, with the red flag waving above them and hosannas to the Russian masters written over the walls. This first feeling of mine had been wholly instinctive, but I soon found that facts supported it. My administrator was waiting at my house to tell me that all my properties had been confiscated: the castle, the woods in Poeni Moldavia, and my little farms. Soon Anton called to say that the household had been cut off from the hospital, where immediately the family portraits had been removed and pictures of Stalin put up instead. The castle had been sealed and was under guard, our house guard had been doubled by the addition of Communists, and no one was allowed to go out of the grounds. It is in this way, I thought, that I am to be treated as a private individual.

Groza had asked to see me, but I was not able to reach him in any way. His secretary told me that the Prime Minister, he thought, had only wanted to assure me that I had nothing to worry about. I felt this was a little ironic under the circumstances, and I resolved that, since Groza had said he wanted to see me, see me he would! I knew that he always took a morning walk, so Bittermann and Badillo set a watch the next day—for, astonishingly enough, my house was not put under any strict surveillance. When they saw him leaving his house, which was about ten blocks from mine, I rushed into the car with Stefan and drove up to a side street.

There we got out and sauntered down as if we also were taking our morning walk, and had quite by chance met the Minister.

Groza greeted me most affably and remarked on what a lovely day it was. I agreed, but I did not let it go at that. I told him all that had happened to me, and when he looked surprised I insisted on things being put right, which he promised to do. I cannot say that he was not pleasant to me, and when I cornered him, which I repeatedly did, he carried out a series of minor improvements, if such they could be called. For example, in Bran the family were allowed to go about freely and to communicate with the hospital staff. Finally I talked with Bodnaras by telephone, but by this time the course of events was so plain that I told him I feared my job was over, and that it might be best for me to go away, too. He said he felt with regret that this was the right thing to do for the time being, but that he was sure conditions would settle down so that I would be able to return. He asked permission for himself and his wife to come to say good-bye to me—something which of course they did not do. Groza I continued to see, and it was through him that the final arrangements for our departure were made.

The government agreed to give us a train in which Elisabeta should travel too. She was then still at her place in the country, but was coming up to town. We were permitted to take only personal belongings—that is to say, clothes, linen, and silver for the use of eight people—but no works of art, as these were "the property of the people," no carpets, and no jewels except those which were indisputably "family jewels" not acquired in recent years. A Control Commission came to watch us carefully so that we should "steal" none of our property—two men in Bucarest and eighteen men in Bran. These men were with us continually, so that there was no question of privacy, even for discussion. They were still to some extent human, so that at my pleading they did make an occasional exception: it is for that reason the statue of St. Benedict stands today in my bedroom, after having been smuggled out "by permission" in window draperies.

It was to me terrible to have these guards always present to witness my parting from friends, a succession of moments which were unbelievably difficult to endure. With each it was the same pain, the same desperate last embrace, the same agony, repeated endlessly throughout the long days. More and more gathered in my house; old and young, high and low. I wept so much that finally I had no more tears left. I felt drained of all feeling except one of immense pain, and only the need to get the children away kept me going, and forced me cold-bloodedly and mechanically to make the necessary arrangements. Had I been alone, I came to realize, I would never have left Romania.

On January 6, 1948, all was at last ready for me to go to Bran and collect the children and our luggage there. If it had not been for the kindness of Archbishop O'Hara, who lent me from the Catholic War Relief a truck which the husband of one of my best friends volunteered to drive, I would not have been able to transport to Bucarest what we were to be permitted to take. I was given two days to go to Bran and return, although actually we did not leave Bucarest for Switzerland until January 12, and this arrangement gave me approximately twenty-four hours in Bran. Groza sent with me a secret service man, to "protect" me, although I told the young man that I did not feel my life was in danger except from his own colleagues! I went out of my way, however, to try to win his sympathy, and I succeeded. He was as kind as his difficult position permitted him to be.

It was of course a miracle, and one which I have had more leisure to appreciate since I left Romania, that not only was I able to win Communist permission for much of my work, but that my person was respected and my life spared. There were occasions when to protect others I interfered with the activities of Russian soldiers, with nothing to implement my words except a great and burning indignation, and they retreated. There was little time to be wasted in being afraid, and on only one or two occasions did I actually feel fear for myself. Yet I was not blind to the possibilities. I knew that my secret activities were always in danger of discovery, and could not help but bring swift punishment. I carried with me a poison, and I saw to it that I had enough for the children in case it should be decided that they were to be taken from me and sent to Russia. Would I have used it? How can I know? It seems to me a sufficient comment on conditions that a mother should be forced to think of the possibility of having to make such a decision.

That morning in January my guard and I drove back with Stefan and Badillo, stopping in Brasov to see Mrs. Podgoreanu and Sandu and his wife, but the grief of those partings is quite beyond what I can even now mention.

In Bran I found everyone in a strained state of nerves. No packing had been permitted until I came, and the castle was still locked and sealed, but now the Communist guards opened it. I walked about the rooms, followed always by one or another of our guards, taking farewell of this beloved abode of my mother's and mine. Each object I picked up was immediately pounced upon to see if I was "stealing" something. I tried to see myself in the past, and in this way to wipe out the horror of the present from my mind . . . I do not want to dwell on how I saw Bran for the last time.

There was in the castle a small vaulted chapel my mother had had decorated and blessed long ago. When in 1940 an earthquake had damaged the lovely church in Cotroceni, I had obtained permission to remove from his grave there, and to bring to the chapel in Bran, the remains of Mircea, my youngest brother. He was not quite four years old, and the great love of my heart, when he died in October, 1916, one of the first victims of typhoid in the epidemics during the war. Very soon afterwards the German advance had forced the government to retreat to Jassy, so that the body of Mircea had remained in enemy-occupied country. Now I knelt down in the little chapel and read again the inscription my mother had had carved for his grave when the war was over and we had returned to Bucarest. Translated, it reads:

In this sanctuary of Cotroceni, beside those who in former days were rulers of this land, lies the youngest son of King Ferdinand and Queen Marie, born December 21, 1912,

MIRCEA

died October 20, 1916, in the time of war, while the soldiers of Romania were sacrificing their lives for the dream of centuries.

Two years he remained sole guardian of the home of his parents, over which the country's flag had ceased to float. Mourn for him, for he shared with us the days of suffering, but the days of rejoicing he did not live to see.

Ileana and baby Mircea

Once more Mircea has remained to guard our home. But this time his mother's heart, in the rock across the narrow valley, keeps him company. I had wanted to take it with us, but the marble sarcophagus was so firmly cemented into the rock that we could neither open nor remove it. Then I thought that, after all, it must be my mother's wish that her heart should remain with her people, in the Romanian rocks and soil. Though all the rest of us must go, something of her and of her youngest son would remain; a symbol of the love and faith that I believe no earthly power can destroy.

Anton, the children, and I knelt for the last time at the shrine of the heart, praying deeply and silently. Within myself I promised solemnly that wherever I went I would try to continue my work; that since in my heart Romania's image was engraved, my life would as ever be dedicated to her. From one of the tables in the castle I had taken a lovely old metal box, and pushing aside the snow with my hands, I filled it with Romanian soil. This, of all I carried away with me, is the most precious thing I have here in my home in New England.

The most heartbreaking parting of all was the parting from the hospital. I was only able to go there as it was growing dark, and the children came with me. First we gathered in the staff dining room, and I spoke my last message, choked by tears. Then I went around the wards, where each patient in his or her way gave vent to sorrow and despair. Each parting was like an actual wound in my heart, especially when I came to the soldiers, for at first they would try to look manly and behave with correct fortitude, but they could not continue so. One even fell at my feet, and burying his face in my apron he sobbed hopelessly. Then there were the children, the small orphans gathered in my nursery. They did not understand what was happening, and when I knelt down to take them into my arms they made designs on my face with my tears. At last I broke away from them. I gave one last look into the operating room, which seemed in its gleaming whiteness to stand for all the love and service I had given to the hospital. Was it possible that I would never work there again? Never?

Nothing now remained but the simple act of saying good-bye and parting from my co-workers and my friends. We knelt down and said a prayer for God's blessing upon the continuance of the work, and upon one another in this hour of parting. Other words were useless. I opened the door and crossed the beloved threshold for the last time, and the dark night swallowed me up.

Bran Castle—the door to the chapel where Mircea is buried

Ileana 1951

TWENTY-NINE

January 7, 1948: 3:30 P.M.

A last farewell to our dear, small house; to my room with its loved pictures and comfortable bed; to the well-known tables and chairs. Good-bye, dear home, good-bye to your warmth and friendliness. I shall never see you again. This is the last time. Never again shall I enter under your roof or see the dawn from your windows.

As one condemned to die I left it, knowing that this in very truth was the end. Outside my room in the narrow passage stood the weeping servants. They kissed my hands and wept as if I were already dead. I tore myself away from them and, gathering the silent and frightened children together, went with them and Anton into the courtyard. The three cars and the truck lent to us were ready to start.

The hospital staff were there to say good-bye once more, and some of the patients with them. On the street the guards had seen to it that no one stood about or watched. I went up to each one who waited: my patients, my friends, and those with whom I had worked so hard and so well. Words failed us, but we let our tears run unshamed down our faces. I kissed each in turn, a kiss of peace, of friendship, of farewell. Only with one did I not exchange this embrace, for in this hour truth was too naked, and I knew his would be a Judas kiss. I was far beyond resentment. I could forgive, but I could not pretend.

At the gate stood my old friend the publican, whom I had been often warned against because he was a Communist. He strode past the guard, ignoring him, and throwing his arms around me he kissed me heartily, while his tears mingled with mine.

"Remember you are our *Ilenuta draga*: nothing can ever change that: our dear child!"

I could but press the old man's hand. Turning once more to the others I tried to smile, then I entered the waiting car. We drove out, and as we did so the gendarme at the gate, in spite of orders, presented arms and called "Sa tariti, Domnitza!" as he had always done.

When we crossed the bridge, there at the village side stood a great mass of peasants and of the students home on vacation. They had waited there, where they were fairly sure the guards could not prevent their doing so. As many as could come, with so short a notice, had gathered even from the most distant villages. They crowded around the cars and I got out. They kissed my hands and the hem of my uniform; they handed me fir branches, the evergreen that stands for the eternity of love, life, and faith. Then the multitude knelt down before me and asked for my blessing, and I lifted my hand and made the sign of the cross over their bent heads.

Once more I entered the car. The people drew aside, still kneeling, to let us pass, and a great sound of wailing went up from them. I felt that I was helping with the rites at my own funeral. The afternoon was drawing to a close, and my heart lay within me like a dead weight. The road was still heavily blocked with snowdrifts, so that we had to make a detour through Tohan, a village of factory workmen considered entirely "Red." Here, too, the road was partly impassable. We tried driving through the fields which the wind had swept clear of snow, but there had been a thaw. Two of the cars and the truck sank into the damp earth and we could not move them. At this hour the workmen were returning on foot from the factory not far away.

"I will go and ask them for help," I said. Those who were with me, especially the Communist guards, felt this was imprudent, and were afraid of the consequences, but I had no fear as I went over to some of the workmen and requested their help. Silently they acquiesced, and came to our rescue. With great efforts, by digging, pushing, and pulling, and only after getting themselves wet and muddy, they got the cars on the solid ground again, and to a point from which we could regain the road. The work had been done efficiently and well, but in unusual silence.

"I must go back to them and thank them," I told the guards.

"That would be most unsafe! It is getting dark, and they might do you harm," I was warned. Nevertheless, I retraced my steps to where the little knot of taciturn men still stood.

"Thank you," I said to them. "Please take this and divide it among you. I know it is little, but it is all I have." And I held out to them what money had been left to me.

The men looked at one another, and then one stepped out from among them.

"No, Domnitza," he said to me sorrowfully. "No, Domnitza, not today will we take a gift from you. Have you not been at our beck and call night and day? None has knocked at your door without being received. We have rendered you so small but so sad a service—see, the very earth is loath to let you go! But one request we still have of you. Will you kneel down with us and say a prayer for King and country, and for your return?"

And there in that muddy field, as the sun slowly set behind the Carpathians and filled the world with a last glow of splendor, I knelt down, joining in prayer with the factory workmen and those who till the soil. "Our Father, Who art in heaven . . ."

The sun was setting: but it rises again!

AFTERWORD

I feel it is necessary to stress that this book is my own personal story. It makes no pretense of being either a political or a historical work, but merely tries to portray what recent political and historical events did to an individual—to me. My motive in trying to tell this story has been twofold. It comes from my deep conviction of the life-and-death nature of the present struggle for a free world, and it comes from my strong and abiding love for Romania. I do not need to defend my conviction to any thinking person: I would like to say a little more about my country both to my fellow Romanians and to those who are interested in my story.

For Romania in her two-thousand-year fight for independence as a nation, and for the Romania Mare—the Greater Romania—who achieved this independence, I feel both love and pride. Deeper and more impossible to put into words are the love and pride I feel for Romania during her years of stress. There was a remarkable solidarity: a brotherhood that in better times we had not known. In those days of darkness and despair, in spite of spies and denunciations we stood together. No one would have refused shelter to one who knocked at his door. Political opinion was of no importance. We were Romanians, standing as one against the oppressor and the powers of darkness.

If, then, I do not appear vigorous enough in my condemnation or defense of some to satisfy those who have viewed events from outside the country, it is partly because I have experienced this brotherhood. It is also because, as I have said, this is my personal story, and as a person I have always been able to see the other man's point of view. Human hopes and joys and sorrows have moved me deeply because I have always seen the individual as a human being rather than as an exponent of any creed or belief, and pity has been my strongest emotion toward friend and foe alike. This has in no sense made me tolerant of evil, but it has given me an understanding which separates the individual from the evil, instead of presenting the one as the personification of the other.

I have lived for a long time beyond fear and pain, and since then values for me have changed. I wish to judge no man, but I stand uncompromisingly on the side of freedom and justice. I will fight the powers of darkness in whatever form I meet them, and to the death. Resentment and hatred I feel none of. These are weaknesses in which we have no right to indulge today. They waste both strength and energy, and we can afford to waste neither. Having been a nurse, I was concerned most often with the sick and the dying, and they have no political color, race, or faith to distinguish them in a hospital ward. My first concern was to help them, and not to let personal feelings or political opinions overshadow the service I was there to perform. Therefore I made it my business to work with all authorities as long as this did not conflict with my religious convictions.

In this book, also, I have made no attempt to record all the splendid humanitarian work done by the different welfare societies in Romania, each of whom has its own story to tell. This is a personal record in which I tell only what I personally witnessed and can vouch for, except for the barest skeleton of historical framework necessary to explain the setting of the events. In these days when so much is repeated from hearsay, I think each person should be careful to tell only the truth for which he can personally take responsibility, for with truth alone can we combat the powers of darkness overshadowing a large part of the world. I must leave untold, then, the efforts made by others in which I had no part, but I remind you that I tell my story not as unique but as characteristic of life in a period of national strain and danger. Even within these limitations, I must leave much unsaid to protect those still behind an Iron Curtain.

I wish here to thank those who helped me to bring this book, as we say in Romania, *la bun sfarsit*—to a good finish. I have no way of thanking my collaborator, Dorothy Kuenzli Hinckley, for she has become almost part of me, but we both thank her husband, Dr. Edward B. Hinckley, who painstakingly read each chapter through, and who advised and criticized without discouraging us. Thanks are due, too, to our respective families, who patiently bore with our neglect of our motherly and housewifely duties in the interests of "the book": to Stefan, Maria-Ileana, Alexandra, Dominic, Maria Magdalena, and Elisabeth; and to Marjorie, Edward Charles, and Lois Vivian Hinckley. It was my son Stefan who drew the map and who reminded me of many of the events in which he had a part.

I am grateful to Dr. John D. Montgomery, who read the manuscript, and to Mr. Georges Duca, Mr. Ray Baker Harris, Colonel Carroll Krichbaum, and Mr. Wilmer Park for their kindness in lending photographs and snapshots to illustrate this book, since mine of course are lost. I am grateful also to Mr. Brutus Coste, who supplied me with dates for many historical events, and who put at my disposal notes and documents by which I could guide and correct my brief political and historical references. All reactions to these, however, are my own personal feelings.

In deciding upon an English spelling for Romanian words I have aimed for ease in reading rather than for consistency. Thus in names like "Brasov" and "Peles," where the Romanian "s" has a cedilla and would be pronounced "sh" in English, I have not tried to indicate this, but have used the spelling common to most atlases, since, after all, these pronunciations do not differ a great deal. Where the Romanian "t" with a cedilla is used, however, I have written the English "tz" to indicate the pronunciation, as in "Domnitza" and "Constantza." There are many other accent marks on Romanian names and I have omitted all of them. Except for one explanatory reference, I have used the English version for the name of my nephew, King Michael, since it is more familiar here in that form than is the Romanian "Mihai." My spelling of "Romania" is to me not only nearer the Romanian spelling, but also indicates its direct derivation from "Rome" and "Roman." "Bucarest" also seems to me nearer the Romanian "Bucuresti" (the final "i" is not pronounced) than the more common English form, "Bucharest."

In making this explanation and these acknowledgments of gratitude, I do not feel that I can fail to mention my consciousness of the help given me by the thoughts and prayers of my people, both in exile and still in bondage. To the extent that I succeed in contributing to a more conscious appreciation of freedom as something that must be defended, and to a better knowledge of my freedom-loving country, I speak for these Romanians unable to speak to you themselves.

Massachusetts, U.S.A.
1951

EPILOGUE

The evening sky was a wide dual ribbon of deep-sea blue and the golden light of a waning sun as our jet plane began its landing into Regina, Saskatchewan. I was silently repeating the lines from Psalm 103(104): "You made the moon to tell the seasons, the sun knows when to set; you bring darkness on, night falls," the psalm recited every evening in Orthodox Christian monasteries—a psalm thus well-known to the author of *I Live Again*. In preparation for the landing, I closed my companion reading book, *I Live Again*, authored by Ileana, Grand Duchess of Austria and Princess of Romania and of oh, so many wondrous titles. I was on my way to a city named after her great-grandmother, Victoria, Empress Queen of England, to visit the oldest Romanian community in this capital city of Saskatchewan. This lovely "Queen City," which once even had the honor of a visit from the author herself, was very distant in time from the war-beleaguered Romania of seventy years ago that she described in the pages of *I Live Again*.

I had read the book several years before and had taken it with me on my trip to refresh my memory. Princess Ileana, writing in 1951, a very few years after she had left Europe, poured out her heart to the American public in *I Live Again*. In the book, she states: "I want to spend most of the time [in writing] on the events that led to my country's loss of freedom, on the resistance put up by my people; on their great suffering and on their great courage" (p. 195). Not only did she put her thoughts into words, but she also drew sketches at the heading of each chapter.

As a young priest-monk, I had occasionally served the monastic community of the Orthodox Monastery of the Transfiguration in the earlier days of its founding. Her monastery is nestled in the rolling hills near Ellwood City, Pennsylvania, an area not unlike parts of Transylvania. There was no resident priest, and thus on various feast days and holidays, particularly during the Lenten season and the Feasts of Pascha and the Nativity of Jesus Christ, we would leave our own little community in Michigan to provide the Orthodox services for the very small community of nuns. It was during these visits that I came to know Princess Ileana—of course, at this time, Mother Alexandra, abbess and foundress of the community. My relationship with her is as unique to me as were those of other priests who also served the community, hearing confessions, listening to stories about life in Romania as the youngest daughter of King Ferdinand and Queen Marie, of her concerns for her children and grandchildren, leaving us wondering, and yes, maybe questioning, how a princess came to leave family and society to embrace the restrictive life of a monastic. What moved her to make this choice, to live this kind of life?

Princess Ileana—and I use her title because such she was when she wrote her book and such she remains—was raised by her mother, Marie, Queen Mother of Romania, to serve her nation. Born on January 5, 1909, the eve of the Orthodox Feast of the Theophany, "God's self-revelation," Ileana was the youngest daughter of seven children born to Ferdinand I, King of Romania, and Marie, his wife and queen. *I Live Again* is not about her life as a princess royal but about a woman with a message concerning others, the Romanian people and the domination of that nation by atheistic communism. Her book is not only about what her mother had trained her to do and to be—a servant of the people—but what she chose to do, heart and soul. In addition to this theme of *noblesse oblige*, we catch glimpses of her personal spiritual growth as she reflects on her actions and responses in facing the trying demands of this period of her life.

From childhood, Ileana was taught service to her people, which meant, of course, service to the nation, its language, traditions, and history, as well as to its principal faith, the Eastern Orthodox creed. Her father was Roman Catholic and her mother Anglican; their children were baptized and raised in the Eastern Orthodox faith. Perhaps this spiritual tie to the people bestowed on her a special depth of understanding, of care and respect for the lives of the peasant as well as the intellectual. It was this faith that sustained her through the years of war tribulations and her abusive expulsion from her nation. She was known by all as a believing soul. In a particularly trying time during the war, a friend once chided her, when she was concerned that there was a lack of bed sheets for her hospital, "But you who have so much faith—do you limit the power of God when it comes to sheets?" (p. 209). Ileana took this to heart.

That the author is thoroughly Romanian is shown in the depth of her knowledge of the nation. She grew up in Romania, and she identified with the nation; she was Romanian, she remained Romanian all her life. She loves and lauds the people and then reflects on their faults. She carries them in her arms and then tries to help them stand on their own. Romania, a land of charm and mystery, of traditions and wealth; a land shaped by suffering from invading armies and reshaped by the determination of its people to remain who they were and who they had always been, and who they would be. Ileana felt this as a child and throughout her life to the end. She adorned herself in national costumes to cheer up the wounded soldiers whom she nursed, because she knew that this was a touch of home. She brought them little presents at traditional holiday times to make them feel as though they were in a family again. She witnessed, all the while, the strength of the people to endure suffering founded on the hope that the God of their faith would not abandon them to more invaders.

It was this thread of service to her fellow and trust in a higher Power winding throughout her life that slowly drew her to pursue a new life, a life far removed from the life in a palace of marble, to a modest wood structure that she would call her monastic home. When communist officials denied her participation in a special memorial service for her much beloved mother, a service of particular importance to Orthodox Christians, she was extremely sorrowful, then angry, but finally came to an understanding that "Such things did not matter . . . [they] were there simply to be overcome, . . . for us to use in building the staircase of life"

(p. 232). Ileana would learn to do without many other things as well.

This volume of the heart is as valid today as it was when it was written sixty-five years ago. Princess Ileana could not have foreseen the decades of suffering the Romanian people would endure until 1989, when the so-called revolution took place. In 1990, she traveled to Romania, her first and only visit since the ruling officials forced her to leave. Perhaps she was aware of her impending death the next year. She reflected that little had changed in her homeland; she would today be concerned for the nation, just as she had been when she wrote her book. The Romanian nation continues to be pressured from the north by Russia and from the west by Hungary. The geopolitical reality of Romania cannot change. Only when the "great powers" pawn her lands to her enemies in exchange for their support is there a temporary change. As the author herself knew, the mantra in World War II Romania was, "*Vine americanii!* The Americans are coming!" But they did not come, nor was she successful in persuading them to come.

America and Americans and how they would perceive her thoughts, how they would relate to the depth of the suffering of the people of Romania, was foremost in her mind as she wrote this book. Ileana was certainly hopeful that the American public would react to her story and become a catalyst to convince the American government to help her country. She was intent on relating how her own life had been a real part of the fabric of the life of her people, a people who for centuries had suffered numerous invasions and who were then enslaved by a new invasion, atheistic communism; the nation absorbed into the Soviet Russian hegemony in Eastern Europe. "Vine americanii?" No.

Mother Alexandra, Princess Ileana, spoke to me of some of her many wartime experiences, and in particular, of the one person with whom she was most disgusted: Ana Pauker, one of the first powerful women communists in Romania. She described her as one who "showed me the cold and dehumanized brilliance by which she had reached the powerful position she occupied" (p. 310).

The purpose of the book is to reveal the broken heart of the author and to be a reflection on the bruised heart of her people. How does a grand duchess and princess reflect the suffering of her own people? How does she accept exclusion from the life of the nation she represented and served? She was given no choice but a command: "Leave the country!" "Perhaps you can understand the shock of an end to all these things coming, not naturally, but as if a knife had rudely cut through a whole life in a moment. It condemned me, not to death, but to a living death"—words reflective of her conversation with Ana Pauker (pp. 367–368).

Persons who are not interested in studying history cannot learn from it. Princess Ileana knew world history as well as the history of her country. She not only knew its past, but she realized that she was living what would become the past. She knew that darkness challenges light and that knowledge of the past could help one shape one's life; and most importantly for her, would shape the lives of her loved ones, especially of her children. I either had not read or did not recall her statements that I had just come upon about her fear of being taken into Soviet Russia or about her children being separated from her and taken away. What maternal concern drove her to reveal in this book, "on only one or two occasions did I actually feel fear for myself. Yet, I was not blind to the possibilities. I knew that my secret activities were always in danger of discovery, and could not help but bring swift punishment. I carried with me a poison, and I saw to it that I had enough for the children in case it should be decided that they were to be taken from me and sent to Russia. Would I have used it? How can I know?" (pp. 376–377). What a tremendous burden for a mother to consider!

We Americans, I would venture to say, are not accustomed to read about the heartaches of a royal princess in regard to her personal concerns for her people. We would expect talk about balls and romances, jewels and palaces, cutting ribbons to new buildings; but concerns about nursing injured soldiers and struggling with finding food, clothing, and hospital bedsheets, housing and benzene to run the automotive transportation of a household? Really! This is what the chapters of the book reveal, a woman born into royalty yet brought face to face with the worries about how her six children could be educated. A grand duchess making dresses for her daughters from draperies? Is *I Live Again* about personal regrets, about loss of things, objects resting on bitterness, going from riches to rags? It reveals the story of how one person, a person of privilege, responded to the choices life put in front of her. From plenty to austerity and from palaces and castles to suburban residence, from fairy-tale Austria and mystical Romania to Yankee New England—this is the road along which Princess Ileana traveled, finally putting down roots in rural Pennsylvania, USA.

During the difficult war years, World War I and World War II, the years of invasion and subjection, Princess Ileana was in continual contact with people suffering in various trying situations. Her royal dignity was present always, but her human frailty sometimes caught her unawares. "I remember my angry and inconsiderate remark. It has made me try humbly ever since not to speak quickly any words which may hurt someone unnecessarily" (p. 198). The effort to consider the other, one's neighbor, was good preparation for her years as a speaker in America, but most of all as abbess of her small community.

Of course, Princess Ileana was not alone in serving the Romanian nation; there were many others. She was cautious not to reveal the names of friends who were still in communist Romania out of fear for the lives of those who might still be alive. She states this not once but often (e.g., pp. 258, 284, 367). Remember that this book was written in 1951, shortly after she left her country in 1948 and came to free America. The Cold War was in place, the Iron Curtain blocking outside help for her country. She remains concerned for what is happening over there while establishing a new life for her family in New England. From 1950 to 1961, she traveled extensively, lecturing against communism. Indeed, she carried on in America, as she had been encouraged to do by a friend. Pressing a silver priest's cross into her hands to save it from confiscation and destruction, the woman whispered in her ear, "God bless you and carry on wherever you may be" (p. 132). Ileana carried on for her family while continuing her work to expound the needs of the enslaved people of Romania.

When finally forced to leave Romania, this grand duchess and princess stooped down to the snow-covered ground at the chapel at Bran, Transylvania, and scooped up a handful of Romanian soil, "the most precious thing I have here in my home in New England" (p. 379). This handful of soil is now in the Romanian Orthodox Episcopate museum in Grass Lake, Michigan. As she made her way out of Bran and her fairy-tale castle, people, young with the old, gathered along the road and knelt down, asking for her blessing. "I lifted my hand and made the sign of the cross over their bent heads," she writes (p. 382). Bishops bless; priests bless; parents bless their children. No action could have better shown the relationship between this traveler-exile and those remaining home than that of a mother and her children blessing each other.

Earlier, I stated that Ileana had drawn sketches to illustrate the book. There are also wonderful photos of her and her family, her beloved children. "I am so grateful . . . for their kindness in lending photographs and snapshots to illustrate this book, since mine of course are lost" (p. 387). By these few words, we can understand how a princess's life was made void of the simplest and yet most personal possessions, her photographs of better times.

"Love that is eternal; one Friend who never leaves us, however imperfect and sorrowful we may be: God," she wrote, and "when I was, I believe, giving the utmost of myself spiritually, intellectually, and physically—and all of that was wiped off the face of the earth as a sponge washed off a blackboard. It was not easy to find my balance again; to live again; and when I did I was bitterly lonely. It was only when I had turned entirely to God and forgotten myself and my pain that I found I was neither lost nor alone" (pp. 235-236). Thus, she who felt dead came to live again! Perhaps another of her gifts to her neighbor was to be a witness to the courage and great effort to set aside the decades of trial and tribulation to show others that one can overcome the oppressive burdens of life, to come into a new and sharing life, a life caring for others not in material support with food and bandages, but as a witness that death can be overcome and new life embraced. Having lived in the dark night of suffering, she has come into the light of a new dawn to live again.

"One thing I know: the golden thread that binds a life together is love in its many and wondrous forms; love of beauty, love of children and of mankind, love of home and country, and ultimately love of God—whose perfect Love includes all others" (p. 237).

+NATHANIEL, *Archbishop of Detroit*
The Romanian Orthodox Episcopate of America
April 3, 2016–Sunday of the Holy Cross

POSTSCRIPT

I remember Princess Ileana from the time I was a boy. She respected my parents, Fr. Eugene and Preoteasa Eleonora, as friends. We visited her in her Massachusetts home. She visited and slept in our Indiana parish house, a fact that was hard for my classmates to believe. "Really? There's a princess in your house?"

As prim and proper as she could be, she was also so warm and personable. She was interested in you and wanted you to feel comfortable with her, in a friendly, motherly fashion. In time, after my ordination to the diaconate, while I was still in seminary, she even honored my wife Anita and me by visiting the third-floor attic apartment we were renting. And as she stood there in our kitchen, now in her black monastic garb as Mother Alexandra, she gave me a small silver cross from around her neck, a remembrance I will always treasure. She said, "You will be a priest. Pray for me."

As a child she was gifted to actually see her guardian angel! And in her lifetime she experienced more than any of us could imagine: the pomp of royalty, the joy and sorrow of motherhood and of caring for the people of Romania and the wounded victims of war, the shock and hardship of exile and the challenges of beginning life again in America (her beloved adopted country), the spiritual efforts and deep peace of the tonsured life, the struggle of establishing an Orthodox monastery in America—a blessed oasis of spiritual peace for generations to come. And after all she had endured and accomplished in life, when my wife and I visited to pray for her on what proved to be her deathbed, she spoke quietly only of love and thankfulness to God.

Ultimately, Ileana, lovingly remembered by so many as the beautiful Princess of Romania, blossomed beyond her royal status into the ever-memorable Mother Abbess Alexandra, who now dwells with the King of All in the Throne Room of Paradise. *I Live Again?* Indeed she does. Forever.

I commend her Orthodox Monastery of the Transfiguration for reprinting her wonderful book, the story of her life.

Protopresbyter Laurence Lazar, Dean
St. George Romanian Orthodox Cathedral, Southfield, Michigan

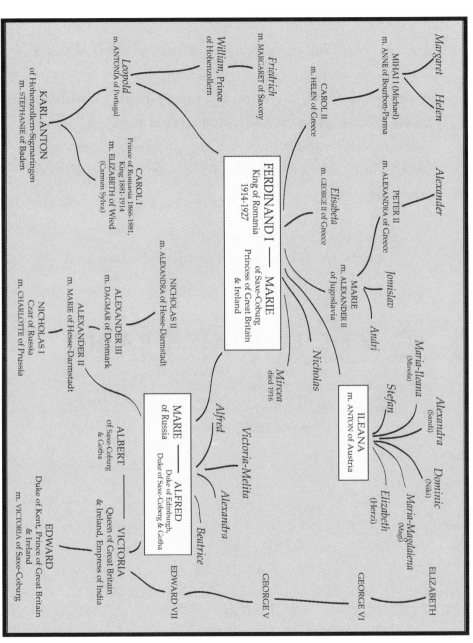

Princess Ileana's family tree (read bottom to top)

Ancient Faith Publishing hopes you have enjoyed and benefited from this book. The proceeds from the sales of our books only partially cover the costs of operating our nonprofit ministry—which includes both the work of **Ancient Faith Publishing** and the work of **Ancient Faith Radio**. Your financial support makes it possible to continue this ministry both in print and online. Donations are tax-deductible and can be made at **www.ancientfaith.com.**

To view our other publications,
please visit our website: **store.ancientfaith.com**

ANCIENT FAITH RADIO

Bringing you Orthodox Christian music, readings,
prayers, teaching, and podcasts 24 hours a day since 2004 at
www.ancientfaith.com